D0464608

The New Urbanism

Library Square, Downtown
Hayward, California
(Solomon Architecture and
Planning; 1992). Drawing
by Thai Nguyen.

Peter Katz

Afterword by
Vincent Scully

Essays by
Todd W. Bressi
Peter Calthorpe
Andres Duany
and Elizabeth Plater–Zyberk
Elizabeth Moule
and Stefanos Polyzoides

The New Urbanism
Toward an Architecture of Community

McGraw-Hill, Inc.

New York San Francisco Washington, D.C.
Auckland Bogotá Caracas Lisbon London Madrid
Mexico City Milan Montréal New Delhi San Juan
Singapore Sydney Tokyo Toronto

Library of Congress Cataloging-in-Publication Data

Katz, Peter.
    The new urbanism : toward an architecture of
community / Peter Katz ; afterword by Vincent
Scully ; essays by Todd Bressi ... [et al.].
        p.   cm.
    ISBN 0-07-033889-2
        1. Architecture–United States–Human factors.
    2. Architects and community–United States.
    3. Architecture–Canada–Human factors.
    4. Architects and community–Canada. I. Scully,
Vincent Joseph. II. Bressi, Todd W. III. Title.
    NA2542.4.K38 1994
    720'.1'03–dc20   92-47474
                                                    CIP

Copyright © 1994 by Peter Katz. All rights reserved.
Except as permitted under the United States Copyright
Act of 1976, no part of this publication may be
reproduced or distributed in any form or by any means,
or stored in a data base or retrieval system, without the
prior written consent of the publisher.

0   1IMP/1IMP   9

ISBN 0-07-033889-2

The sponsoring editor for this book was Joel Stein,
the editing supervisor was Jane Palmieri, the
production director was Geraldine Fahey and the
production manager was Tom Kowalczyk.

The book was designed and composed on an Apple
Macintosh computer system by Peter Katz and Clifton
Lemon. The typeface, Monotype Bembo, is a variation
of a roman letter originally cut by Francisco Griffo for
the Venetian printer Aldus Manutius. Its first known
use was in 1495. The Bembo type family was selected
for this book because its design, combining classic
structure and humanistic warmth, has kept its appeal
through nearly five centuries of changing printing and
typesetting technology.

This book was printed in Hong Kong
through Print Vision, Portland, Oregon.

To the memory of Doris Katz,
a dedicated mother, designer and educator.
She taught me and countless others
about the importance of design and its power
to enhance the quality of our lives.

Contents

Preface

Peter Katz

By the summer of 1991, when I began this project, it seemed evident that a new urban design movement was taking shape. Publications as diverse as *The Atlantic, Travel & Leisure, People* and *Smithsonian* had all featured what was then being called "Neo-traditional" planning. Several television networks had covered it as well. The architectural press was slower to come around; this story didn't fit neatly into their well established celebrity system.

For me, an extensive article in *Time Magazine* on the work of Andres Duany, Elizabeth Plater-Zyberk and Peter Calthorpe was the clincher. A new architecture and urban design movement had already gone mainstream, yet few of the architects that I knew were even aware of it. This book had to be done.

The New Urbanism is a movement that I feel will be of great relevance to future planning efforts in this country. It addresses many of the ills of our current sprawl development pattern while returning to a cherished American icon: that of a compact, close-knit community.

For most of human history, people have banded together for mutual security or to be close to critical resources—water, food and, more recently, ports, rail hubs and employment centers. The advent of the automobile and a host of other factors provided an opportunity to disperse—to go beyond the limits of one's own walking range or that of a streetcar line. The crowding, crime and disease which plagued center cities in the past offered reasons enough to leave. In the postwar era, suburbia became the lifestyle of choice for most Americans.

While this new way of living had many advantages, it also fragmented our society—separating us from friends and relatives and breaking down the bonds of community that had served our nation so well in earlier times.

Despite the increasing sophistication of our physical and electronic networks (highways, telephones, television, etc.), we remain today a fragmented society. Networks, alas, are no substitute for true community.

In my view, the New Urbanism couldn't have come at a better time. There is a growing sense that the suburban paradigm, which has dominated since the 1940s and 1950s, cannot sustain another generation of growth.

The costs of suburban sprawl are all around us—they're visible in the creeping deterioration of once proud neighborhoods, the increasing alienation of large segments of society, a constantly rising crime rate and widespread environmental degradation. Though gradual, and for that reason unnoticed by many, these changes have altered our world in ways that we are just now starting to understand.

The Geography of Nowhere, an excellent book by James Howard Kunstler, provides a comprehensive look at the crisis of place in America's

A telecommute work facility occupies the upper floor of a neighborhood center in Southport, West Sacramento, California. A child-care center, convenience store, cafe and newsstand are on the street level.

Planners Andres Duany and Elizabeth Plater-Zyberk proposed several such centers within the town. Drawing by Charles Barrett and Manuel Fernandez-Noval.

suburbs. Kunstler finds no shortage of causes–the auto and petroleum interests, the greed of developers and the shortsightedness of civic officials among them. The "joyride" that he feels we've been on since the 1940s has devastated our built environment. Now that the ride is over, we must deal with its consequences.

The New Urbanism addresses that challenge. It may not be the American Dream as it was constituted in our parents' generation, but it could ultimately offer a better option for those of my own–the baby-boom generation. We've been teased by the promise, yet denied the benefits of this so called "dream."

The proposals of the New Urbanism, for example, include several forms of housing that haven't been built since my grandfather's time. Since then, they've been systematically eliminated. I'm referring to truly high-quality apartments and townhouses, boarding houses that were respectable places to live; also accessory units, duplexes and quadruplexes of every kind. All of these proven options from the past seem again suited to the needs of a diverse society.

The New Urbanism, though, is not just a revival. While it borrows heavily from traditional city planning concepts–particularly those of the years 1900-1920 (now coming to be regarded as a watershed era in the history of urban design)–the New Urbanists acknowledge that many realities of modern life must be dealt

with: automobiles and "big-box" stores, to mention just a few.

Far from suggesting we turn our backs on the benefits of modern living, the return to community that they advocate may, in fact, be *empowered* by new technology. Telecommuting with the aid of computers and modems from a home office or neighborhood work center is one such example. The advantages of time and money saved by *not* driving long distances to work and having increased time available for family and friends are evident. Where pilot programs have been started (Washington State sponsored one such effort), employees jumped at the chance to work closer to home.

In his book *Penturbia*, economist Jack Lessinger predicts that such changing work patterns will make suburbs obsolete and trigger a boom in the rural areas where people now vacation or retire. A recent article in *The New York Times* suggests that such a shift may well be occurring: It cites reports of population growth in some rural areas for the first time in 60 years.

While the effects of such rural dispersion could be even more catastrophic than the recent suburban exodus, one hopes that land-efficient New Urbanist planning methods could help avert such a fate. On this point, it is important to note a major philosophical division among the practitioners of the New Urbanism that is reflected in this book's two-part structure:

Some believe that land at the region's edge shouldn't be developed until all infill possibilities have been exhausted; others feel that since current economic and political realities favor growth at the edge, it is better to mold such new growth into a more sustainable development pattern that will not drain the vitality of nearby established urban centers.

These two approaches are mentioned here, not to promote divisiveness but rather to illustrate how the principles of the New Urbanism, articulated in the three essays which follow, can be applied to a variety of situations–both new development and infill–at a range of densities and scales and in all regions of the country.

The prospect of a new century raises serious concerns about the quality of life that can be expected in a future era of diminished global resources. In that light, all of the strategies in this book should be examined, tested and tested again in relation to prevailing development models. If the New Urbanism can indeed be shown to deliver a higher, more sustainable quality of life to a majority of this nation's citizens, we can only hope that it will be embraced as the next paradigm for the shaping of America's communities.

The Region

Peter Calthorpe

The New Urbanism is concerned with both the pieces and the whole. It applies principles of urban design to the region in two ways. First, urbanism—defined by its diversity, pedestrian scale, public space and structure of bounded neighborhoods—should be applied throughout a metropolitan region regardless of location: in suburbs and new growth areas as well as within the city. And second, the entire region should be "designed" according to similar urban principles. It should, like a neighborhood, be structured by public space, its circulation system should support the pedestrian, it should be both diverse and hierarchical and it should have discernible edges.

The first application is a simple but unique contribution of this movement. Urbanism is now well understood in the city, but rarely applied to the suburb. Although there have been many transgressions over the post war period, the principles of urbanism have clearly reemerged since Jane Jacobs, Vincent Scully, Aldo Rossi, Leon Krier and many others have articulated the traditions. What is new is the application of these principles in suburbia and beyond. Too often we think of these aesthetic, spatial and programmatic principles in terms of density and the inner-city context. But the New Urbanism demonstrates how such ideas can be realized in the contemporary suburban condition and formalized at any density. It

shows that the relationship between architecture and public space can be "urban" regardless of building height or mass; that spatial hierarchy and connectedness can be rendered regardless of land-use intensity; and that pedestrian life can exist in single-family neighborhoods as well as on tenement streets. Applying these principles in the unlikely areas of the modern suburb, while coping with its economic and social imperatives, is one important contribution of the New Urbanism.

The second application acknowledges that the city, its suburbs and their natural environment should be treated as a whole—socially, economically and ecologically. Treating them separately is endemic to many of the problems we now face, and our lack of governance at this scale is a direct manifestation of this disaggregation. Seen as a whole, the American metropolis should be designed with much the same attitude as we design a neighborhood: There should be defined edges (i.e., Urban Growth Boundaries), the circulation system should function for the pedestrian (i.e., supported by regional transit systems), public space should be formative rather than residual (i.e., preservation of major open-space networks), civic and private domains should form a complementary hierarchy (i.e., related cultural centers, commercial districts and residential neighborhoods) and population and use should be diverse (i.e., created by adequate affordable housing and a jobs/housing balance). Developing such an architecture of the region creates the context for a healthy urbanism in neighborhoods, districts and at the city center. The two forms of urbanism work together.

The Crisis of Growth

To understand how the New Urbanism works in a regional context, the evolution of the modern American metropolis must be understood (even if in sketch form as it must be here). For the last 40 years growth has been largely directed by suburban flight, highway capacity and federal government mortgage policy. The typical development cycle started with bedroom communities pioneering the most remote sectors of the metropolitan region.

With federal and state highway investments, such seemingly remote suburbs and small towns became commute-accessible to the existing major job centers. They offered low-cost land and affordable housing for the regional work force. Retail, services, recreation and civic uses followed in proportion to the demand created by the housing.

When they reached critical mass, the new suburban areas began to attract jobs. "Edge Cities," as author Joel Garreau calls them, were soon formed. As these new decentralized job centers grew, the process began again—creating another layer of sprawl extending out from the decentralized job centers. Today, the suburb-to-suburb commute represents 40 percent of total commute trips while suburb-to-city comprises only 20 percent.

Out of this evolution of the modern metropolis there has grown a profound sense of frustration and placelessness. A homogeneous quality overlays the unique nature of each place with chain-store architecture, scaleless office parks and monotonous subdivisions. Even these qualities are easily blurred by the speed at which we move and the isolation we feel in our cars and in our dwellings. At their extreme, the new forms seem to have an empty feeling, reinforcing our mobile state and the instability of our families. Moving at a speed which allows only generic symbols to be recognized, we cannot wonder that the man-made environment seems trite and overstated.

Americans initially moved to the suburbs for privacy, mobility, security and home ownership. What we now have is isolation, congestion, rising crime, pollution and overwhelming costs—costs that ultimately must be paid by taxpayers, businesses and the environment. This sprawling pattern of growth at the edge now produces conditions which frustrate rather than enhance daily life. Meanwhile, our city centers have deteriorated because much of their economic vitality has decanted to the suburbs.

Ironically, the American Dream is now increasingly out of sync with today's culture. Our household makeup has changed dramatically, the workplace and work force have been transformed, family wealth is shrinking and grave environmental concerns have surfaced. But we continue to build post–World War II suburbs as if families were large and had only one breadwinner, the jobs were all downtown, land and energy were endless and another lane on the freeway would end traffic congestion.

Settlement patterns are the physical foundation of our society and, like our society, they are becoming more and more fractured. Development patterns and local zoning laws segregate age groups, income groups, ethnic groups and family types. They isolate people and activities in an inefficient network of congestion and pollution, rather than joining them in diverse and human-scaled communities. Our faith in government and the fundamental sense of commonality at the center of any vital democracy is seeping away in suburbs designed more for cars than people, more for market segments than real communities. Special interest groups now replace the larger community within our political landscape, just as gated subdivisions have replaced neighborhoods.

Our communities historically were embedded in nature, helping set both the unique identity of each place and the physical limits of the community. Local climate, plants, vistas, harbors and ridge lands once defined the special qualities of every memorable place. Today, smog, pavement, toxic soil, receding natural habitats and polluted water contribute to the destruction of neighborhood and home in the largest sense.

We threaten nature and nature now threatens us in return: sunlight causes cancer, air threatens our lungs, rain burns the trees, streams are polluted and soils are toxic. Understanding the qualities of nature in each place, expressing it in the design of communities, integrating it within our towns and respecting its balance are critical to making the human place sustainable and spiritually nourishing.

A Taxonomy of Growth

The problems of growth are not to be solved by limiting the scope, program or location of development. They must be resolved by re-thinking the nature and quality of growth itself, in every context. People argue heatedly about growth: where, how much, what type, what density and if it is really necessary at all. Sprawl is bad, infill is good (if it is not in our neighborhood), new towns destroy open space, master-planned communities are sterile and urban redevelopment is fine for "other people." Any region with a high growth demand has several options. It can 1) try to limit overall growth;

2) let the towns and suburbs surrounding the metropolitan center grow uncontrollably until they become a continuous mass; 3) attempt to accommodate growth in redevelopment and infill locations; or 4) plan new towns and new growth areas within reasonable transit proximity of the city center.

Every region needs to find an appropriate mix of these very different options. Each strategy has inherent advantages and problems, which need to be understood.

Limiting growth on a local level without the appropriate regional controls often spreads development into remote areas that are more receptive to sprawl. This increases commuting distances and creates our well known hop-scotch land-use patterns.

Sometimes called "managed" or "slow" growth, this strategy is often used by a jurisdiction seeking to avoid its fair share of affordable housing or the expansion of transit. Unless there is a strategy for limiting growth at a regional level, local attempts will only extend and displace the problem.

At the other extreme, allowing the uncontrolled growth of existing suburbs and towns is our most common growth strategy. It has the most familiar results: sprawl, traffic and a loss of the identity for what historically may have been distinct neighborhoods, villages and towns. And it is an approach which seems inevitably to lead

to powerful citizens' no-growth movements and growth limitations, thus fueling the cycle of regional sprawl.

Infill and Redevelopment

The best utilization of existing infrastructure and the best opportunity to preserve our open space will come from infill and redevelopment. Therefore it should always be a central part of a region's growth policy. But to expect infill sites to absorb all or even most new development is unrealistic. This is sometimes because there are not enough sites to accommodate the demand, and partly because no-growth neighborhood groups often resist such infill. Once again, without a political force to balance the larger economic and environmental needs of a region against the anti-infill tendency of individual communities, there is little hope such growth will reach even its limited potential. Both urban and suburban infill sites have special concerns and constraints beyond the generic and widespread political problems of NIMBYism (not in my backyard syndrome).

Over the last 30 years, urban infill and redevelopment has been a prime objective for most cities. There have been some successes but many failures. The list of problems and constraints is long: racial tension, gentrification, economic stagnation, bureaucracy, deteriorating schools and red-line appraisals to name a few.

There are many ways to resolve or reduce the magnitude of these constraints, and they all need to be considered in future urban infill efforts. But it is clear that such strategies are falling short and additional means to advance urban infill are needed.

Portland, Oregon, is an example of a city and region which has gone beyond the traditional programs for urban infill and revitalization. It has successfully supported infill in two progressive ways: an Urban Growth Boundary (UGB) and zoning that supports a transit system that is focused on the central city. The UGB is a state-mandated limit to growth around the metropolitan region which was established in 1972. Both strategies are central to the thesis of a New Urbanism–that a regional system of open space and transit complemented with pedestrian-friendly development patterns can help revitalize an urban center at the same time it helps to order suburban growth. Downtown Portland, because of its light-rail system, sensitive urban planning and regional limits is now growing in a healthy relationship to its suburbs. Both the UGB and Portland's expanding light-rail system have helped to direct new development and economic activity back into its thriving downtown.

Suburban infill represents a different set of problems and constraints. Typically, no-growth and slow-growth neighborhood groups inhibit the density and mix of uses while driving the cost of suburban development ever upward. The existing street systems and zoning codes stand as further blocks to creating walkable communities. Finally, the density and configurations typical of suburban sprawl make transit a heavily subsidized safety net rather than a real alternative to the car. If we are to have significant growth as suburban infill, much needs to change. Foremost, local citizens must understand that there are options beyond no-growth or sprawl. Local concerns must be tempered with regional needs–an equitable distribution of affordable housing and jobs, preservation of open space and agriculture lands and a viable transit system. This calls for policies and governance which can both educate and guide the complex interaction of economics, ecology, technology, jurisdiction and social equity.

New Growth and Satellite Towns

When urban and suburban infill cannot accommodate the quantity or rate of growth of a region, new growth areas and satellite towns may be considered.

New growth areas are the easiest to develop with transit- and pedestrian-oriented patterns. However there is one caveat: They also may spread the city's size. Satellite towns are typically larger than new growth areas and provide a complete spectrum of shopping, jobs and civic facilities. But both, if well planned and transit-oriented, can complement infill and help to structure and revitalize the metropolitan region.

An effective transit system accomplishes many things. It can invigorate downtown, as transit invariably focuses on the central business district. Adding more sprawling suburbs to a metropolitan area only increases pressure for parking and freeways downtown, while competing with the city for jobs and retail activity.

By contrast, transit delivers people to the heart of our cities, reducing the need for parking and avoiding destructive urban freeway projects. Adding transit-oriented new growth areas and satellite towns can reinforce the city's role as the region's cultural and economic center. The transit system that is supported at the edge with new growth can also become the catalyst for redevelopment and infill at the regional center.

Recent experiences with "new towns" and new growth areas (sometimes called master-planned communities) have given such developments a bad name. In Europe, with some notable exceptions, new towns are predominantly sterile and suburban in character. In America they are sterile, suburban and–even worse–economic failures. But the questions remain: Are these qualities inherent or products of a dysfunctional design philosophy? And if new towns could be designed more intelligently, would they be justified or necessary?

To answer these questions it is useful to understand the history of new town planning. At the turn of the century and during the great depression the theory of new towns evolved in several directions. Ebenezer Howard and the Garden City movement defined a Luddite's vision of small towns built for workers surrounded by a greenbelt, combining the best of city and country. These towns were formed around rail stations and formally configured with a combination of the Romantic and Beaux Arts urban traditions: powerful civic spaces surrounded by village-scaled neighborhoods. In the same period Tony Garnier developed the first Modernist approach to town planning, segregating industry, isolating different uses and freeing buildings from the street. His was the first such vision of the 20th century city. During the depression Le Corbusier and Frank Lloyd Wright expanded this vision in the urban and suburban context while retaining fundamental Modernist principles: segregation of use, love of the auto and dominance of private over public space. In these utopias (which after World War II came to guide our development patterns) the street as the community's habitable common ground disintegrated. Even in the most progressive of the post-World War II new towns and master-planned communities, these basic Modernist concepts have compromised, if not completely destroyed, their ability to evolve

into vital communities. The task of the New Urbanism is to learn from these failures, avoiding their sterile and suburban character while defining a form of growth which can help mend the metropolis.

Urbanism of the Pieces

The specific nature of a metropolitan region will dictate which growth strategies are necessary and useful. Some regions with a very slow growth rate may only need incremental infill. Some regions with fast growth and much undeveloped suburban land may benefit from both infill and new growth area projects. Other regions may require all three strategies, including satellite towns, to absorb massive growth without destroying the identity of existing places. One thing is certain: With any blend of these forms, it is the quality of development, not just its location or size, that is the principal problem and opportunity of growth.

Sprawl is destructive in any growth strategy. Contemporary suburbs have failed because they lack, as do many of the so-called "modern" new towns and edge cities, the fundamental qualities of real towns: pedestrian scale, an identifiable center and edge, integrated diversity of use and population and defined public space. They may have diversity in use and user, but these diverse elements are segregated by the car. They have none of the places for casual and spontaneous

interaction which create vital neighborhoods, quarters or towns. Unless urban infill sites, suburban new development areas and satellite towns embody the qualities of the New Urbanism, they will fail too. In every context, therefore, the quality of new development in a region should follow town-like principles— housing for a diverse population, a full mix of uses, walkable streets, positive public space, integrated civic and commercial centers, transit orientation and accessible open space.

Urban infill often succeeds because those urban qualities pre-exist and need only be preserved, not necessarily created. Nevertheless we see many urban infill projects which succeed in destroying these desirable pre-existing qualities. For smaller parcels in existing urban neighborhoods the task is to complete the mix of a community while honoring the unique qualities of the place. For suburban sites, even with the political constraints, mixed-use neighborhoods can be infilled. Far from being blank slates, these suburban infill sites sometimes offer rich histories to build on as well as debilitating sprawl to overcome.

Satellite towns at the outer edge of the metropolitan region can easily afford features that more expensive areas cannot provide— greenbelts, transit and affordable housing to name a few. At the same time they buffer their own edges with greenbelts, they can help establish permanent edges for the region. Without greenbelted satellite towns or stable Urban Growth Boundaries, a fast growing region will continually expand into and threaten close-in natural edges and open space. Additionally, satellite towns can help manage the growth of older suburbs and towns by absorbing excess development.

Urbanism of the Whole

The way these pieces are woven together into a whole is also part of the New Urbanism. Beyond resolving the balance between new growth and infill, and controlling the urban qualities of both, there is the challenge of creating a truly urban metropolitan form—oriented to public rather than private space, diverse, hierarchical and pedestrian-scaled.

Clearly, the Urban Growth Boundary is the regional equivalent of a defined neighborhood edge. These boundaries create identity for the whole and express the need to preserve nature as a limit to human habitat. Similarly, major open space within the region can be seen as a "village green" at a mega-scale. This internal commons, like the boundaries, establishes the ecological and conservation values which can help form the basis of regional character.

Urbanism at the regional scale has other parallels. Pedestrian scale translates into transit systems. Transit can order and formalize the region in much the same way a street network orders a neighborhood. It supports the life of the pedestrian throughout the region.

Diversity is a fundamental component of urbanism at both the neighborhood and regional scale. At the regional scale it is too often taken for granted—but diversity without connections (segregated diversity) is not urban at any scale. The diverse population and functions within a region should have a connecting fabric which makes the region vital and inclusionary. Our freeway and arterial networks now seem to privatize and isolate the components of a region more than connect them.

Finally, urbanism articulates the hierarchy of public and private, of civic and commerical. At the regional scale this means that the diversity and differences throughout the region should find a complementary and grand order. By this I mean that neighborhoods and districts should not just repeat one another but, much like the private and civic buildings of a neighborhood, find appropriate locations to express relative focus and importance.

These two dimensions—urbanism within neighborhoods and urbanism as regional form giver—are meant to inform and direct interventions within the existing framework of our cities, suburbs and towns. Infill, new development or reconstruction can and inevitably will shape the principles of a New Urbanism.

The goal is to apply the best of urban design to both the region and the neighborhood—applying them to a new context and at a new scale. The New Urbanism is not just about the city or the suburb. It is about the way we conceive of community and how we form the region—it is about diversity, scale and public space in every context.

The Neighborhood, the District and the Corridor

Andres Duany and Elizabeth Plater-Zyberk

The fundamental organizing elements of the New Urbanism are the neighborhood, the district and the corridor. Neighborhoods are urbanized areas with a balanced mix of human activity; districts are areas dominated by a single activity; corridors are connectors and separators of neighborhoods and districts.

A single neighborhood standing free in the landscape is a village. Cities and towns are made up of multiple neighborhoods and districts, organized by corridors of transportation or open space. Neighborhoods, districts and corridors are urban elements. By contrast, suburbia, which is the result of zoning laws that separate uses, is composed of pods, highways and interstitial spaces.

The Neighborhood

The nomenclature may vary, but there is general agreement regarding the physical composition of the neighborhood. The "neighborhood unit" of the 1929 New York Regional Plan, the "quartier" identified by Leon Krier, the "traditional neighborhood development" (TND) and "transit-oriented development" (TOD) share similar attributes. They all propose a model of urbanism that is limited in area and structured around a defined center. While the population density may vary, depending on its context, each model offers a balanced mix of dwellings, workplaces, shops, civic buildings and parks.

Like the habitat of any species, the neighborhood possesses a natural logic that can be described in physical terms. The following are the principles of an ideal neighborhood design: 1) The neighborhood has a center and an edge; 2) The optimal size of a neighborhood is a quarter mile from center to edge; 3) The neighborhood has a balanced mix of activities–dwelling, shopping, working, schooling, worshipping and recreating; 4) The neighborhood structures building sites and traffic on a fine network of interconnecting streets; 5) The neighborhood gives priority to public space and to the appropriate location of civic buildings.

The neighborhood has a center and an edge. The combination of a focus and a limit contribute to the social identity of the community. The center is a necessity, the edge not always so. The center is always a public space, which may be a square, a green or an important street intersection. It is near the center of the urban area unless compelled by some geographic circumstance to be elsewhere. Eccentric locations are justified if there is a shoreline, a transportation corridor or a place with an engaging view.

The center is the locus of the neighborhood's public buildings, ideally a post office, a meeting hall, a day-care center and sometimes religious and cultural institutions. Shops and workplaces are usually associated with the center, especially in a village. In the aggregations of multiple neighborhoods which occur in a town or city, retail buildings and workplaces may be at the edge of the neighborhood, where they can combine with others and intensify commercial and community activity.

Neighborhood edges may vary in character: they can be natural, such as a forest, or man-made, such as infrastructure. In villages, the edge is usually defined by land designated for cultivation such as farms, orchards and nurseries or for conservation in a natural state as woodland, desert, wetland or escarpment. The edge may also be assigned to very low-density residential use with lots of at least 10 acres. When a community cannot afford to sustain large tracts of public open land, such large private ownerships are a way to maintain a green edge.

In cities and towns, edges can be formed by the systematic accretion between the neighborhoods of recreational open spaces, such as parks, schoolyards and golf courses. It is important that golf courses be confined to the edge of neighborhoods, because fairways obstruct direct pedestrian ways to the neighborhood center. These continuous green edges can be part of a larger network of corridors, connecting urban open space with rural surroundings, as described in the 1920s by Benton McKaye.

In high-density urban areas, the neighborhood edge is often defined by infrastructure, such as rail lines and high traffic thoroughfares that best remain outside the neighborhood. The latter, if generously lined with trees, become parkways that reinforce the legibility of the edge and, over a long distance, form the corridors connecting urban neighborhoods.

The optimal size of a neighborhood is a quarter mile from center to edge. This distance is the equivalent of a five-minute walk at an easy pace. The area thus circumscribed is the neighborhood proper, to differentiate it from the green edge, which extends beyond the discipline of the quarter mile. The limited area gathers the population of a neighborhood within walking distance of many of their daily needs, such as a convenience store, post office, community police post, automatic bank teller, school, daycare center and transit stop.

The stop's location among other neighborhood services and within walking distance of home or work makes the transit system convenient. When an automobile trip is necessary to arrive at a transit stop, most potential users will simply continue driving to their destinations. But the neighborhood, which focuses the required user population within walking distance of the stop, makes transit viable at densities that a suburban pattern cannot sustain.

Pedestrian-friendly and transit-oriented neighborhoods permit a region of cities, towns and villages to be accessible without singular reliance on cars. Such a system gives access to the major cultural and social institutions, the variety of shopping and the broad job base that can only be supported by the larger population of an aggregation of neighborhoods.

The neighborhood has a balanced mix of activities— dwelling, shopping, working, schooling, worshipping and recreating. This is particularly important for those who are unable to drive and thus depend on others for mobility. For instance, the young are able to walk or bicycle to school and other activities, freeing their parents from the responsibility and tedium of chauffeuring. The size of a school should be determined by the number of children who can walk or bicycle to it from adjacent neighborhoods.

And the elderly, who relinquish their willingness to drive before they lose their ability to walk, can age in place with dignity rather than being forced into specialized retirement communities, which are the attendant creations of the suburban pattern.

Even those for whom driving may not be a burden enjoy secondary advantages. The proximity of daily destinations and the convenience of transit reduces the number and length of trips, decreases the private stress of time in traffic and minimizes the public-borne expenses of road construction and atmospheric pollution.

The neighborhood's fine-grained mix of activities includes a range of housing types for a variety of incomes, from the wealthy business owner to the school teacher and the gardener. Suburban areas, which are most commonly segregated by income, do not provide for the full range of society. The true neighborhood, however, offers a variety of affordable housing choices: garage apartments in conjunction with single-family houses, apartments above shops and apartment buildings adjacent to shopping and workplaces. The latter's transitional sites are not provided within the suburban pattern whose rigorous, sanitized segregation of uses precludes them.

But the greatest contribution to affordable housing may be realized by the neighborhood's ability to reduce multiple automobile ownership and many of its associated costs. By enabling households to own one less vehicle, the average annual operating cost of $5,000 can be applied toward an additional $50,000 increment of mortgage financing at 10 percent. No other action of the designer can achieve an improvement in the availability of housing for the middle class comparable to the sensible organization of a good neighborhood plan.

The neighborhood structures building sites and traffic on a fine network of interconnecting streets. Neighborhood streets are configured to create blocks of appropriate building sites and to shorten pedestrian routes. They are designed to keep local traffic off regional roads and to keep through traffic off local streets. An interconnecting pattern of streets provides multiple routes that diffuse traffic congestion.

This contrasts to the easily congested single trajectories standard to the suburban pattern: culs-de-sac spill onto collector streets, which connect at single points to arterials, which in turn supply the highways. The suburban traffic model is more concerned with speeding traffic through a place than with the quality of the place itself; the pedestrian is assumed to be elsewhere on separate "walkways" or nonexistent.

Neighborhood streets of varying types are detailed to provide equitably for pedestrian comfort and for automobile movement. Slowing the automobile and increasing pedestrian activity encourages the casual meetings that form the bonds of community.

The neighborhood gives priority to public space and to the appropriate location of civic buildings. Public spaces and buildings represent community identity and foster civic pride. The neighborhood plan structures its streets and blocks to create a hierarchy of public spaces and locations for public buildings. Squares and streets have their size and geometry defined by the intention to create special places. Public buildings occupy important sites, overlooking a square or terminating a street vista.

The suburban practice of locating government buildings, places of worship, schools and even public art according to the expediencies of land cost is ineffective. The importance of these civic and community structures is enhanced by their suitable siting, without incurring additional costs to the infrastructure.

The District

The district is an urbanized area that is functionally specialized. Although districts preclude the full range of activities necessary for a complete neighborhood, they are not the rigorously single activity zones of suburbia: the office parks, housing subdivisions or shopping centers. The specialization of a district still allows multiple activities to support its primary identity. Typical are theater districts, which have restaurants and bars to support and intensify their nightlife; tourist districts, which concentrate hotels, retail activity and entertainment; and the capitol area and the college campus, which are dominated by a large institution. Others accommodate large-scale transportation or manufacturing, such as airports, container terminals and refineries.

Although a degree of specialization for certain urban areas enhances their character and efficiency, in reality, few pure districts are really justified. Thanks to industrial evolution and environmental regulation, the reasons for segregating uses recede with time. The modern North American workplace is no longer a bad neighbor to dwellings and shops.

The organizational structure of the district parallels that of the neighborhood and similarly, for a good fit within the greater region, relies on its relationship to transit. An identifiable focus encourages the formation of special communities: a park for workers at lunch, a square for theater-goers to meet, a mall for civic gatherings. Clear boundaries and dimensions facilitate the formation of special taxing or management organizations. Interconnected circulation supports the pedestrian, enhances transit viability and ensures security. And like the neighborhood, attention to the character of the public spaces creates a sense of place for its users, even if their home is elsewhere.

The Corridor

The corridor is at once the connector and the separator of neighborhoods and districts. Corridors include natural and man-made elements, ranging from wildlife trails to rail lines. The corridor is not the haphazardly residual space that remains outside subdivisions and shopping centers in suburbia. Rather, it is an urban element characterized by its visible continuity. It is defined by its adjacent districts and neighborhoods and provides entry to them.

The corridor's location and type is determined by its technological intensity and nearby densities. Heavy rail corridors are tangent to towns and traverse the industrial districts of cities. Light rail and trolleys may occur within a boulevard at the neighborhood edge. As such, they are detailed for pedestrian use and to accommodate the frontages of buildings. Bus corridors can pass through neighborhood centers on conventional streets. All of these should be landscaped to reinforce their continuity.

In low-density areas, the corridor may be the continuous green edge between neighborhoods, providing long-distance walking and bicycle trails, other recreational amenities and a continuous natural habitat.

The corridor is a significant element of the New Urbanism because of its inherently civic nature. In the age of the metropolis, with villages, towns, neighborhoods and districts aggregated in unprecedented quantity, the most universally used public spaces are the corridors that serve connection and mobility. Of the three elements—the neighborhood, the district and the corridor—the latter, in its optimum form, is the most difficult to implement because it requires regional coordination.

Conclusion

The conventional suburban practice of segregating uses by zones is the legacy of the "dark satanic mills," which were once genuine hazards to public welfare. The separation of dwelling from workplace in the course of the last century was the great achievement of the nascent planning profession and remains institutionalized in zoning ordinances. The suburbs and cities of today continue to separate the naturally integrated human activities of dwelling, working, shopping, schooling, worshipping and recreating.

The hardship caused by this separation has been mitigated by widespread automobile ownership and use, which in turn has increased the demand for vehicular mobility. The priority given to road building at the expense of other civic programs during the last four decades has brought our country to the multiple crises of environmental degradation, economic bankruptcy and social disintegration.

The New Urbanism offers an alternative future for the building and re-building of regions. Neighborhoods that are compact, mixed-use and pedestrian friendly; districts of appropriate location and character; and corridors that are functional and beautiful can integrate natural environments and man-made communities into a sustainable whole.

The Street, the Block and the Building

Elizabeth Moule and Stefanos Polyzoides

The form of the New Urbanism is realized by the deliberate assembly of streets, blocks and buildings. In the American urban tradition, the cutting of a grid is the first presence of urban structure in the landscape. In this act of making a place, space is allocated for both public and private use—for buildings and for open spaces. Shaping this void in the city is an act of demo-cratic responsibility. A plan is laid down by a governing body regulating private and public initiative in the construction of its parts. Public bodies, citizens and entrepreneurs slowly gene-rate streets, squares and parks. Single buildings incrementally introduced into blocks eventually determine the character of the open spaces. It is at this most elemental scale, every day in a myriad of fleeting and poignant moments, that architecture and urbanism define each other.

This very simple American city-making model has been virtually abandoned in recent years. For the last half century, the building of the public realm has been handled with little regard for those it serves and for the quality of life that it generates. Increasingly, architecture has become the instrument of excessive self-expression. Individual buildings are often con-ceived as solely private, self-referential objects incapable of generating the public realm. Conversely, our public regulation system of zoning that controls the growth of the city has become overly verbal and complicated and incapable of accurately guiding physical form (especially because everything is negotiable). Zoning conflates issues of use, density and form to such an extent that it has spawned the unpre-dictability and visual chaos typical of the Ameri-can city. Moreover, transportation-dominated infrastructure engineering has so preferred the accommodation of the car over human beings, that the intended users of the public realm have been driven out. What many confuse as an unregulated and unfriendly urban landscape is actually the result of wrongly coded and uncritical design.

Because our current society has become so adept at creating and fetishizing those things which are private, we shall focus on the prob-lem of making that which we hold in *common*. In city-making parlance, this is called the public realm. It is that shared space in society which brings people to gather together, to relate to one another and/or to be separate.

The New Urbanism seeks a fresh paradigm to guarantee and to order the public realm through individual buildings. Buildings, blocks and streets are interdependent. Each one con-tains to some degree the ingredients of all the others. Any decision to design streets in a particular manner seals the formal fate of blocks and buildings. Blocks of a specific character determine correspondent streets and buildings. Buildings of particular qualities dominate the blocks that contain them and the streets that surround them.

The matrix for addressing the totality of street, block and building principles of the New Urbanism is *design*–not policy planning–and amounts to an aesthetic position. But this position is not about the definition of style, particularly revivalist style. Nor is it about diminishing design freedom. Instead, it is a method of design that is rooted in first causes and historical precedent. It is an attitude of expression that values the cultural variety inherent in climatic, social, economic and technical difference. It is also a professional ethic that stresses the integration of all architectural, engineering and design disciplines, the active collaboration among their practitioners and the participation of the public in the design process.

Above all it is about ensuring that there *is* a public realm. A city is a human artifact which is a collection of places and things. It is what we are born into and what we leave behind. What we hold in common is not only that which we share with the living, but that which we share with those before us and those after us. The city is therefore based on permanency.

An accessible (socially and physically) and truly shared place can be guaranteed at the most elemental scale through the following urbanist principals. These tenets prefer the human scale over that of the auto, balance private interests with public interests and employ simple and physically determined methods over those that are complicated and solely legal-minded.

The Street

Streets are not the dividing lines within the city. They are to be communal rooms and passages.

Pattern - A single given street is always to be part of a street network. Connectedness and continuity of movement within such a network will encourage the mixing of uses in the city. A variety of alternative paths connecting various destinations shall minimize the traffic load on any one street.

Hierarchy - There is to exist a variety of streets based on their pedestrian and vehicular loads. Under no circumstances will a street be abandoned solely to vehicular traffic. Conversely, assigning streets solely to pedestrian use will sap their vitality. Distances between intersections will favor the walkability of streets and a proper rhythm of building form on given blocks.

Figure - The architectural character of streets is to be based on their configuration in plan and section. Building heights are to be proportionally related to right-of-way widths. The number of traffic lanes will balance vehicle flow and pedestrian crossing considerations. Shifts in scale within street sections are to be accomplished by the design of the landscape, building edges and other vertical streetscape elements.

Detail - The design of streets shall favor their proper use by pedestrians. The governing principles are: minimized block radii to slow cars at intersections, allowing easy crossing by pedestrians; landscaped medians to reduce apparent street widths; two-way streets that improve pedestrian crossing safety; properly designed curbs and sidewalks at intersections that accommodate the impaired. In addition, street parking protects pedestrians from the actual and perceived danger of moving traffic.

The Block

Blocks are the field on which unfolds both the building fabric and the public realm of the city. A versatile, ancient instrument, the traditional block allows a mutually beneficial relationship between people and vehicles in urban space.

Size - Blocks are to be square, rectangular or irregular in their shape. In their best historical dimensions, they vary between a minimum of 250 and a maximum of 600 feet. This dimensional range allows single buildings to easily reach the edges of blocks at all densities. It also forces parking to be located away from the sidewalk, either underground, in the middle of the block or in the street.

Configuration - Independent of shape, city blocks are to be lotted so that all of their sides can define public space. A variety of widths and depths of individual lots determine the range of building types and densities that will eventually establish the intended city fabric. Initial lotting shall plan for this. Alleys shall absorb parking and servicing loads and allow the outer faces of blocks to become more intensely pedestrian.

Streetground - At its perimeter, each block is to be divided into parkway, sidewalk and setback. Within each block, lobbies, major ground floor interior spaces and public gardens of all kinds and sizes are to be understood as an extension of the public space of the city.

Streetwalls - The predominant visual character of all built fabric depends on several attributes of building envelopes: Their height, mandated setbacks and projections define the enclosure of the street. Their maximum width along with their height define a building's mass. Setback lines and the percentage build-to at their edges establish the fundamental rhythm between open space and built form on each block. Threshold elements at the setback line, such as arcades, porches, stoops, stairs, balconies, eaves and cornices, loggias, chimneys, doors and windows, are the means by which buildings interface with and determine the life of the street.

Parking - The omnipresence of cars within the public realm threatens the vitality of cities. Accommodating the pedestrian is the first order of priority for parking. Cars are best accommodated in the middle of blocks or underground. Parking garages are acceptable as long as their ground floors at the sidewalk are occupied by pedestrian-related uses. Parking garages are to be regular buildings and, as such, need significant public faces and the built-in spatial redundancy necessary for a future use other than parking. Where parking lots are inevitable, they should double up as significant public gardens.

Landscape - Regularly planted trees along blocks shall establish the overall space and scale of the street as well as that of the sidewalk. These artifacts from man's historical contact with nature remain a psychically critical element of urbanism. The choice of particular species of trees and the patterns of their placement affect light and shadow, color, views—all significant aspects of the experience of place. Public open-space types (civic parks, neighborhood parks, etc.) shall be designed to be inhabited, not solely viewed. Semi-public ones (quads, courtyards, patios) are to give life and internal character to urban blocks.

The Building

Buildings are the smallest increment of growth in the city. Their proper configuration and placement relative to each other determines the character of each settlement.

Use - Neither of the two opposing extreme views of architectural use put forward by the Modern movement—functionalism and universal flexibility—adequately addresses the making of a city or town. They have resulted in exclusive zoning and the fragmentation and disconnection of parts of the city from each other.

Buildings are to be designed by reference to their type, not solely their function. This allows for some changes in use and for multiple adaptations over time without compromising a building's form or rendering it obsolete. This is also critical from an environmental point of view.

Building types are to be organized by reference to dwelling, employment or institutional first uses. Their definition is based on their common architectural ingredients.

Density - Floor Area Ratio (FAR) zoning regulations are totally abstract and favor the design of buildings as singular objects. They are to be replaced with building envelope guidelines that link entitlements with predictable physical and architectural definitions of the public realm. Density regulations shall be stated independently of building use and parking. Parking requirements shall be established on a neighborhood and district basis as opposed to building by building. They are to be phrased by their intended architectural and urban consequences, not just numerically.

Form - There exist two kinds of buildings: fabric and monumental. Fabric buildings are to conform to all street and block-related rules and are consistent in their form with all other buildings of their kind. Monumental buildings are to be free of all formal constraints. They can be unique and idiosyncratic, the points of concentrated social meaning in the city.

Built form and landscape form are mutually dependent. The relationship of buildings to the public realm is to be reciprocal. Frontality shall allow three scales of architectural expression: One that emphasizes the public character of streets; another that reflects the semi-public nature of open spaces interior to the block; and a third that responds to the service nature of alleys and backyards.

Each building and garden is of a particular formal type. Each formal type is defined by reference to a set of determining formal characteristics. Adjacent buildings and gardens sharing some of these characteristics generate a sense of a cohesive framework within the city. The hand of the individual designer acting on stable types is the source of all architectural variety.

Architecture is deeply bound within the culture of each region of the country. Building types, not building styles, are to be the source of historical continuity in our towns and cities. Further design should be based on research that establishes the viability of historic, regional types; and also suggests newly created or imported types that may have possible local applications. It is from the mix of time-tested and new architectural models that authentic regional building differences can emerge.

The social content of buildings establishes their character and their scale. Far from being mere objects of consumption, buildings can be used for a variety of social ends: forming the public realm, expressing the importance of our public shared institutions and improving the daily working and home life of a citizenry.

Individual buildings shall become ecologically sensitive in their use of materials and energy. Regionally proven methods of building and easily available local and recyclable materials are to be favored over international technogeneralizations. Where economically possible, labor intensity in the building process shall be preferred. Low-energy consumption and pollution-free operations must be pursued.

Buildings are instruments for constructing time and place, not items to be consumed and discarded. For all practical and symbolic purposes, they are permanent fixtures in the landscape and the city. They should be designed with enough material and technical quality to allow their continuing renovation and reuse well beyond the expiration of their mortgage.

Coding

Specific street, block and building design rules for public or private developments shall be typically designed and presented in the form of a code. These codes are to be simply written and illustrated. They shall be brief and intensely physical in their prescriptions. Their content amounts to a covenant among the owners, designers and users of particular projects. Eventually their individual interests and actions will incrementally but inevitably generate the public realm.

The judicious application of codes is to result in a diverse, beautiful and predictable fabric of buildings, open space and landscape that can structure villages, towns, cities and, indeed, the metropolitan region. Architecture and urbanism shall not be separated; nor shall formal, social, economic and technical/functional issues be considered in isolation.

The process of coding operates fully within the American urban tradition of safeguarding the public realm while allowing significant freedom for the designers of individual buildings. It is in the balancing of such public and private interests and concerns that the future quality of life in the American city lies.

Planning the American Dream

Todd W. Bressi

What is the "New Urbanism" that the projects in this book embody? In one sense, it represents a rediscovery of planning and architectural traditions that have shaped some of the most livable, memorable communities in America–urban precincts like Boston's Back Bay and downtown Charleston, South Carolina; neighborhoods like Seattle's Capitol Hill and Philadelphia's Germantown; and traditional small towns where life centers around a courthouse square, common, plaza, train station or main street. For planners and architects who embrace the New Urbanism, places like these provide both inspiration and countless practical lessons for the design of new communities.

But the New Urbanism is not a romantic movement; it reflects a deeper agenda. The planning and design approaches explored in this book revive principles about building communities that have been virtually ignored for half a century: Public spaces like streets, squares and parks should be a setting for the conduct of daily life; a neighborhood should accommodate diverse types of people and activities; it should be possible to get to work, accomplish everyday tasks (like buying fresh food or taking a child to day care) and travel to surrounding communities without using a car. The projects in the following pages show how these traditional approaches to building communities are being applied anew in suburbs and urban infill projects, places that until recently have been regarded as being altogether different from traditional communities.

The New Urbanism also represents a new chapter in the history of American city planning. For a century, this reformist profession has been guiding urban redevelopment and suburban expansion with the goals of eradicating the crowding, poverty, disease and congestion that threatened to overwhelm industrial cities, and of creating a rational, efficient framework for growth that all but rejected traditional patterns of city and town development. The result of these efforts is a metropolitan landscape that is beset by an altogether different set of problems–traffic congestion, poor air quality, expensive housing, social segregation and neighborhoods whose physical character amounts to little more than the confluence of standard development practices and real estate marketing strategies. The New Urbanists are confronting these problems with an energy and creativity that had eluded planners until now.

The planners and architects whose work is shown in this book are at the forefront of a growing group of designers who are taking up this agenda. Their work is not clouded in theory and rhetoric. It is attracting the attention of not only critics and scholars but also people who can make change happen: citizen advocacy groups, local and regional planning agencies and

The automobile and the single-family home emerged as icons of the American dream. Government highway construction programs and housing policies promoted a landscape (left) and lifestyle (below) that repudiated traditional urbanism.

even private developers. There is little question that the approaches these designers advocate will be shaping the form of American cities and suburbs for decades to come.

From City to Suburb: A Century of American Planning and Urban Design

The suburban dispersal American cities have experienced in the last century has been remarkable in several ways. First, the magnitude of growth and the range of social and economic groups that have emigrated to the suburbs are unprecedented. Second, suburbs have evolved beyond their original role as "bedroom" communities; they now offer shopping, work and cultural activities, rendering suburbanites less reliant on central cities. Finally, this dispersal has been accompanied by the invention of new typologies for houses, commercial buildings and public spaces that contrast sharply with traditional forms—typologies that have been injected into center city projects as well.

This unprecedented suburban expansion has paralleled the unprecedented expansion of America's middle class and its desire to rise above urban, working-class conditions. The most powerful icon of the middle class, the single-family detached house surrounded by ample yards, has roots in Victorian-era mythology: The house was seen as a cradle, nurturing (and cultivating) the emerging independent

nuclear family, and as a bulwark, insulating women and children from the industrial city's evils. The house nurtured the family by providing specialized places for socializing, private life and household work, and by offering an opportunity, through landscaping and interior decoration, for the expression of individual taste. And the house, protected in its residential enclave and surrounded by spacious yards, offered privacy and protection from outside contamination. Suburban neighborhoods and houses also offered the middle class a new connection with nature: Romantic, picturesque site planning with curved streets and lavish plantings demonstrated the proper balance between nature and human artifice; irregular house forms like

porches and bay windows were considered a sign of organic complexity; and the yard was a garden that demonstrated the family's connection with the earth.[1]

The middle class's ability to move to suburban single-family homes was facilitated by transportation innovations. Before the 1920s, most suburbs grew in tandem with the extension of streetcar and railroad lines. Generally, they were compact clusters extending as far as a person might comfortably walk between home and a streetcar stop, and platted on tight grids that made land subdivision and sale efficient. Houses usually were put up by small builders who followed local practices or chose from the myriad of easily available plans. Houses came in a range of styles and typologies, depending on the region and the resident's taste and wealth—from Philadelphia's rowhouses and double homes to stately midwestern Victorians to California Craftsman bungalows.

After World War I, suburban growth was shaped by automobiles, which became the second icon of suburban life: Cars provided an unprecedented level of mobility, freeing people to determine their own travel patterns, and strengthened the suburbs' middle-class nature by excluding those who could not afford purchase and maintenance costs. Automobiles opened vast amounts of land for development, and the business of making and sustaining them

Increasing reliance on automobiles has resulted in troubling changes to the design of houses, whose appearance and plan are dominated by garages.

Kohler, Wisconsin, an industrial town designed by Werner Hegemann and the Olmsted brothers, is an example of early 20th century town planning efforts.

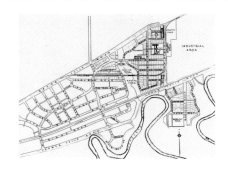

boosted the economy more than efficient streetcars ever could.

As auto ownership skyrocketed, government eagerly built networks of boulevards, parkways and expressways that served as armatures for dispersing development ever more widely and thinly. Car owners found the single-family detached house especially convenient because it offered easy possibilities for storing autos. When cars were novelties, garages appeared as backyard outbuildings; as cars became household fixtures, they attached themselves to the sides of houses; and as families acquired whole fleets of vehicles, garages moved to the front. Along the way, garages doubled or tripled in size; now they can be the most dominant visual element of a house's facade or an entire streetscape.

By the 1920s the profession of city planning was becoming institutionalized. Planners sought to remake cities from within through administrative reforms, such as building codes, and aggressive actions like clearing and rebuilding blighted areas. They also sought to foster orderly suburban growth by devising plans for efficient metropolitan regions in which residential districts were safely segregated from commercial and manufacturing activities but easily accessible to them via highway networks.

The boldest attempts at restructuring cities dated from Chicago's 1893 World's Columbian Exposition, which demonstrated how a combi-

nation of Baroque planning and Neoclassical architecture could impose a sense of order, civility and purpose on chaotic industrial cities. These efforts, which borrowed heavily from France's Beaux Arts school of architecture, were christened "City Beautiful" here. City Beautiful plans typically sought to establish formal civic centers, in which architecture and public space were conceived as a unified whole, and efficient networks of arterial streets to speed traffic through traditional street grids.

The most ambitious planners, inspired by British Garden City projects and their experience designing new communities for war industry workers, sought commissions for the design of entirely new towns. They, too, found inspiration in the architecture and planning of historic European towns, meticulously documented in books such as Camillo Sitte's *Town Planning According to Artistic Principles* and Werner Hegemann and Elbert Peets' *The American Vitruvius*. But few of their proposals, outside of industrial or resort towns, attracted backers of sufficient wherewithal; the most notable surviving examples are Venice, Florida; Mariemont, Ohio; and Kingsport, Tennessee.

A concept that had more impact on suburban planning was architect Clarence A. Perry's "neighborhood unit." This idea reinforced the Victorian notion that a neighborhood was a protective domestic enclave requiring insula-

tion from commerce, work and traffic, and held that the functional and literal center of a neighborhood should be an elementary school. Each neighborhood would be surrounded by arterial streets wide enough to handle through traffic; internal streets would be designed to facilitate circulation within the neighborhood. Local shops would be located along the arterials, preferably at traffic junctions and adjacent to similar districts.[2]

Planners found it easiest to establish regulatory frameworks in which private developers could make their own decisions about neighborhood design. Subdivision regulations governed the process by which buildable lots could be created out of undeveloped tracts of land–typically dictating lot sizes and shapes, street widths and block lengths, and open-space setasides. Zoning prescribed the activities that could take place on a lot; the size of a building that could be developed; dimensions for front, back and side yards; and requirements for functional matters like parking.

Agencies such as the U.S. Commerce Department and New York's Regional Plan Association promulgated model subdivision and zoning laws that were replicated in countless communities, often with little modification for local conditions. These mechanisms did not presume any one type of design, but they imposed a new level of uniformity on suburban development

Defense housing projects,
such as Linda Vista outside
San Diego, set the tone for
postwar mass production in
the home-building industry.

As more Americans moved
to the suburbs in the 1950s,
shopping and workplaces
followed. Southdale (left),
near Minneapolis, the first
enclosed, climate-controlled
shopping mall in the U.S.
(Victor Gruen Associates,
architects; constructed 1957).

Connecticut General Life
Insurance Company
headquarters (bottom) in
Bloomfield, Connecticut
(Skidmore, Owings &
Merrill, architects; con-
structed 1954-7).

by creating classification systems that treated hundreds or thousands of properties alike. Usually, their underlying purpose was to protect land values, foster family environments and maintain a degree of economic and social exclusion. In practice, zoning often separated commercial and residential uses, sanctified single-family homes by isolating them from apartments and imposed liberal setback rules that required large lots, thereby driving up housing costs.

As traffic volume increased, these standards were modified to make auto travel more safe and efficient while protecting the character of residential areas. Eventually, they called for streets wide enough to accommodate both parking and traffic, turning radii so generous that service and emergency vehicles could negotiate any cul-de-sac, and T-configured intersections that minimized traffic conflicts. Planners distributed traffic through hierarchical networks of arterial, collector and local streets. Grid systems fell out of favor because they allowed through traffic on residential streets, and culs-de-sac were enshrined in the standards because they prevented through traffic.[3]

New Deal reforms that promoted home ownership and stimulated the housing industry encoded these design principles more than local planners could ever have. These reforms required unprecedented standardization—of the terms under which money would be lent, methods by which property was appraised and criteria used to determine whether a loan could be insured. In essence, a set of national criteria determined the worth and bankability of a house; these evolved into standards for house design, lot and yard configurations and street layouts that became patterns for the home building industry. Again, single-family detached homes had a special advantage—the mechanics of lending for them were much simpler than creating ownership opportunities within multi-family buildings.[4]

This standardization was complemented by changes in the home-building industry, which learned mass production techniques while building housing for war workers and had a large pool of demobilized GIs eager to step up to suburban living (thanks to New Deal and veterans housing programs). Before 1945, the typical contractor put up 5 or fewer houses a year; by 1959 the average was 22.[5] Today, developers typically bring more than 100 acres through the approval process at a time and spin off sections to different builders, who rarely undertake projects with fewer than 150 houses or 100 apartments because of the economics of planning, building and marketing. To simplify production, most builders offer only a handful of models, and regional or national builders might repeat the same models in several places.[6]

Since World War II suburbs have taken on a more diverse character; functions once unique to center cities began to follow their customers and labor pools outward. Industrial activities were lured by the ability to spread out in low-slung buildings on large pieces of land and the easy access to the rapidly expanding network of interstate highways. Regional shopping centers began to flourish in the suburbs in the early 1950s. In the 1970s, white-collar "back-office" functions found new homes in the suburbs as companies tapped into a new labor market: Suburbs were full of underemployed women, many of whom were well-educated, not union members and eager for a paying job.

Nevertheless, this development occurred piecemeal at best. Bankers, builders and plan-

Downtown urban renewal projects like San Francisco's Golden Gateway tore out historic urban fabric (foundations of demolished buildings in foreground) and replaced it with superblocks designed in the "International style."

(Wurster, Bernardi and Emmons, architects; constructed 1965.)

ners evolved standards that extended the framework of separated uses and hierarchical, auto-friendly traffic networks to these new types of development. Efficient land-use approval processes encouraged each commercial and residential project to be considered on its own, with little regard to the development that surrounded it. As a result, malls, offices and housing tracts simply leapfrogged to less congested areas near arterials or freeway interchanges and demonstrated little visual or spatial connection with their surroundings.

Urban renewal programs provided federal funds and legal tools for injecting these suburban approaches into cities, where architects and planners advocated tearing out "blighted" housing and industrial buildings and replacing them with modern apartment and office towers. While the ostensible rationale of these efforts was to improve urban social and economic conditions, they also cleared the way for massive infusions of capital investment by wiping out complex street, ownership and leasing patterns.

Following the ideas of architect-planners like Le Corbusier, urban renewal buildings disdained traditional urban forms and stood as isolated objects surrounded by plazas, park-like open spaces or parking lots. Cities also were reconfigured to accommodate auto traffic: Side streets and alleys were closed to create large "superblock" compounds free of cars; other streets were widened and straightened to serve as high-speed arterials. Loop and spur freeways were wrestled through central cities to pump even larger volumes of cars in and out.

What has the last century of suburb building and city planning wrought? By and large, these efforts have accomplished what they set out to do. They have liberated many people from crowded, unhealthy living conditions. They have established a social, economic and regulatory framework that unleashed enormous amounts of metropolitan development. But the land-use and transportation patterns that emerged have created problems of their own—many of which seem even more intractable than those posed by industrial cities.

Home ownership, a cornerstone of suburban life, is out of reach for an increasing number of households. Most do not fit the archetype of working husband, housewife and two children, rendering the traditional single-family, large-lot house increasingly irrelevant. The infrastructure costs for low-density, single-family development are staggering; in northern California, where such costs can add almost $30,000 to the cost of a new house,[7] even two-income households cannot afford the ideal three-bedroom, two-bathroom, three-car-garage house on a quarter-acre lot. Compounding this is the steep cost of automobility: keeping two cars can cost upwards of $10,000 a year.[8]

Sprawled, low-density suburban development is compromising the quality of life suburbs often promise. First, more and more leisure time is being spent on commuting. A one-hour commute consumes ten hours a week; congestion and mismatched housing and job locations force some people to commute two or more hours each way. Second, reliance on cars has a devastating impact on people who cannot drive or afford them: Children cannot travel to school or organized activities unless driven by somebody; teenagers, who need cars to have independent social lives, take after-school jobs to pay for their cars, cutting into studying and social time; elderly people who lose their drivers' licenses can no longer shop, visit or see doctors. Third, while suburbs might have once offered a healthy antidote to grimy industrial cities, cars are now generating tremendous air pollution, particularly in suburban metropolises like Denver, Los Angeles and Houston. Finally, attractive rural landscapes are being lost in region after region; even John Steinbeck's storied Salinas Valley is threatened.

Most problematic is the effect suburban dispersal and urban renewal have had on civic life. Social scientists debate the extent to which physical design creates or reflects social conditions. But current metropolitan settlement patterns have clearly exacerbated social, class and racial segregation and diminished the

How low-density sprawl compares to traditional development. Diagram by Andres Duany and Elizabeth Plater-Zyberk.

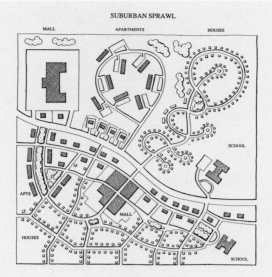

importance of common ground on which people of different backgrounds and outlooks might encounter each other. They have heightened, not ameliorated, urban social and economic decline and created vivid new symbols of urban distress. By isolating people in houses and cars and by segregating households into homogeneous enclaves, the late 20th century suburban metropolis has done little to replace the urban vitality it so aggressively replaced, and little to foster desperately needed civic responsibility in our increasingly diverse society.

The New Urbanism at Work

The deceptively simple responses the New Urbanists propose to these problems are based on one, equally simple principle: Community planning and design must assert the importance of public over private values. This principle serves as a reference for making the layers of decisions involved in creating a new community–from how the design of buildings relates to the streets they face to how land-use and density patterns are coordinated with regional transit routes. These planning and design approaches are being applied with equal vigor to new communities on the suburban edge, exurban towns and inner-city infill sites:

The center of each neighborhood should be defined by a public space and activated by locally oriented civic and commercial facilities. These places should not

be relegated to leftover sites at the edge of neighborhoods, and their form and image should be strengthened by surrounding building form, architecture and street patterns.

Each neighborhood should accommodate a range of household types and land uses. A neighborhood is a place for living, shopping and working. It should include building types varied enough to accommodate this range of activities and flexible enough to be easily adapted as different uses for them emerge.

Cars should be kept in perspective. Land-use patterns, street layouts and densities should make walking, bicycling and public transit viable alternatives to driving, especially for routine, everyday trips. Streets should be safe, interesting and comfortable for pedestrians. Improving traffic flow should be only one of many considerations in platting streets and designing neighborhoods.

Architecture should respond to the surrounding fabric of buildings and spaces and to local traditions. Buildings should not be conceived as objects

isolated from their surroundings; they should contribute to the spatial definition of streets, parks, greens, yards and other open spaces.

The New Urbanists draw upon a range of design traditions for inspiration. Their ideas about the relationships between planning and architecture reach back to the City Beautiful and Town Planning movements, which in turn reach back to Renaissance and Classical cities. Their ideas about connections between land use and transit draw on practices that shaped the development of streetcar suburbs and ideas that were advocated by regional planners in the early decades of the century.

One can even find a trace of 1920s "city efficient" and "city functional" influence in the New Urbanists' thinking. Peter Calthorpe and Andres Duany/Elizabeth Plater-Zyberk, whose projects and ideas have received the most attention, implicitly acknowledge that there should be some standard increment of suburban growth and that the proper focal point of any new community should be a public space that provides a locus for civic activities, local commercial uses and a transit stop connecting the neighborhood to the region. This underlying structure, they believe, gives a perceptible sense of order and identity at a range of scales.

The basic template of Peter Calthorpe's regional plans is the "transit-oriented development" or TOD, which channels growth into

Calthorpe Associate's TOD (transit-oriented development) concept combines regional transportation and land-use strategies with detailed plans for proposed transit-oriented communities (bottom and right).

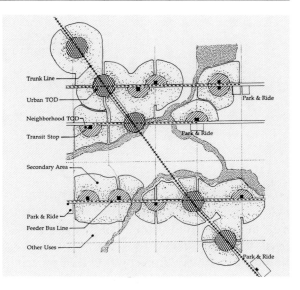

discrete nodes along light-rail and bus networks. A TOD, which is like a streetcar suburb-meets-edge city, exploits a basic relationship between transportation and land use: Put more origin and destination points within an easy walk of a transit stop and more people will use transit. Each TOD would be a dense, tightly woven community that mixes stores, housing and offices in a compact, walkable area surrounding a transit station. Calthorpe has written that in theory 2,000 homes, a million square feet of commercial space, parks, schools and day care could fit within a quarter-mile walk of the station, or about 120 acres.[9] In the same space a typical suburban developer might build just 720 single-family homes.

Closest to the station would be space for retail and service businesses, professional offices, restaurants, health clubs, cultural facilities and public uses—making jobs, goods, entertainment and services easily accessible to TOD residents and transit riders without requiring auto usage. Buildings near the center could have large floorplates to accommodate back-office and bulk retail uses. They could rise several stories, enabling a mix of commercial, office and even residential uses. And they could require less parking because of their location near transit and housing and because businesses with different peak periods (such as movie theaters and offices) can share parking.

Near the commercial area would be a mix of small-lot single-family houses, duplexes, town-houses and apartments—suitable and affordable for families, singles, empty-nesters, students and the elderly. Housing would be clustered around courtyards or parks that would link with larger public spaces, day care and recreation facilities. A final ring of development, in the quarter mile surrounding the core, would consist of single-family detached homes or larger-scale commercial enterprises. Although this sounds like typical suburban development, Calthorpe would encourage minimum average densities of 10 to 15 units per net acre (enough to support a bus line) and focus neighborhoods around shops, day-care facilities and parks.

Calthorpe's plans for Portland, Sacramento and San Diego propose a range of TODs: An "urban TOD" is located directly on a main transit route and is suitable for job-generating and high-intensity uses like offices, retail centers and

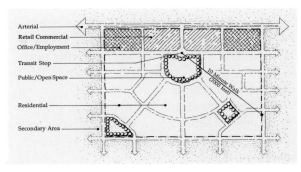

high-density housing. A "neighborhood TOD," located on a feeder bus line, would have a residential and local-serving shopping focus. TODs could be located not only in new growth areas but also in infill or redevelopment sites, which could evolve from auto-oriented to pedestrian-oriented places. Rio Vista West, a TOD proposed for San Diego, incorporates a 120,000-square-foot discount retail operation.[10]

The "traditional neighborhood development" (TND) approach conceived by Andres Duany and Elizabeth Plater-Zyberk (their firm is known as DPZ) and others operates at a smaller scale, includes more fine-grained regulation and varies more in response to local conditions than Calthorpe's TOD approach, but it is rooted less strongly in convictions about regional planning and the importance of transit. TND-like master plans have been proposed in a range of scenarios, from resort communities (Seaside and Windsor, Florida) to redeveloping shopping centers (Mashpee, Massachusetts) to mobile home parks (Rosa Vista, in Mesa, Arizona) to traditional suburban settings (Kentlands, in Gaithersburg, Maryland).

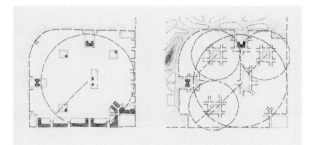

Architects Duany and Plater-Zyberk's TND model proposes a five-minute walk (no more than one-quarter mile) for one's daily needs and a three-minute maximum walk to neighborhood parks.

The basic building block of DPZ's community plans is the neighborhood, which is sized (from 40 to 200 acres) and configured (a radius of no more than one-quarter mile) so that most of its homes are within a three-minute walk of neighborhood parks and a five-minute walk of a central square or common. There, a meeting hall, child-care center, bus stop and convenience store are located. Each neighborhood would include a variety of housing types suitable for different household types and income groups.

In most DPZ projects, neighborhoods are nested and layered into larger units called villages or towns; what makes each community unique is that the patterns of overlapping and connection never repeat from one place to the next. Groups of neighborhoods form villages, which generally are separated from each other by greenbelts but connected by major streets. A village school might be located in a place where several neighborhoods come together. Civic and commercial uses that serve the village (such as recreational facilities or a cinema) or a broader area (such as a fire station, conference center or retirement home) often are located along main streets and next to public spaces.

A town, which might comprise several villages and neighborhoods, can include an even larger variety of commercial or institutional uses. Avalon Park, in Orlando, includes several

towns that are specialized according to the regional services they provide. One contains a university campus and cultural facilities; another features a large component of office space and related services; others incorporate the retail activity associated with a regional mall and with a typical commercial strip.

An equally important characteristic of the New Urbanists' proposals is the way neighborhoods and communities are knit together. DPZ is a forceful advocate of platting neighborhoods with grid-like street patterns, as was common practice through the 1920s. Street networks with frequent connections, they argue, ease traffic congestion by providing a choice of paths for any trip, yet tame cars by requiring frequent stops. Such networks make pedestrian and bicycle movement easier by slowing auto traffic and making trips shorter than in places with hierarchical street systems; combined with requirements for mixing land uses, they could produce communities in which walking is a realistic choice for most everyday trips. Moreover, networks with intersections at regular intervals create a sense of scale and order not evident in typical subdivisions, improving one's sense of orientation.

The imagery of the grid does not imply that all streets will be designed similarly. DPZ's codes sometimes call for a dozen different types of streets—boulevards, streets, courts, roads, lanes,

alleys and others—each with its own dimensions and specifications for street and sidewalk width, tree planting, on-street parking, traffic speed and pedestrian crossing time. Consequently, each street's character reflects more precisely its location and use, as opposed to the uniform, overscaled local and collector streets found in typical suburbs. Calthorpe's TOD plans often include a layer of radial streets emanating from the core. Radial streets, he argues, are efficient for pedestrians because they make the trip to the center of the community shorter. They serve as a powerful contrast to local streets, adding a civic presence and grandeur rarely found in suburbs, and they reinforce the clarity and identity of the center.

Just as important in Calthorpe's plans is the way TODs are connected to the region—each neighborhood is accessible to others and to existing communities through a network of light-rail and bus routes. No matter how walkable each neighborhood is, no matter how many shopping and job opportunities it provides, people in this highly mobile society will not live their entire lives within the confines of one community. Nowadays, suburban travel patterns resemble a tangled web, not a hub-and-spoke pattern with all trips leading to central cities and back. But when these diffuse travel patterns are spread over low-density areas, transit is impossible. By directing development

Calthorpe Associates' plan for the city of San Diego demonstrates how the TOD concept operates on several scales at once.

The plan starts by recognizing a proposal to expand San Diego's immensely popular light-rail line throughout the city and demonstrating how nodes of transit-oriented development can be dispersed along the network (below left).

However, such development will encourage transit ridership only if there are a variety of land uses (housing, retail and employment centers) with easy pedestrian connections to transit.

Comparative plans contrast conventional development with TOD proposals. Near Tecolote Road (center, below and bottom), parking areas, arterials and culs-de-sac would be replaced with a fine-grained street network that converges on a transit stop and an adjacent park.

At University Town Centre (right, below and bottom), a shopping mall parking lot is filled in to create a pedestrian environment between a transit stop and the mall.

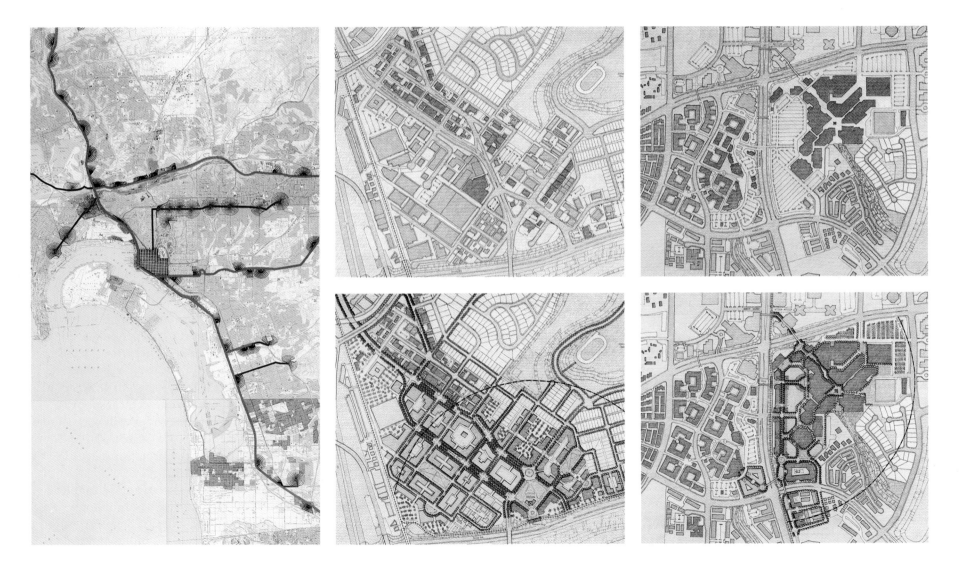

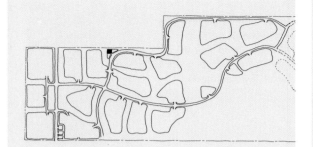

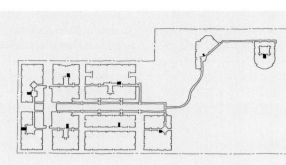

Typical suburban sprawl (left) contrasted with a New Urbanist proposal (right). The street system organizes a collection of defined neighborhoods. Churches and other civic buildings anchor community open spaces rather than float in parking lots.

Studies by Dover, Correa, Kohl, Cockshutt, Valle for Florida's Treasure Coast Regional Planning Council.

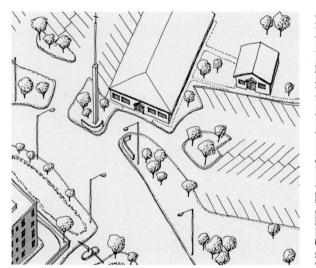

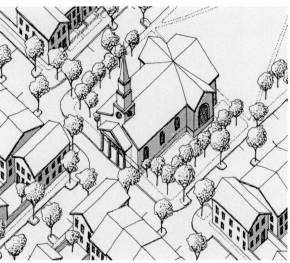

into denser nodes, the New Urbanists channel more trips into discrete corridors that could be served by transit.

What most distinguishes the neighborhoods proposed by the New Urbanists is the importance accorded to public spaces like greens, plazas and parks. Like traditional town commons or courthouse squares, these spaces are regarded as the civic focus for neighborhoods. They are located in central, prominent places, feature local commercial uses and are often connected to major streets. Community facilities (such as day care, churches, schools or meeting rooms) are assigned special positions adjacent to these spaces, underscoring the

importance both the institution and public space play in community life.

Many design strategies are used to reinforce the identity and stature of these spaces. They might be treated as figural elements; their location, shape and volume made distinct and identifiable. Buildings surrounding the space might be subject to special urban design guidelines, particularly streetwall and setback requirements that ensure they help define the volume of the space. The green in Kentlands' Old Farm neighborhood has several distinctive characteristics: adjacent to it are renovated farm buildings that convey a sense of history; lines of row-houses and tightly arranged detached houses

create enclosure on two sides; it sits at a high point in the neighborhood; and it incorporates a dramatic pre-existing stand of mature trees.

The same principles apply to street design. The New Urbanists reposition the detached house to better define the space of both the public street and private yard: A row of houses with regular setbacks can turn the street into a positive space. DPZ's codes dictate the proportion of building heights to street width, ensuring that each type of street has a distinct spatial character. In commercial and multi-family areas, buildings face public spaces such as streets and parks; parking lots are tucked behind or, if that is not possible, to the side—but not between the street and the building.

Streets also are designed to be comfortable, safe and interesting for pedestrians. At Laguna West, the main street runs perpendicular to a pre-existing six-lane regional artery so traffic, noise and pollution do not invade the central shopping and office area. Residential streets, narrower than those in most typical suburbs, slow traffic and allow for wider walkways. Trees planted in parking lanes also slow traffic and convey the sense that the street is a succession of smaller, human-scaled spaces.

The New Urbanists also pay close attention to architecture—particularly to a building's siting on its lot, massing and exterior detail—arguing that only certain types of buildings and spaces

Single-family houses are reconfigured so that they are better connected to the public life of the street and private spaces are more useable. Diagram by Dover, Correa, Kohl, Cockshutt, Valle.

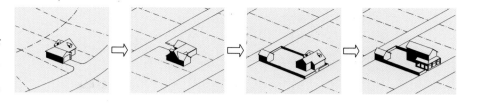

can create the range of public and private spaces that successful communities require. Most suburban zoning, for example, generates houses that are suited only for nuclear families and configures open space to surround houses and isolate them from other houses and the street. These Victorian-era legacies leave few of the well-defined neighborhood gathering places that can be found throughout traditional towns and cities, and they provide housing for a decreasing proportion of American households.

The neighborhoods proposed by the New Urbanists generally include a richer mix of building types than can be found in conventional suburban neighborhoods–from sideyard houses, rowhouses, semi-detached houses, cottages, secondary units, courtyard apartments, mid-rise apartments to shopfronts and offices with apartments above. Development is controlled by designating for each lot the building type that might be put there, and setback regulations are used to create functional open spaces and a strong relationship between buildings and streets.

The most detailed level of planning found in the New Urbanists' work is architectural design guidelines. DPZ's codes are the most elaborate and tightly drawn—sometimes dictating the thickness of mortar bands between bricks. The codes, which vary from town to town and often are based on historic styles and local vernacular,

can cover the design and placement of elements such as windows, garage doors, balconies and decorative columns; the selection and combination of materials; the massing and pitch of roofs; and more. These rules seem to exert an extraordinary level of control (particularly for mass-market housing) and generally reveal a tilt toward romantic and picturesque townscapes. But their purpose is to force greater attention to detail, thereby invigorating suburban architecture and imparting a greater level of civility to the streetscape.

Building the New American Dream

Given the enormous power that financial institutions, state highway agencies (one of them, Caltrans, has been nicknamed "the California Pentagon"), landowners and developers wield over local planning decisions, how influential will the New Urbanists be?

Remarkably, significant public sentiment is gathering behind them. In 1989, when a Gallup poll asked people what kind of place they would like to live in, 34 percent chose a small town, 24 percent a suburb, 22 percent a farm and 19 percent a city.[11] Dissatisfaction with suburban life surely contributes to this sentiment: Polls of San Francisco area residents routinely find traffic congestion and the lack of affordable housing are the most significant quality of life concerns.[12]

As unhappiness with congestion, development of sensitive lands, housing costs and air quality mounts, public agencies are being strong-armed into action. One outcome has been the unraveling of the political consensus that growth is good. Citizens routinely vote against development proposals because they expect growth will only worsen their quality of life; many communities are implementing growth controls or outright moratoria. Ironically, new development consequently occurs in ever more haphazard patterns, exacerbating these problems.

At the same time, a number of statewide and regional planning initiatives are lending credence to the New Urbanists' ideas. Air quality boards in Los Angeles and Sacramento are forcing local governments to reconsider land-use patterns that generate excessive automobile use. Washington State's tough growth management law has Seattle studying how to accommodate growth in TOD-like "urban villages" along its proposed light-rail system. Virginia's Loudoun County, responding to residents' fears that its rolling farmland would be converted into the next ring of Washington, D.C. suburbs, approved TND-style zoning that encourages traditional hamlets and villages. Recent California legislation requires localities to accommodate secondary units in some form. That state's voters have approved several local

The Regional Plan Association uses images like these to show alternative growth scenarios for the New York City metropolitan region. A commercial strip (far left) is contrasted with more compact, clustered development (left).

Duany and Plater-Zyberk relies on carefully drawn and colored renderings to convey a romantic, historicist impression of its proposals. This drawing of a proposed community in northern California (bottom) evokes the character of an Italian hill town.

building community support. During a charette, the firm confers with local officials, community leaders and interest groups; stages public meetings and presentations; and calls in local architects, planners and citizens to collaborate. The focused program becomes an event, capturing attention in ways that typical planning activities never do.

The New Urbanists place an enormous importance on communicating their proposals in terms that decision makers and everyday citizens can easily grasp, and their presentations are as strong on style as on substance. Calthorpe and Duany can be charismatic and compelling public speakers. DPZ's proposals are often accompanied by captivating if overly romantic perspectives (drawn by Charles Barrett and

tax increases to pay for building new mass transit systems, and there is talk of lining some of them with TOD-like development.

Advocacy groups are pressuring for development policies that echo New Urbanist ideas. California's Local Government Commission published a primer, *Land Use Planning for More Livable Places*, that incorporates many of these suggestions. The Regional Plan Association, a business-sponsored research and advocacy group, is urging municipalities in the New York/New Jersey/Connecticut metropolitan region to plan TOD-like "compact clusters" along regional commuter lines; one rail agency, New Jersey Transit, is studying how to promote transit-friendly development near its stations. The citizens' group 1,000 Friends of Oregon commissioned Calthorpe to develop a regional TOD plan along Portland's MAX light-rail system; similarly, The Treasure Coast Regional Planning Council asked Dover, Correa, Kohl,

Cockshutt, Valle (DCKCV), a Miami-based design and planning firm, to create a regional plan based on TND principles.

The New Urbanists believe the best way to change suburban development patterns is to change the rules of the game. They have concentrated on crafting subdivision regulations, zoning codes and regional plans—and on building the consensus necessary to win grassroots and political approval for their proposals. Their success has resulted from several factors: an inclusive approach to preparing plans, unusually powerful and carefully targeted presentations, a well-honed ability to advance their proposals as straightforward solutions to difficult problems, a persistence derived from their conviction and commitment toward their ideas and a pragmatism that enables compromise.

DPZ's on-site charettes, which concentrate most of the work for a project into several days of intense activity, have proven invaluable in

Intensive charettes led by Duany and Plater-Zyberk (left) involve local officials, community leaders, residents and local designers in preparing plans for new communities. This helps solidify the constituency for each project.

Dover, Correa, Kohl, Cockshutt, Valle prepares crisp computer simulations to help communities understand the future impact of its proposals. This view of a one-quarter-mile study area in Davie, Florida (left), reveals large gaps in the town's present urban fabric.

That same area (below) is shown to accommodate much greater density, when redeveloped according to New Urbanist principles.

colored by Manuel Fernandez-Noval) that emphasize the picturesque quality of the firm's town plans and architectural visions. DCKCV prepares realistic simulations that meld computer technology and photography in depicting existing and proposed build-out conditions.

Unlike purely visionary proposals, the New Urbanists' work demonstrates a practical concern with how they will be implemented. One DCKCV study explains how a project platted as a series of traditional neighborhoods on a grid could be developed in small components by numerous builders over many years–just like any other large-scale project. Some DPZ proposals incorporate a "regulating plan" that enables local government to reassert street platting and subdivision prerogatives that were ceded to private developers decades ago for efficiency's sake. The typical regulating plan is made up of three layers of rules; the more a proposal follows, the fewer discretionary reviews it will face. The DPZ-inspired TND-ordinance is a prototype planning document that local governments can adopt and developers can implement without staging an intensive charette. The ordinance follows the legal precedent of the planned unit development but is designed to produce traditional neighborhood layouts and architectural forms.

Nevertheless, businesses and public officials have erected their share of hurdles. Early

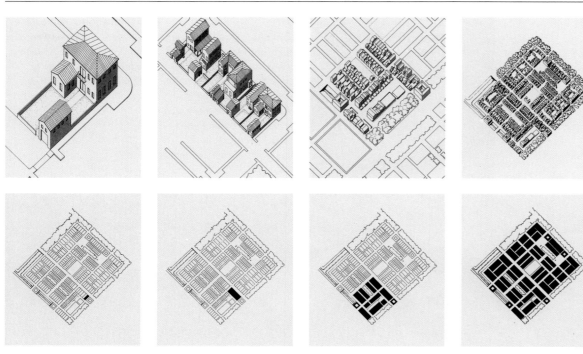

This series of drawings by Dover, Correa, Kohl, Cockshutt, Valle shows that New Urbanist proposals can be parceled to independent builders in the same increments as those used in conventional suburbs.

The options include (from far to near left) one lot at a time, a half block, a ward or a complete neighborhood.

versions of the TOD developed by designer-educators like Calthorpe, Douglas Kelbaugh and Daniel Solomon did not include a "secondary ring" of detached homes; Calthorpe introduced this feature to accommodate developers' demands for a greater proportion of single-family detached housing. When Laguna West's developers asked that the grid be replaced by a standard cul-de-sac arrangement, Calthorpe compromised again but designed pedestrian connections where through streets would have been. At Kentlands, DPZ planned a two-story day-care center to frame a nearby civic space, but no national day-care chain would agree to operate it—one-story buildings require less staff and have lower insurance costs. (A local operator ultimately agreed to move in.) The city balked at streets less than 20 feet wide, fearing that fire trucks would not be able to get through, until builders agreed to install fire sprinklers in houses along those streets.[13]

At a larger scale, it has been difficult to integrate TODs with transit. In Santa Clara County, California, where the existing light-rail line is expanding, developers have been unable to accumulate large tracts of land near stations and local officials have been reluctant to use their redevelopment powers to assemble sites. In Sacramento, although there are long-range plans for light rail to serve Calthorpe's Laguna West project, there is no guarantee. This means that transit may not be implemented until after development occurs, or that transit-oriented development may lag decades behind the extension of a transit line.

Nevertheless, one could argue that with either transit or TODs in place, it is more likely that a link between transit and denser development eventually will emerge. This is happening now around stations on the San Francisco region's BART system, where dense station-area development had been resisted for decades.

Now cities like Concord, Pleasant Hill and Hayward are planning for a new generation of growth around their stations.

Prospects for the New Urbanism

The projects presented in this book hardly reveal the extent to which principles of the New Urbanism are influencing American city and suburban design. Countless firms and planning agencies are embracing these strategies in redevelopment plans, design review guidelines and zoning laws. Toronto, for example, is studying how zoning and design guidelines can encourage small-scale infill projects along its main streets, which already are pedestrian-oriented transit corridors. For a decade, New York City has been rewriting its Le Corbusier-influenced "tower-in-the-park" zoning ordinances to encourage shorter, squatter buildings more like its fabled brownstones, Park Avenue apartments and "wedding cake" office towers.

Just as Seaside put the TND concept on the map, the 1979 master plan for Manhattan's Battery Park City (Alexander Cooper and Stanton Eckstut) showed how traditional street patterns and building forms could be introduced on urban infill and redevelopment sites. Numerous similar plans are now proceeding, most notably in Los Angeles (Playa Vista—Moule & Polyzoides; Moore Ruble Yudell; DPZ; Hanna Olin), San Francisco (Mission Bay—EDAW; ELS;

A plan for the community of Southport in West Sacramento, California, by Duany and Plater-Zyberk proposes a unique implementation strategy. It links the ease of obtaining permits with a developer's willingness to follow a highly detailed regulating plan.

This "carrot" approach outlines three levels of compliance. Level I of the plan (below left) determines the form of all streets, blocks and public spaces.

Developers seeking approval for such plans would face a modest fee and a six week wait for permitting. This contrasts with the lengthy, expensive environmental review and public approval process that is the norm for development in most areas of California.

Level II (below center) requires that major streets, retail centers, public buildings and parks be sited according to the master plan. Conforming projects would require a six-month wait and a somewhat larger fee.

Level III developments (below right) are similar in scale to most "pod" projects now seen in the suburbs. This approach locates only the largest collector streets, activity centers, school sites and greenbelts between each developed area.

Developers in this scenario would face the "normal" battery of review for such projects. This typically means years of delay plus often onerous fees for consultants, lawsuits and mitigation of project impacts.

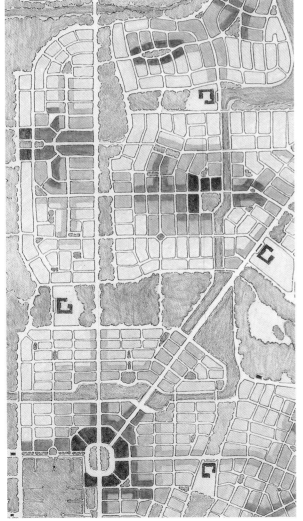

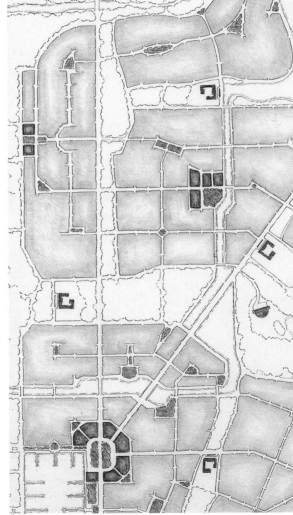

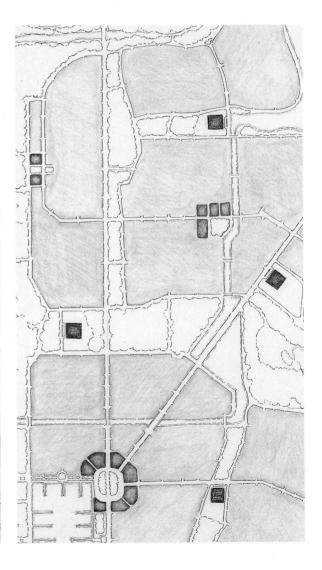

Mission Bay (below), a proposal for redeveloping a large industrial site in San Francisco, builds on the city's pattern of blocks, rowhouses, neighborhood commercial streets and figural open spaces.

Ghent Square (bottom left) in Norfolk, Virginia, is a redevelopment project that integrates with an existing historic neighborhood. (Harry Weese and Associates, 1970-90)

At Harbor Point in Boston (bottom center), a partly abandoned public housing project (bottom right) was converted to mixed-income housing. Infill rowhouses and a new street network create a better relationship between buildings, streets and other public spaces.

Battery Park City (right) extended New York's street grid to a waterfront landfill site and called for apartment buildings whose massing and appearance are evocative of Manhattan's historic apartment districts.

Baltimore's widely praised Oriole Park (right and bottom left) is regarded as a planning success because it reasserts the importance of downtown within the larger region, it respects the city's street plan and nearby historic fabric and it connects to public transportation.

Gateway Cleveland, a downtown revitalization effort (bottom right), includes a similarly designed stadium. Projects like these mediate thoughtfully between large-scale, auto-dependent uses and traditional urban scale.

Solomon Inc.; Skidmore Owings and Merrill) and Boston (Harbor Point–Goody, Clancy). In New York, Peterson/Littenberg's Clinton redevelopment plan injects innovative new interior block public spaces into the original Manhattan grid.

Even new baseball stadiums are being designed with principles of the New Urbanism in mind. Baltimore's Oriole Park at Camden Yards (HOK Sports), for example, fits snugly within the city's existing grid (reinforcing the public space of the street), connects to nearby light-rail and commuter railroad lines (providing an option to auto travel) and is within a short walk of a range of housing, retail and office facilities (adding to the local diversity of activities). Projects like this and Cleveland's new downtown plan and baseball stadium (Sasaki Associates) reinforce the role of center cities as regional activity centers, and their design reverses decades of building fortress-style stadiums surrounded by acres of parking.

While it is likely the design precepts embodied in the New Urbanism will influence the shape of new communities for years to come, their impact on peoples' lives will be less certain, for several reasons. First, some critics contend New Urbanist projects (particularly DPZ's) emphasize visual style over planning substance. There is a danger that the movement will be characterized by houses designed in

historic styles and neighborhoods planned to have a small-town feel, while more substantial planning ideas are abandoned out of frustration or indifference. (A flip through the real estate section of any newspaper reveals that many new developments are adopting New Urbanist design approaches only superficially, as motifs to enhance their marketing strategies.)

Second, the New Urbanists' large-scale suburban and exurban proposals have been criticized for providing a justification for promulgating sprawl, whatever the improvement in planning and design. In fact, while the isolated, dispersed projects that are likely to be built will improve peoples' lives at the neighborhood scale, the impact of the New Urbanism at a broader scale could be minimal unless regional planning initiatives like those in Sacramento, San Diego, Portland, Seattle and Toronto are followed through, and unless these principles are applied routinely to urban infill projects.

Similarly, the New Urbanism has not yet fully tackled some fundamental metropolitan development issues. It responds only minimally to ecological concerns at the local and regional scales (Calthorpe plans to address this in a forthcoming book). Moreover, the projects in this book have taken only tentative steps, at best, to cope with America's sharpening economic and social divisions. For example, they expand housing opportunities only in a limited way; housing for low-income households and groups with special needs will require additional government initiatives.

Finally, the types of communities the New Urbanists envision are unlikely to emerge from design initiatives alone. Once a project is completed, layers of community organization will evolve. Will the beautifully drawn neighborhood open space be controlled by a private home owners' association, or will it be truly public? Will community facilities, such as day-care centers, churches and meeting rooms be available to all? Could cooperative systems of ownership (as practiced in European co-housing and mutual housing models) provide an even stronger basis for community cohesion?

The New Urbanism is a welcome step forward, but it is only a step. At best, the movement has refocused the public's attention more strongly on how the design of our communities has a very real impact on our lives. If the presence of projects in the landscape can inspire a broadened, sustained public debate about the nature of American communities; if Seaside, Laguna West, Riviera Beach and their descendents can create vivid alternatives to current atomized, privatized development patterns, then the New Urbanism might truly begin to reshape the American dream.

Notes

1. Gwendolyn Wright, *Building the Dream: A Social History of Housing in America* (Cambridge, MA: MIT Press, 1981), and Robert Fishman, *Bourgeois Utopias* (New York: Basic Books, 1987).
2. Clarence A. Perry, "The Neighborhood Unit," in Committee on the Regional Plan of New York and Its Environs, *The Neighborhood Unit* (New York, 1929), pp. 34-35, as excerpted in Christopher Tunnard, *The Modern American City* (New York: D. Van Nostrand, 1968), pp. 163-164.
3. Spiro Kostof, *The City Shaped: Urban Patterns and Meanings Through History* (London: Thames and Hudson, 1991), p. 80.
4. Kenneth T. Jackson, *The Crabgrass Frontier* (New York: Oxford University Press, 1985), pp. 205-206; Kostof, *The City Shaped*, p. 82.
5. Peter G. Rowe, *Making a Middle Landscape* (Cambridge, MA: MIT Press, 1991).
6. Jackson, *The Crabgrass Frontier*, p. 239; Peter Calthorpe, *The Next American Metropolis* (New York: Princeton Architectural Press, 1993).
7. "Fees Cast Shadow on Affordable Housing," *Housing and Development Report* (San Francisco: Bay Area Council), October 1991.
8. Calthorpe, *The Next American Metropolis*.
9. Peter Calthorpe, "Pedestrian Pockets: New Strategies for Suburban Growth," in *The Pedestrian Pocket Book* (New York: Princeton Architectural Press, 1989), p. 11.
10. Much of this description comes from Calthorpe, *The Next American Metropolis*.
11. Andres Duany and Elizabeth Plater-Zyberk, "The Second Coming of the Small Town," *The Utne Reader*, May/June 1992.
12. See various issues of *Housing and Development Report* (San Francisco: Bay Area Council) that report on the annual Bay Area Poll.
13. Todd W. Bressi, "Cities to Walk In," *Metropolis*, March 1990; and Edward Gunts, "Plan Meets Reality," *Architecture*, December 1991.

Establishing the Urban Pattern

*We shall not attain to cities and villages
that are beautiful until we learn artistically to
plan them. Transformations may help us
greatly, as London and Paris and some
examples at home show; but a mended article is
never as good as one well made at first.*

Charles Mulford Robinson,
The Improvement of Towns and Cities, 1907

Seaside

Walton County, Florida, 1981

The Seaside plan (below) was designed to optimize waterfront access and views for all of the town's residents, not just those with beachfront homesites.

The community's porch-lined streets (opposite) and walkways all lead eventually to the beach or the town center. The semi-octagonal form of the town center (bottom center in plan) faces out to the Gulf of Mexico across the main road which passes through town.

Seaside's principal public places include (far left in plan) a school site, the town hall (cross-shaped building) and square, an open-air market (north of the town center) and a tennis club (upper right).

Only 10 years old and occupying a mere 80 acres (approximately that of an average-sized regional shopping mall), the coastal town of Seaside on Florida's panhandle has nevertheless come to assume a place of great importance in American urbanism. Though dismissed by some critics as "too cute" and not a "real town," this new community-in-the-making has been the focus of constant media attention since its founding. Recognized in 1990 by *Time* magazine as the "Best of the Decade" in design, Seaside has also appeared in *U.S. News & World Report*, *Smithsonian*, *Travel & Leisure*, *People* and *The Atlantic Monthly*. Numerous television networks have featured the town, as did Prince Charles in his BBC television show and subsequent book on architecture.

Seaside's high visibility and innovative planning concepts have already helped to spark a broad rethinking of the design of America's new communities. Differing in more than just its outward appearance, Seaside also represents a departure in terms of the urban principles and working methods that led to it.

The town's principal designers, architects Andres Duany and Elizabeth Plater-Zyberk, pursued one overriding goal in the conception of the town—that of fostering a strong sense of community. This emphasis seeks to reverse a trend toward alienation that the designers have observed in many aspects of contemporary

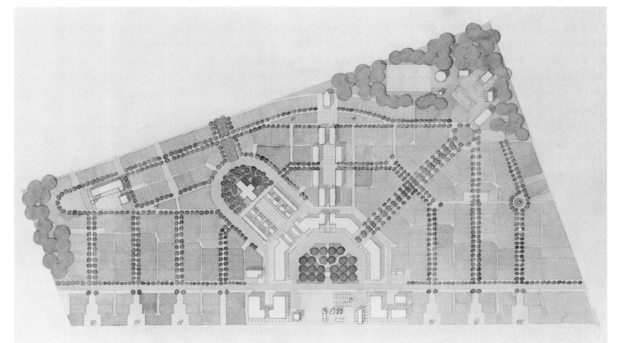

Private houses, condominiums, apartments and retail businesses dominate the waterfront along Florida's north gulf coast (left), a place referred to by some as the "Redneck Riviera." Like many beach areas, this region has suffered from years of poor planning.

While gulf coast beaches are among the finest anywhere, most communities in the vicinity of Seaside have made little provision for public access and enjoyment of this natural asset.

More than 40 drawings exploring the formal possibilities of Seaside's different building types (example, right) helped the design team refine the criteria for the town code.

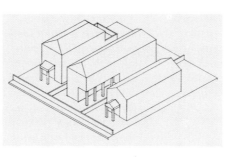

Seaside's design places an emphasis on the town's public spaces (opposite), which range from its main square to the pedestrian-only footpaths at the center of blocks.

suburban life. In their view, such alienation and related social ills result from the increasing privatization of the public realm that used to exist in towns and cities. They proposed that Seaside take an opposite course by consciously asserting the primacy of public *over* private space.

Consistent with that approach, Duany and Plater-Zyberk first defined the town's public spaces—not just what is commonly thought of as public spaces, like parks or squares, but also the streets, boulevards, walks and natural features of the site, such as the beach and dunes. Then, by using an innovative coding strategy, private buildings are allowed to gradually fill in around the public spaces, bringing greater definition to the plan as it reaches completion. This additive process contrasts with the erosion of public space that typically occurs when growth takes place in a more suburban context.

To encourage community interaction, Seaside's compact layout follows the principle of the "five-minute walk"–the time it takes most people to cover a quarter mile on foot. With all one's daily needs inside that distance, the town becomes a more pedestrian-friendly place. It reduces car dependence and promotes casual social encounters among residents.

Seaside's projected population of 2,000 compares in size to a typical American small town or city neighborhood from the 1920s or 1930s, as does its mixture of uses. The town will eventu-

ally contain 350 houses along with about 300 other dwelling units including apartments, outbuildings and hotel rooms. Its principal public facilities include a school, a town hall, an open air market, a tennis club, a tented amphitheater and a tiny post office. Shops and offices are also part of the plan.

Originally designed to be an inexpensive beachfront vacation community, Seaside today feels more like an upscale resort. The town has seen a tenfold increase in residential lot prices in the decade since it was founded, attracting the interest of developers worldwide. That figure is even more impressive when one considers that land prices in adjacent areas have remained stable or even dropped during the same period. All of the community's homesites are sold and 225 houses have been built. The town now stands at 70 percent completion. Since much of the remaining build-out involves Seaside's civic and commercial areas, it may still be too early to determine how well the town works as a complete community.

What's indisputable is that Seaside has become more widely known and influential than anyone, including its developer or designers, thought it would be. Calling the town's success a "stroke of providence," Plater-Zyberk insists that she and her partner Duany did not set out to "solve all of America's urban problems" in their design for Seaside. She credits the town's

viability as a model for other new developments to the extensive research undertaken in collaboration with the firm's unusually supportive client, developer Robert Davis.

Soon after Davis decided to develop the site, he, his wife and architect Duany roamed the region, exploring old southern towns to determine what makes them work so well. They gradually synthesized a design approach for the town based on what they observed in their travels as well as research into other classic planning models from the past.

The pivotal event of Seaside's design process was a two-week, on-site work session involving many individuals—client, staff, fellow designers, local officials and other consultants. This was the firm's first use of the "charette" methodology for participatory planning. Duany and Plater-Zyberk, along with several other firms, have since adopted this way of working as a standard technique.

To ensure variety within the town, the planners left the design of individual buildings to others. Although Seaside has become known as a showplace for both well-known and up-and-coming architects, many of its most successful residential designs have been the product of builders or home owners.

The town's urban code, a simple one sheet poster, may be responsible for the ease with which nonprofessionals have been able to

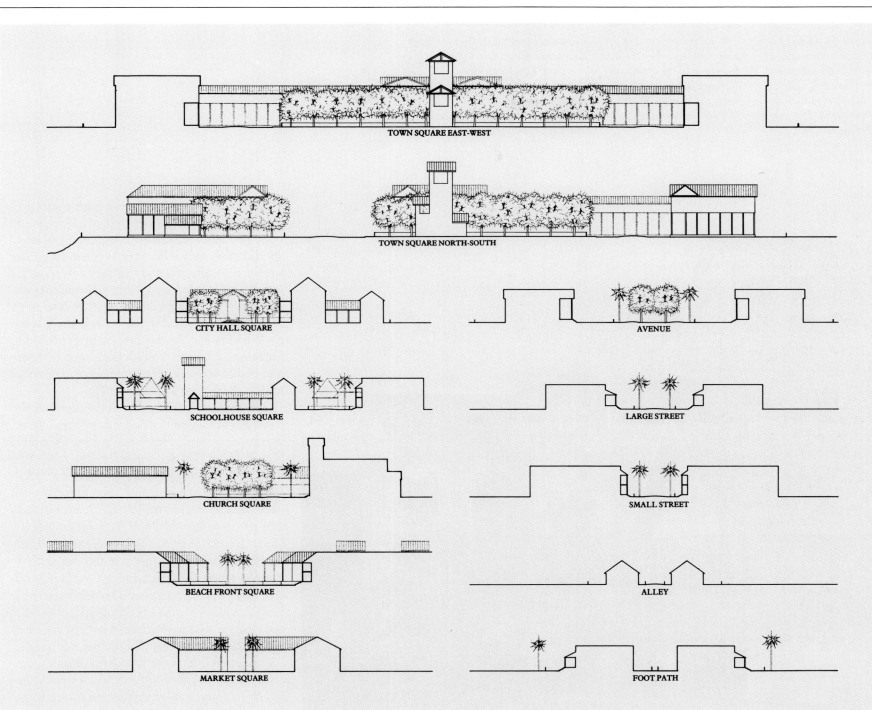

TOWN SQUARE EAST-WEST

TOWN SQUARE NORTH-SOUTH

CITY HALL SQUARE

AVENUE

SCHOOLHOUSE SQUARE

LARGE STREET

CHURCH SQUARE

SMALL STREET

BEACH FRONT SQUARE

ALLEY

MARKET SQUARE

FOOT PATH

Seaside's much touted sense of community is largely a result of the closeness of houses to one another and the street (below). The town code mandates that all private buildings follow a consistent build-to line, thus helping to define the public space of the street.

On north-south streets, this uniform setback preserves view corridors out to the sea. Front porches of a minimum size and proximity to the street are another element of Seaside's urban code.

Within the restrictions of its zoning, architectural and landscape regulations, considerable variety nevertheless exists at Seaside. Each house is unique, with designs spanning a wide range of architectural styles.

conceptualize and implement their own designs. Prescriptive, rather than proscriptive, the code describes what form a building can and should take, rather than the reverse. Its guidelines are communicated through a series of simple diagrams and captions that physically describe a specific building type. Several of the ideas first developed in the Seaside code were the basis for the Traditional Neighborhood Development (TND) Guidelines used by Duany and Plater-Zyberk on later projects (several of which are featured in this book).

The designers take pride in the fact that the town has achieved the desired strong sense of community while closely following its intended physical plan. Unlike other recent master-planning efforts, many of which resemble a "catalogue" of the architectural styles popular during each decade of their build-out, Seaside's resilient urban structure seems to transcend such issues. Evidence of this is the way it graciously accommodates buildings of many disparate styles—Victorian, Neoclassical, Cracker, Modern, Postmodern and even Deconstructivist.

And while its unique combination of stylistic and programmatic elements may not together constitute a "real town" in the strictest sense, it's undeniable that the powerful ideas about community put forward at Seaside have already imparted some important lessons about the future of urbanism in America.

An aerial photo of Seaside (below), taken in 1989 shows the completed grid of streets. Blocks on the east side of town were nearly built-out, while the western part had only a few houses.

Streets (bottom), originally surfaced with crushed shells, ultimately were covered with brick pavers. Sheet metal, Seaside's predominant roofing material (right), is one of several options suggested in the town code.

Seaside has the unmistakable character of a beach community. A network of sand walkways (opposite) cuts through the middle of blocks, enabling one to walk comfortably to the beach in bare feet.

Named "Krier walks" after the architect Leon Krier who suggested them, these walkways are sometimes the main access to outbuildings at the rear of lots.

Beachfront development at Seaside accommodates both public and private uses. Unlike other states, Florida doesn't limit private oceanfront building. Nevertheless, the plan maintains a predominantly public beach.

A group of six identical rental units known as the "Honeymoon Cottages" (below left) and a few single-family houses (example, bottom left) are the only private dwellings located on the beach side of the main coastal road.

Other structures, such as the pavilions and boardwalks (below right and overleaf) and the beach itself, are considered to be public facilities for the use of all residents and visitors.

Seaside's distinctive beach pavilions reflect developer Robert Davis' keen interest in architecture and design. Referred to as "follies," their primary function is to mark beach entrances and terminate views from streets in the town.

Some of the follies also serve as cabanas with facilities for beach-goers. All of them have seating where one can enjoy a view of the gulf.

The boardwalks that connect the pavilions and beach were added later to the program—they respond to recent state legislation aimed at preserving sensitive beach-front and dune areas.

The Pensacola Street beach pavilion (below left), designed by Tony Atkin, is topped by a weather vane in the shape of a pelican. It is now being used as the town's chapel.

The East Ruskin Street beach pavilion (below) was designed by Stuart Cohen and Anders Nereim. Tupelo Street's beach pavilion (bottom and opposite), designed by Ernesto Buch, was Seaside's first folly.

Civic and commercial places are where people gather at Seaside. The town's market area (below) uses shipping containers as a basic module of construction. Their industrial character is softened by the addition of gable roofs, wooden columns and fabric canopies.

Seaside's first commercial buildings (right) were designed by Deborah Berke and Steven Holl. Berke's building (left in photo) is a market; Holl's (center in photo) includes shops and offices with dwellings above.

Seaside's post office (bottom right) is a modest facility situated at the focal point of the town plan. Designed by Robert Davis with Robert Lamar, its Neoclassical design and strategic location have made it an architectural symbol for the town.

The parking lot of the motor court (left), designed by Scott Merrill, is the largest single aggregation of parking spaces within Seaside. A canopy of trees makes this a comfortable place for both people and cars.

Throughout the town, one is able to perceive axial relationships between special structures and public spaces. The town's water tower, visible on the horizon (below), terminates a street vista from Tupelo Circle, the site of a small gazebo.

These relationships contribute significantly to one's sense of orientation within Seaside. Elements of consistency and variety combine to create a townscape that is active without being overly complex.

While many architects regard Seaside as a mecca for contemporary design, the majority of its homes (selected examples, this spread) reflect the indigenous traditions of the region.

Vernacular styles of the southeastern United States and the Caribbean provided the basis for the town's architectural codes. As one would expect, most houses designed by builders and home owners have been simple, direct responses to the town codes.

Early, Cracker-inspired houses at Seaside (example, right) illustrate the planning team's original intentions and expectations. As land prices increased, larger, more elaborate residences (below) became the norm.

Over the years, a number of prominent architects have designed homes at Seaside. Leon Krier, an internationally recognized architect, theorist and town planner, designed this house (opposite, left). Completed in 1989, the house was Krier's first built work.

The Schmidt House (opposite, upper right) by architects Deborah Berke and Carey McWhorter is a contemporary adaptation of a Charleston sideyard house. Berke was Seaside's town architect for several years.

Architect Walter Chatham designed this residence (opposite, bottom right) for his own family. Though it required a variance for its small front lawn (not visible in photo), this house otherwise is in full compliance with the town code.

Seaside's unique mix of styles, building types and uses (below) give it a texture and authentic variety that contrasts markedly with what one usually thinks of as a "planned community."

Eschewing any one overall theme or style, Seaside shows how highly diverse buildings can combine to create a lively, yet coherent place. Its master plan and codes ensure that individual buildings cannot compromise the town's underlying urban structure.

Laguna West

Sacramento County, California, 1990

The primary focus of the Laguna West master plan (below) is its 100-acre town center (opposite and top center of plan). It includes civic and commercial uses as well as several different forms of high- and medium-density housing.

Diagonal boulevards link this dense central zone with a surrounding secondary area of low-density, single-family homes. A 65-acre lake establishes a clear separation between both. Two islands within the lake provide a residential area of intermediate density.

Market conditions dictated the project's phasing, which focused initially on single-family homes in the secondary area. Most of Laguna West's public infrastructure was also completed in the first phase.

It could have been just another collection of forgettable suburban enclaves and office parks. Instead, developer Phil Angelides persuaded his partners and local government to try another approach for the 1,045-acre Laguna West site, 11 miles south of Sacramento.

The alternative design by Calthorpe Associates included all the same revenue-generating elements as a previously approved conventional scheme but reorganized them around defined public spaces and amenities: a village green, town hall, main street and neighborhood parks.

Dubbed a "better suburb" by the *Los Angeles Times*, Laguna West is the first application of Calthorpe's TOD (transit-oriented development) principles, now embraced in the general plan for Sacramento. Though not yet linked to transit, this community of 3,400 units includes a 100-acre town center of sufficient density to justify transit service (a scenario that is precluded with most suburban densities).

Laguna West's innovative planning concepts have helped it to gain a premium niche in the local real estate market. An independent survey recently showed that 84 percent of the community's residents preferred its pedestrian-oriented features over those of a conventional subdivision. While some argue that Californians will never give up their cars, Laguna West's example shows that many would like to live in a place that at least considers another option.

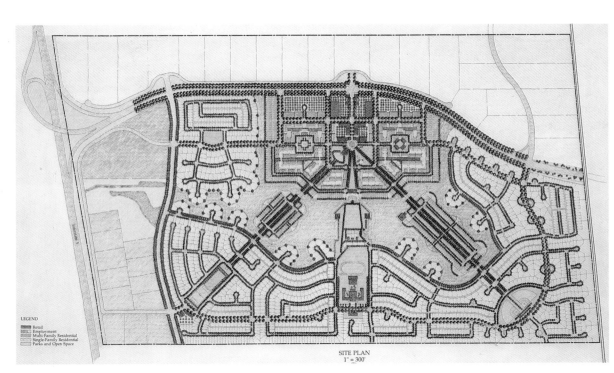

LEGEND
Retail
Employment
Multi-Family Residential
Single-Family Residential
Parks and Open Space

SITE PLAN
1" = 300'

A previous scheme for the property (plan, left) located workplace (shown in purple) and multi-family housing (dark brown) adjacent to the freeway and major arterials in order to buffer the community's lowest-density single-family homes (shown in gold).

By contrast, the current master plan (above) locates its highest-density housing close to shops and services. This enables more of the community's residents to be within walking distance of daily needs.

Laguna West's primary recreation area (opposite, top left and below, center of photo) is bounded on three sides by water. A swim center and running track within this park are shared with an adjacent school (not visible in photos).

Blocks in the town center include both residential and commercial uses. Laguna West's highest-density housing surrounds two residential squares (opposite, bottom left). The town hall and day-care center are located in a larger civic park (opposite, bottom right).

Highly desired water access and views (below and opposite, top right) at Laguna West have been carefully balanced between public use and private development.

A 20-foot easement provides nearly continuous pedestrian access to the lakefront. Custom homesites on small peninsulas extend out into the lake. Compact houses edging the town center face a lakefront promenade.

Laguna West's principal north-south spine (below) organizes the key civic and commercial components of the community. These uses are encountered in a defined sequence as one progresses into and through the town center (from left to right).

Light industrial and office workplace areas (shown in purple) line the north side of Laguna Boulevard, a major east-west arterial connection to nearby highways and a future light-rail station.

A four-block commercial core reconfigures many of the same elements typically found in a suburban retail strip. Anchor stores (indicated in orange) on the outer blocks retain arterial visibility but have been rotated to face toward the community's main street.

Smaller stores on the inner blocks (shown in red) define a nearly continuous street-wall along the main street and Laguna West's central circle. Senior housing (indicated in brown) completes these blocks.

The community's principal civic buildings (indicated in blue) occupy prominent locations around the central circle. A day-care center (at one o'clock) and the town hall/community center (four o'clock) frame one end of the town green.

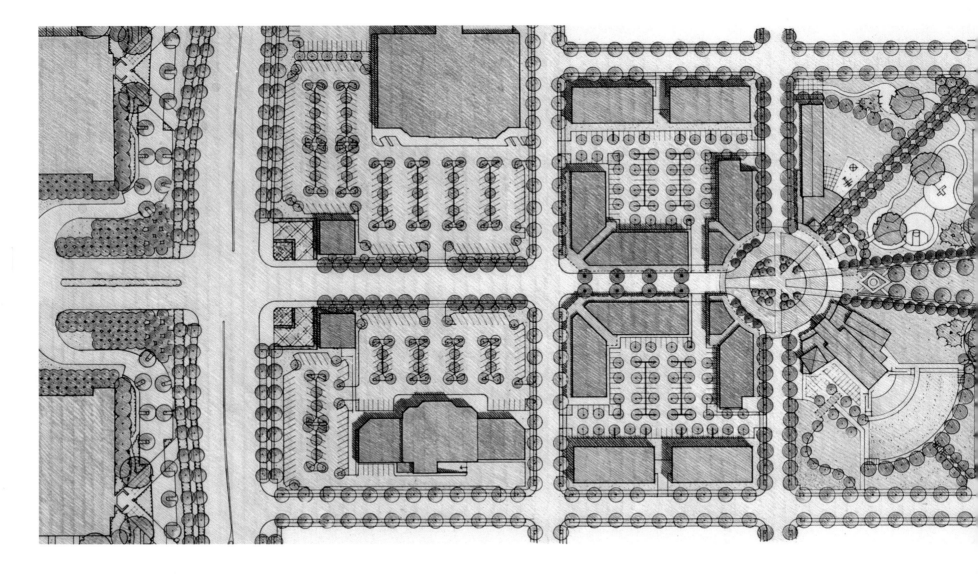

Two- and three-story walk-up apartments (shown in gold) and compact lakefront homes with accessory units (indicated in yellow) form a zone of medium-density housing around the civic and commercial core.

A continuous waterfront promenade lines the outer edge of the the town center. Several small bridges enable pedestrians to reach the community recreation area, swim center (shown in blue), elementary school and single-family residential areas beyond.

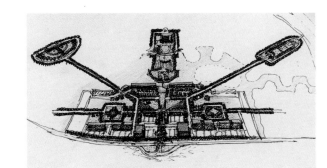

Laguna West's network of streets and public open spaces define the basic structure of the community (left). Two radial boulevards link the town center to neighborhood parks in surrounding single-family residential areas.

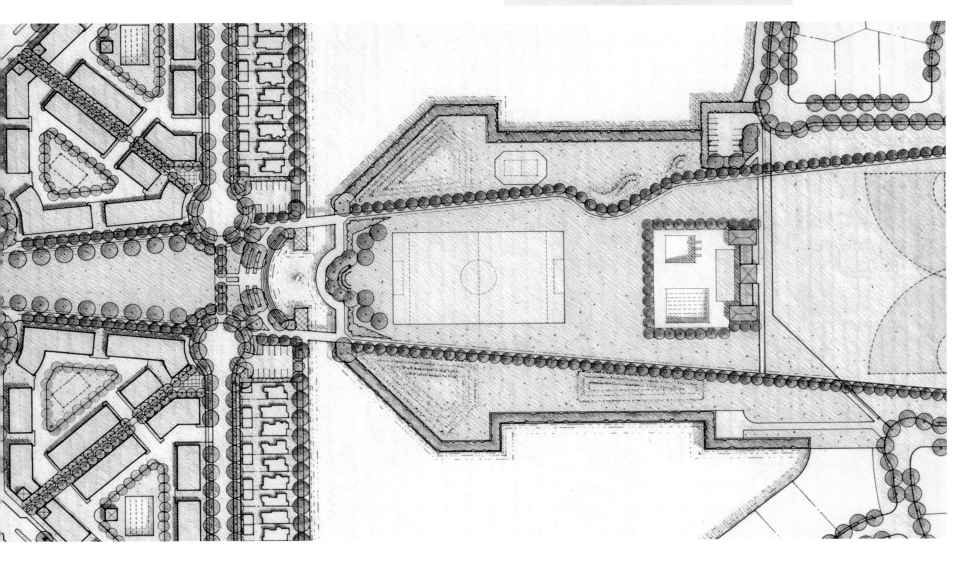

The first housing to be built within Laguna West's town center is a group of 80 compact homes on the lakefront promenade (this spread). With their accessory units, these detached residences achieve densities similar to multi-family housing (14 units per acre).

Four different floor plans are offered. The smallest unit at 1,100 square feet has two bedrooms and two baths on one level. The largest, at 1,800 square feet, includes three bedrooms and two and one-half baths on two floors.

Targeted at a number of different market niches, these houses have attracted the interest of both starter home buyers and "empty-nesters." These otherwise modest homes have a special distinction because of their proximity to water.

The lakefront promenade is the front entrance for these residences. Their porches and elevated stoops promote interaction between residents and passersby.

Two houses share a single driveway and parking court. This reduces the total paved area required for each car. Apartments over garages placed close to the sidewalk help maintain an active street presence at all hours.

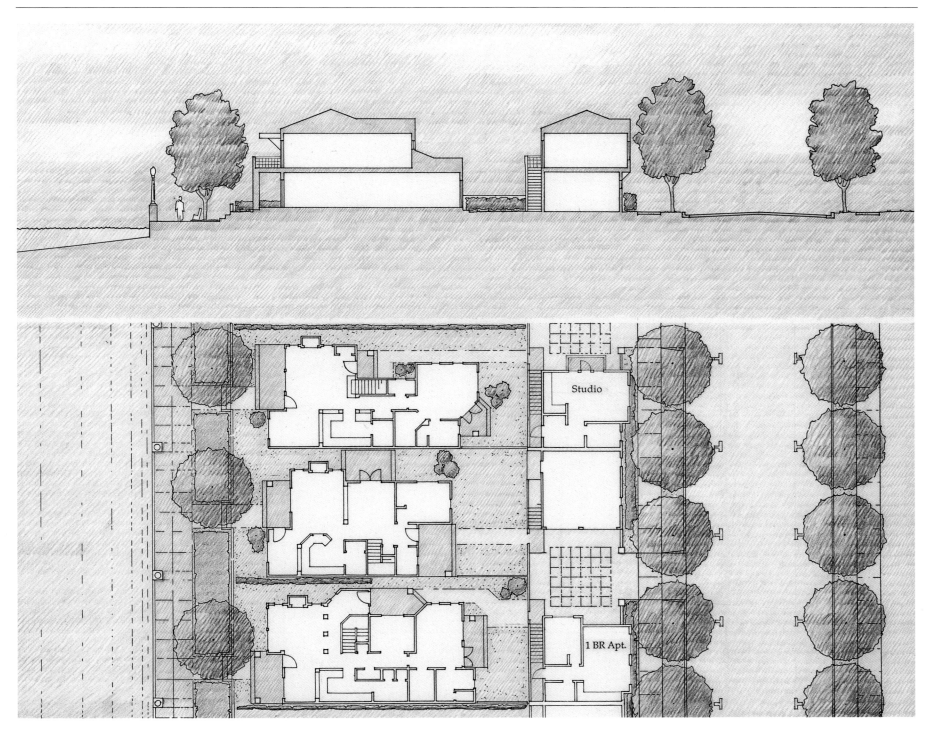

Studio

1 BR Apt.

SOUTHEAST ELEVATION (PARK)

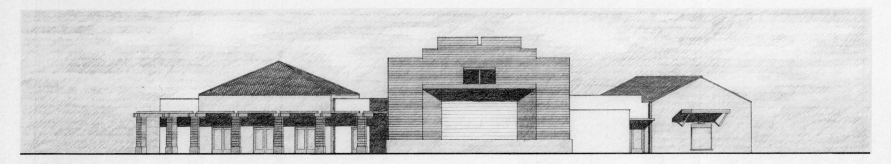

SOUTHWEST ELEVATION (AMPHITHEATRE)

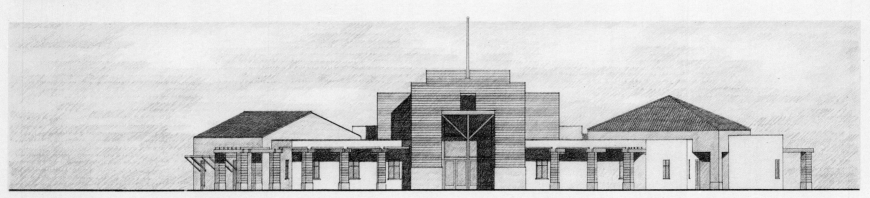

NORTHEAST ELEVATION (PLAZA)

Laguna West's main public building is its Town Hall (opposite and below right). This facility combines offices for the local parks and recreation department, an auditorium, a branch library and an outdoor amphitheater.

A community park adjacent to the Town Hall provides opportunities for both active and passive recreation (below left). Consistent with the development's emphasis on public space, Laguna West's most valuable land is dedicated to civic use.

Apple Computer has built one of its newest plants (bottom left) in the community. Located across an arterial from the town center, it is less than a five-minute walk from most residences.

Houses in Laguna West's secondary areas (this spread) incorporate a number of traditional elements that are considered innovative in the context of contemporary suburban development.

Front porches (below and opposite) are one such feature. A recent independent marketing study showed that 80 percent of the community's residents favored this architectural element, typically associated with older neighborhoods and small towns.

Garages are placed at the rear of most homes. "Hollywood" driveways are used to minimize the paved area in each yard. Carriage houses (opposite, left) are offered by some of Laguna West's home builders.

A broad range of sizes and styles of single-family homes are planned within the community. These range from a modest bungalow (opposite, top right) to more elaborate multi-level houses (opposite, bottom right).

Laguna West's design guidelines control the placement of garages, porches and the house's relationship to the street and its neighbors. The document also suggests ways to establish architectural diversity among the community's homes.

Kentlands

Gaithersburg, Maryland, 1988

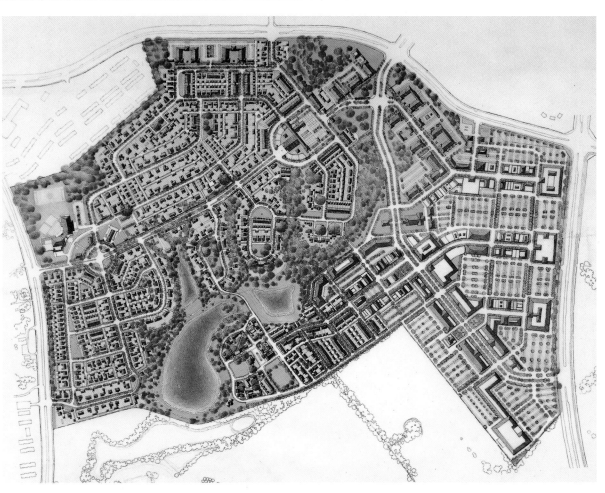

The town of Kentlands is the first application of the traditional neighborhood development (TND) principles to a real, year-round, working community. Unlike Seaside, which some critics dismiss as an isolated resort town and therefore not a true test of the TND concept, this community lies squarely in the path of suburban growth surrounded by housing subdivisions, shopping centers and office campuses.

Located within the city of Gaithersburg, just 23 miles northwest of Washington, D.C., in the heart of what some call the "I-270 technology corridor," Kentlands has been conceived as an authentic town made up of distinct neighborhoods, in the classic American tradition.

The master plan of the community, sited on the 356-acre Kent Farm tract, was the result of a widely publicized design charette led by town planners Andres Duany and Elizabeth Plater-Zyberk. It includes six neighborhoods, each combining elements of residential, office, civic, cultural and retail usage. To encourage diversity both in age and income level, a range of housing types and sizes is planned. For example, carriage houses, which may serve as retirement units, will exist next to single-family homes and townhouses, and rental apartments will be located above shops.

Kentlands includes a variety of civic facilities and public open spaces. A lake and wetland preserve, greenbelts and several small squares

A stately 19th century house (left), originally the focus of the Kent Farm, has been retained on the site. Some of Kentlands' newer homes (opposite) employ similar architectural forms.

The community plan (above) includes six distinct neighborhoods and a large retail center. This version of the retail center (right in plan) has three main streets, each terminated by an anchor department store.

The buildings, gardens and landscape features of the original Kent Farm influenced the design of the Old Farm neighborhood (below).

An early plan proposed the restoration of the farm's ornamental garden (right and center of illustration, below). The site was ultimately used for Kentlands' town commons (page 40).

help to define individual neighborhoods. A school and health club are located in the community, providing additional recreation areas. Clustered at one end of the town commons, several original buildings from the Kent Farm house a new cultural center. This complex is the centerpiece of the Old Farm neighborhood.

The town's principal retail center fronts two major arterials. Though initially conceived as a regional mall with anchor stores connected at its center to the town's main street, the current plan follows a more conventional suburban model—what has become known among retail developers as a "power center."

The ultimate build-out of Kentlands includes 1,600 residential units with a population of over 5,000 total residents. Construction began in 1989, and since then, all roads, water mains, and sewer lines have been completed. The elementary school is now operating, and the town's first church will soon be in use. Several local home builders, along with Kentlands' founding developer, have sold more than 750 lots. At this writing over 300 units are occupied.

Harsh economic times, particularly in the retail sector, have led to a financial restructuring of the development. It is now controlled by the the principal lender to the project, a local savings bank. Despite this change of ownership, the design team's intent is being followed as Kentlands moves steadily toward completion.

A planned cultural center on the site of the old farm is housed in an existing barn and large house (left and right, respectively, in illustration, below).

This civic use was initially proposed during the town's first design charette. The historic buildings have since been donated to the City of Gaithersburg, which will operate the facility.

A particularly prominent tree, known as the "old oak," was preserved as the focus for a small group of homes (left).

A regional retail center at the intersection of two busy arterials occupies a major portion of Kentlands' site. (below and plan, right).

In this early scheme, an otherwise conventional regional mall is connected at its food court entry to the town square. The hybrid center presents an urban face to the town, most of whose residents are expected to arrive on foot.

From nearby arterials the shopping center appears as a typical multi-anchor mall. Large parking areas around the center are shaped into blocks, anticipating possible future development.

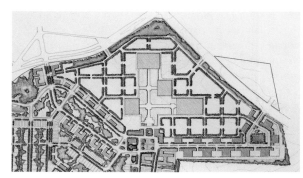

Kentlands' Midtown neighborhood (this page) joins the regional shopping center and the Old Farm neighborhood. It serves the local community with a combination of shops, offices and civic facilities.

As the transition zone between the intense regional retail activity of the shopping center at the town's edge and Kentlands' more residential neighborhoods, Midtown's square and streets provide a true public realm not found in most suburban developments.

Historic towns such as Alexandria, Virginia, and Princeton, New Jersey, offer proven models for the kind of urbanism that is envisioned in this neighborhood.

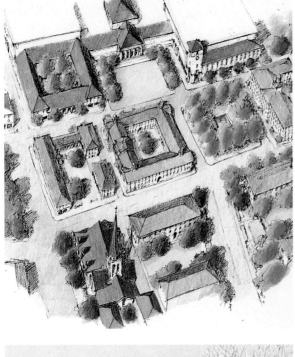

This model view (below) illustrates the fine-grained mix of uses and building types that are interwoven in one of Kentlands' residential neighborhoods.

Known as the "School district," it includes several of the town's key civic and commercial buildings, all located around a prominent circle. A neighborhood child-care center (left edge of photo) is flanked by a church and general store.

Kentlands' elementary school, now completed (photo page 41), is situated behind the child-care center, (just outside photo) on a concentric ring road.

These civic and commercial structures are located in proximity to neighboring residences. While a common feature of older neighborhoods and small towns, Kentlands' integration of uses is considered unusual in today's suburbs.

Each of Kentlands' six neighborhoods offers various housing options. Large single-family houses (below) line the north side of the town commons in the Old Farm neighborhood. Courtyard apartments (bottom) are located near the town square and shopping center.

Among Kentlands' first residences, these townhouses (right) are in the School district. Another townhouse group (overleaf) lines the south side of the town commons, across from the single-family homes mentioned previously.

The provision of public buildings and open space within each of Kentlands' neighborhoods was an important priority for the town's design team.

The expansive town commons (opposite) is anchored by the existing Kent Farm house and barn (center and right, respectively in photo). Both buildings are slated for future use as Gaithersburg's cultural center.

A new house and outbuilding (left in photo) face across a street to the similarly scaled historic farm house.

The elementary school (below) was the first public building completed at Kentlands. The building's classical entry portico terminates the view from a nearby street.

Kentlands' single-family houses (this spread) are provided in a range of sizes, prices and styles. Unlike many suburban areas where large tracts of similar homes are erected by one builder, houses here are produced in a more incremental way.

Working with the town's architectural code, local builders construct residences on individual lots or in small clusters distributed throughout the town.

Similar to the way U.S. neighborhoods and small towns were built in the past, this strategy results in an architectural diversity that is difficult to achieve in single-builder subdivisions.

Kentlands' detached homes are quite similar to their more conventional suburban counterparts in terms of interior layout. There is a great difference, however, in their urban organization.

Houses here sit closer to the street and one another, following build-to lines rather than minimum setbacks. They also occupy much smaller lots relative to their size. Garages are located at the back of lots, accessed from alleys.

Nearly all of Kentlands' residential blocks have alleys at the rear of each lot. Such alleys perform a valuable urban function by providing a place where the servicing needs of a home can be met.

These include auto storage, garbage collection and placement of utility meters and power lines. Most important, rear alleys rid the front of the house of driveways, garages and utility poles, thus creating a better, more spatially defined street.

Kentlands' alleys and their outbuildings (this spread) vary in character, just as the town's streets do.

Kentlands' outbuildings range from simple garages to more elaborate structures with accessory units above. Sometimes referred to as carriage houses, such units offer considerable flexibility in dwelling arrangements. Serving either as an extra bedroom for the main house or as a rental unit for the principal home owner, these units create affordable housing within the community. Because such housing is well dispersed throughout all neighborhoods, the need for large concentrations of conventional multi-unit affordable housing in any one area is lessened.

South Brentwood Village

Brentwood, California, 1991

Conceived as an extension of the existing small town of Brentwood (right) immediately to the north, the South Brentwood Village master plan (below) combines a new residential neighborhood (opposite) with retail and workplace uses on a 140-acre site.

The project is bounded on two sides by local arterials and on another by a canal. The project's fourth side — its principal employment center—fronts an abandoned rail right-of-way. This track may one day become part of a commuter rail system.

Affordable housing is a major issue in northern California; in 1990 only 17 percent of the median income earners in the San Francisco Bay Area qualified to buy an average-priced home.

Home builder Kaufman & Broad, the state's largest, has long catered to buyers caught in this squeeze with its inexpensive subdivision homes. Though it has been successful in such single-use developments, the company recently set out in a new direction at South Brentwood Village, a mixed-use community of 500 homes. While the project includes only detached houses, this plan by Calthorpe Associates differs from the typical suburban subdivision in many respects.

Following local guidelines for jobs/housing balance, 30 percent of the site provides employment-generating uses–light industry, office and retail. A village green, small parks and a church are also found within the community. Tree-lined streets define an open grid of blocks–some with alleys. Many homes built on alley lots have accessory apartments over their garages. These units provide an important form of affordable housing for South Brentwood Village.

These features, its planners contend, will result in a place that looks and feels more like the nearby small town of Brentwood than the many new subdivisions that surround it. For its builder, the success of this project will confirm that cost-conscious buyers want not just affordable homes, but a complete community as well.

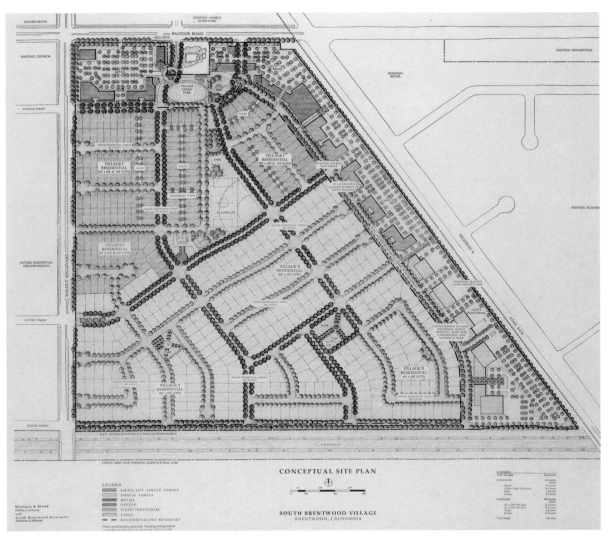

CONCEPTUAL SITE PLAN

SOUTH BRENTWOOD VILLAGE
BRENTWOOD, CALIFORNIA

The community of South Brentwood Village focuses on a main green (below). It is surrounded by retail stores and services, a day-care center, a church and homes.

This key civic space contains seating and a tot-lot at one end. Open lawn areas provide flexibility for gatherings and community events.

More active uses such as soccer, baseball, volleyball and basketball occur in the adjacent "playfield park" and two smaller neighborhood parks.

Design standards for public parks and streets within the development (opposite) have been carefully considered. One innovative element, a gated cul-de-sac (plan, middle row, left; elevation, middle row, center), joins neighborhood streets to adjacent arterials.

Because full vehicular intersections are not permitted in these locations, this alternative enables continuous pedestrian movement throughout the entire grid of streets and arterials.

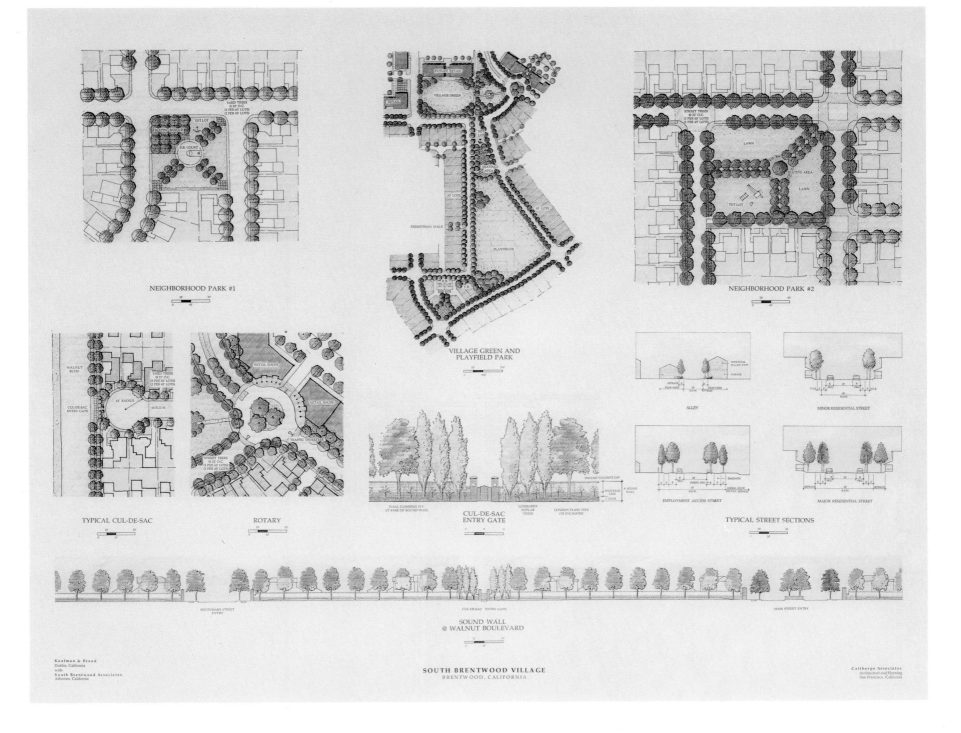

NEIGHBORHOOD PARK #1

NEIGHBORHOOD PARK #2

VILLAGE GREEN AND
PLAYFIELD PARK

TYPICAL CUL-DE-SAC

ROTARY

CUL-DE-SAC
ENTRY GATE

ALLEY

MINOR RESIDENTIAL STREET

EMPLOYMENT ACCESS STREET

MAJOR RESIDENTIAL STREET

TYPICAL STREET SECTIONS

SOUND WALL
@ WALNUT BOULEVARD

Kaufman & Broad
Dublin, California
with
South Brentwood Associates
Atherton, California

SOUTH BRENTWOOD VILLAGE
BRENTWOOD, CALIFORNIA

Calthorpe Associates
Architecture and Planning
San Francisco, California

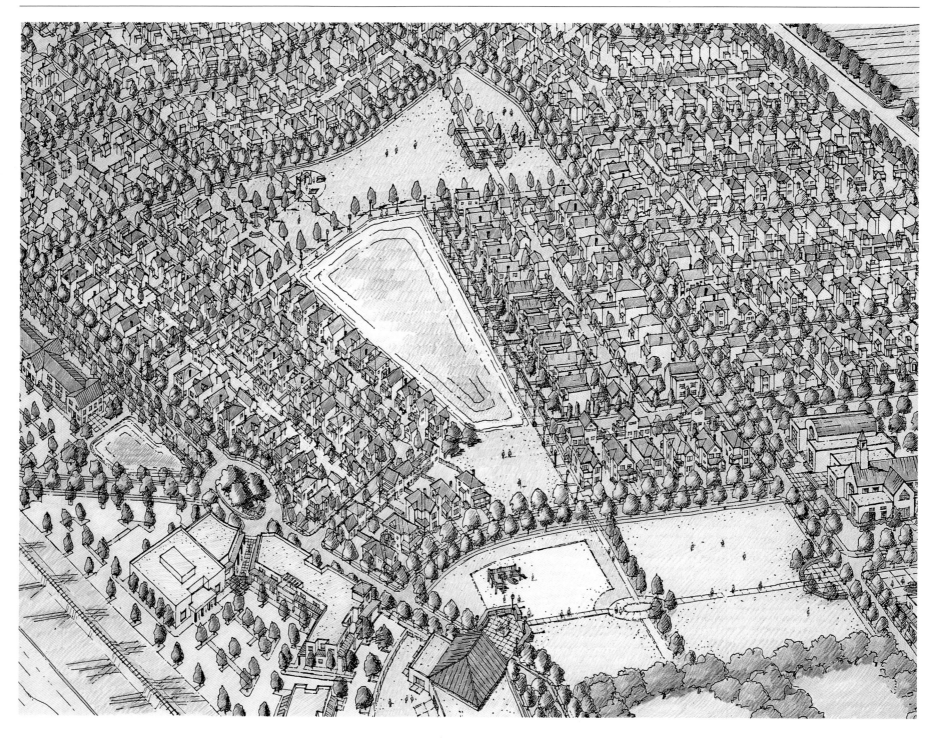

A central lake in this early scheme (opposite) mediates between the village green (bottom right in illustration), designed to serve the entire community, and a smaller park (top center) that is the focus of its surrounding neighborhood.

South Brentwood Village's small-lot, single-family residences (below) provide an affordable option for entry-level home buyers in the San Francisco Bay Area/ Sacramento Region.

Front porches are a prominent architectural element of these homes. Located close to the sidewalk, they contribute to increased activity in front yards and streets—a benefit to neighborhood security and sociability.

Many of the blocks in South Brentwood Village feature rear alleys. Houses in these locations are offered with accessory units above their alley-facing garages.

The "cottage" scale of these houses harkens back to the bungalow—one of America's most revered urban traditions. Bungalows provided affordable housing for a generation of Californians who settled places such as Oakland and Pasadena in the early 1900s.

Bamberton

Mill Bay, British Columbia, 1992

A former cement manufacturing plant (left) dominates the site of Bamberton's proposed lower town center (opposite). The huge scale of these "ruins" influenced the design of the town center.

The industrial character of the existing architecture will be reflected in the design of several new buildings at the water's edge (right in illustration, opposite). A concrete obelisk (foreground) bears a plaque with the history of the plant.

Occupying a dramatic stretch of coastline on British Columbia's Vancouver Island, the new town of Bamberton is intended to be a positive model for ecologically sustainable development. Members of its planning team are committed to building a community that is socially and economically viable within a framework of strict environmental controls.

Bamberton's mostly sloping site is on the Saanich Inlet, just 20 miles north of the provincial capitol of Victoria. Nearly half the town's 1,560 acres will be kept as public open space—greenbelts, parks and wilderness. The plan, by architects Andres Duany and Elizabeth Plater-Zyberk, calls for three villages and a large town center. Each village consists of two to three neighborhoods—a total of 4,900 dwelling units with an estimated population of 12,000.

Bamberton is planned to be self-sufficient, rather than function as a bedroom community. One neighborhood is envisioned as an employment center for the area, while home-based and telecommuting businesses are expected to flourish throughout the town. Many new, and some newly revived traditional, systems for transportation, energy, water use and waste management are being used in the community.

Though conceived in response to local concerns, Bamberton's developers hope that the town's example may ultimately be applicable to broader issues of global sustainability.

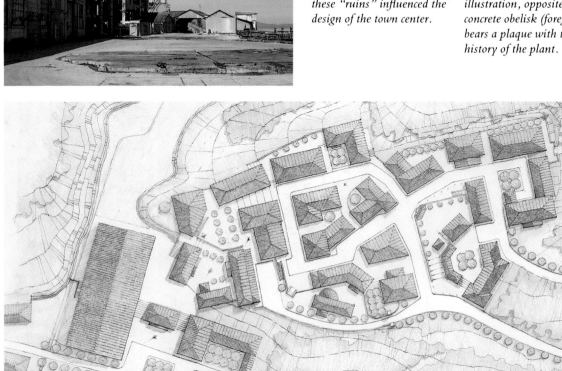

Bamberton's upper town center (plan, above) terraces up the hill from the lower town center. The large gable-roofed "clinker" shed (left in plan, also center of illustration, opposite) functions as an outdoor meeting hall.

The placement of buildings in the upper town center follows the location of existing footings and retaining walls from previous structures. The resulting narrow spaces between many of the buildings lend an almost medieval character to this part of the town.

Bamberton's high school (lower left in plan) is part of the lower town center. Both the upper and lower town centers combine multiple uses; the lower center houses several of the town's cultural institutions.

The plan of Bamberton (right) defines a town center and three villages to be built over 20 years. Most of the site is steeply sloped, providing dramatic views of the Saanich Inlet (below).

The unusual street grid of the villages responds to the extreme gradient of the site. This type of street and block configuration is typical of other hillside towns, such as Sausalito, California. Blocks here are deeper than normal to preserve a layer of intact forest.

A relatively level village called the Uplands (at extreme upper right in plan) is intended to function as Bamberton's employment center because of its easy accessibility for trucks.

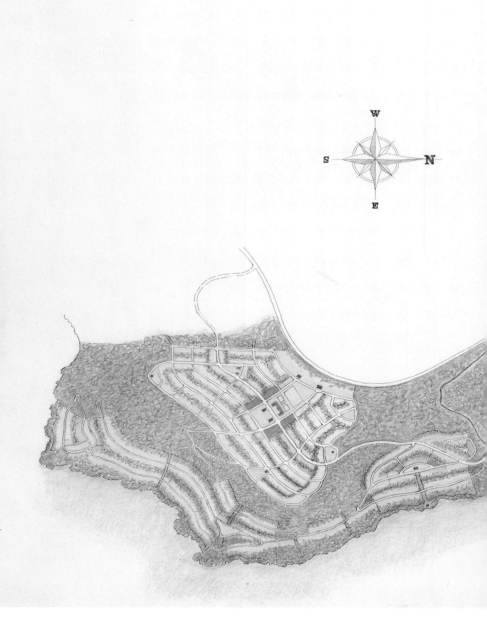

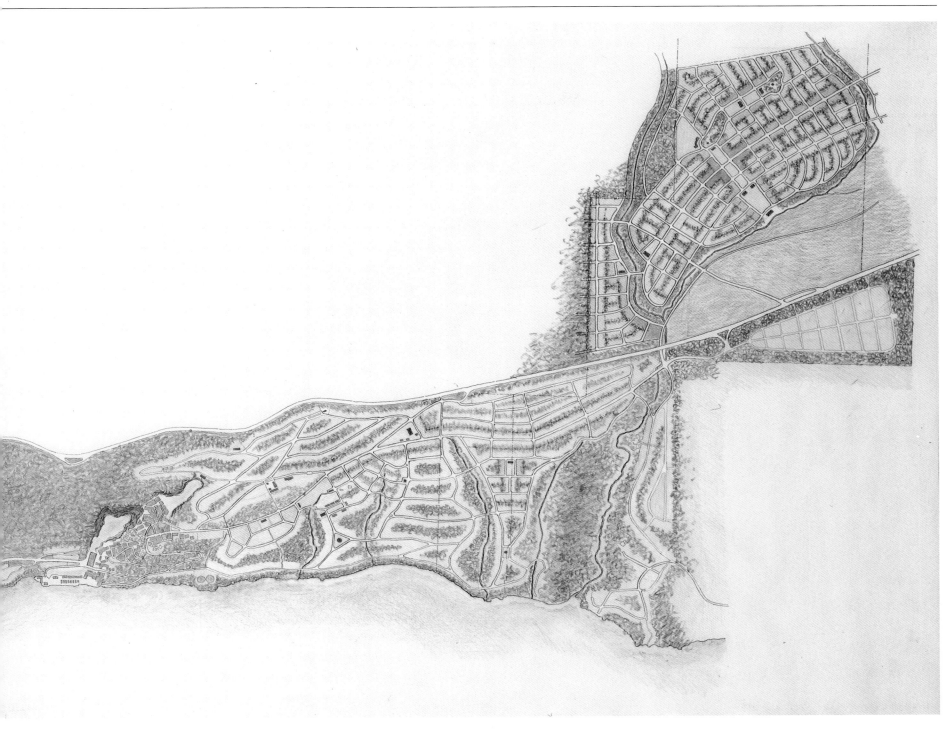

One of Bamberton's village centers (opposite and plan, below) is configured around an existing road and stone wall. A natural hollow to one side of the road is used as the village green.

Though rural in character, this settlement has several row houses at its center. Public buildings include a corner store, post office, meeting hall (to be utilized initially as a project sales center), a telecommute work center (building with spire, opposite) and a pub.

Sites for a school and house of worship have been set aside for future use (upper right in plan).

Other village centers within Bamberton incorporate similar elements but differ greatly in their physical layout. This is due mainly to the unique site conditions affecting each.

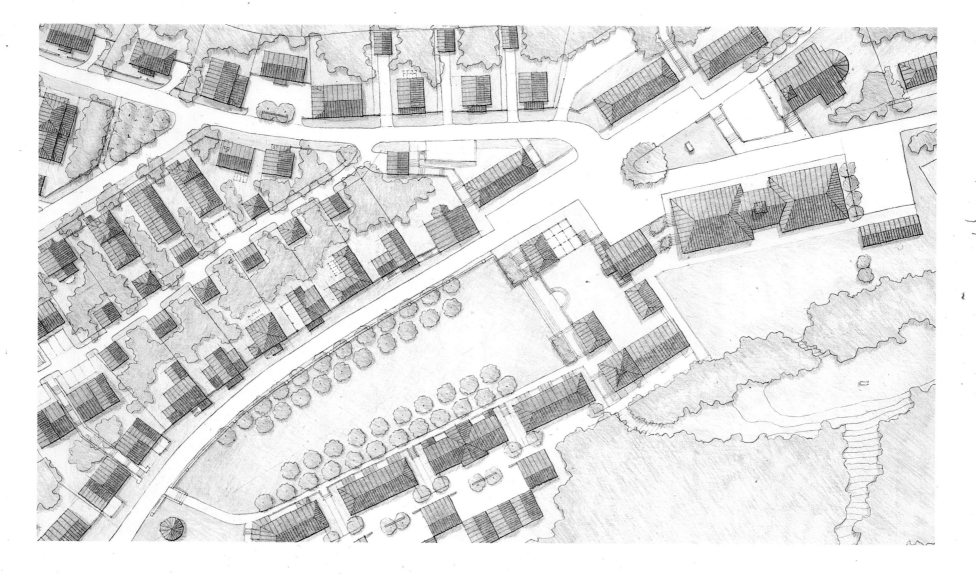

Several appropriate housing types (below) were selected for use within Bamberton's challenging terrain. Since steep slopes preclude alley parking, storage and movement needs of autos affected the design team's choices.

Street elevations (below) combining several different housing types were created as a test of compatibility. Units of varying size and scale seem to work comfortably together, provided that consistent build-to lines and other urban standards are maintained.

Sideyard houses work well on Bamberton's sloping lots. Their long thin footprint does not impede downslope water runoff. Front porches are required on many single-family houses.

A high-density cluster of cottages (left in top illustration) climbs the slope of the block from one street to the next. This type of multi-unit dwelling can be found in Berkeley, Seattle and other west coast cities.

Town houses (below) and detached houses (left) are grouped around shared parking courts. Retaining walls, necessary to create flat land in areas of sloped terrain, double here as the foundations of buildings.

The simple, honest forms of Bamberton's domestic and public architecture recall the American Arts and Crafts movement, popular in the early 1900s. Excellent examples of this style can be seen throughout the Pacific Northwest.

This sober, functional aesthetic defines an architectural identity for the town that reflects its environmental and social aspirations.

Windsor

Indian River County, Florida, 1989

Unique among the case studies in this book, the village of Windsor was conceived from the outset as an exclusive, upscale resort community. Situated approximately 8 miles north of Vero Beach on Florida's Atlantic coast, the village's 416-acre site straddles a narrow spit of scenic coastal land between the Atlantic Ocean and the Indian River.

Inspired by early Caribbean settlements, architects Andres Duany and Elizabeth Plater-Zyberk created a village plan defined by narrow streets alternating with wider boulevards. In contrast to most golf-oriented developments that disperse homes to optimize fairway views, Windsor's homes are clustered into a compact village, "greenbelted" on two sides by the golf course and on another by polo fields. Consistent with Caribbean precedents, most of the community's houses are courtyard and sideyard types. They sit close to the street with walled gardens enclosing the unbuilt portion of each lot. A number of freestanding homes are also planned, but they will be located only at the edge of the village, around the outside of the golf course and along the ocean beach.

In addition to the 18-hole golf course and polo fields, this private community (all home owners are required to be club members) also features tennis courts, an equestrian center, riding trails and a private ocean beach. At the heart of the plan, the village commons serves

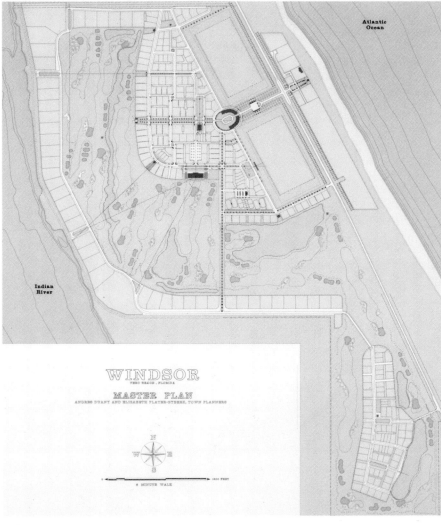

The plan of Windsor (left) locates all of its courtyard, sideyard and townhouse homesites within the internal blocks of the main village and an outlying hamlet to the south. Larger fairway lots face out to the golf course (opposite) designed by Robert Trent Jones, Jr. Windsor's largest lots—its "estate" homesites—are located around the perimeter of the golf course and along the beach.

Streets for the village of Windsor were completed in the spring of 1991, when this photo (left) was taken.

The plan of Windsor integrates two existing polo fields and other landscape features from an earlier, partially implemented site plan. The developers named the village after a favorite polo park in England.

Windsor's street geometry was influenced by the orientation of the polo fields and rows of trees planted as windbreaks for the citrus groves that previously occupied the site.

An early scheme for the village included simple wood bleachers for the polo fields modeled on those at the Oak Brook Country Club near Chicago, built in the 1930s by the father of one of Windsor's founders.

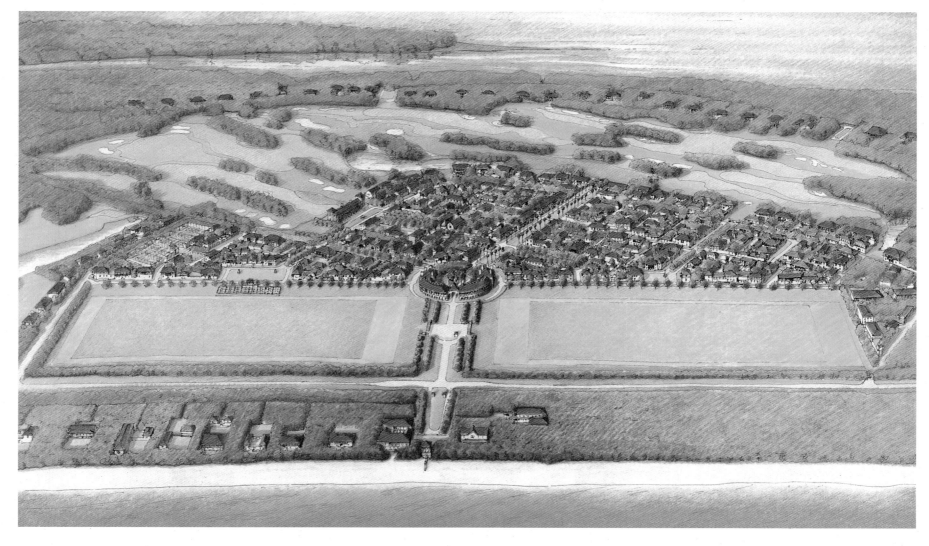

Classical architecture is used to distinguish Windsor's public buildings, which are sometimes smaller than nearby houses.

The village meeting hall (right and bottom left) faces several homes across a green. A polo museum (bottom right) was proposed in an early scheme for the village.

both as a gateway to the community and as a focus for its social and commercial activity. A three-story building on this key site will contain a small inn and several apartments along with a range of shops and services for residents.

Windsor's small-lot courtyard homes are unlike those found in most other U.S. luxury resort developments. In such places, suburban-style large homes on large lots have become the norm. A number of model homes were built to demonstrate the benefits of spaciousness and privacy that can be achieved within the village's modest lots. Because lots are small, the overall character of this part of the community is one of great intimacy and charm. This may be one reason why most of Windsor's home buyers have thus far chosen the village's courtyard designs over freestanding homes located at the edges of the development.

Windsor is being watched closely by planners and developers because it offers a pioneering test of what some have called the "trickle-down" theory of architecture and urban design. If successful, it will indicate that affluent home owners have an interest in, and appreciation of, the benefits of community that result from compact planning. This theory, once con-firmed, will no doubt influence the design of future towns and villages catering to a much broader spectrum of potential buyers–both the affluent and the not-so-affluent.

Street dimensions in the village alternate between narrow (opposite) and wide (right). The wider streets use more generous planting strips on both sides to achieve their greater size.

A typical block at Windsor (below) includes a variety of courtyard and sideyard houses. Each house has a garage and garage apartment that is typically entered from a mid-block alley.

Freestanding homes occupy lots which line the golf course (top edge of illustration, below). To preserve fairway views to the rear, garages for these houses are accessed from off-street parking courts.

Windsor's polo fields (below) and golf course, provide a recreational greenbelt for the community. The manicured landscape frames the village's picturesque composition of forms.

The main entrance to the community (right) is flanked by an allee of oak trees. Four small kiosks in this location were designed by Hugh Newell Jacobsen.

The entry sequence into most of Windsor's sideyard houses (below and right, foreground), brings one first into a walled garden court and then into the main house itself.

Entrances to the village's garage apartments (example bottom, extreme left in photo) can be from either a lane, (as shown here) an alley or a street.

Courtyards of Windsor houses by Andres Duany and Elizabeth Plater-Zyberk (opposite, left) and Clemens Schaub (below) share elements whose architectural expression is regulated by code. These include outbuildings, porches and level changes.

Townhouses designed by Scott Merrill share a continuous street facade (opposite, top right). Single-story wings (opposite, bottom right) project rearward to provide greater privacy for each unit.

Exterior architectural treatments of most Windsor courtyard and sideyard homes give little indication of the diverse character of the private spaces within.

Sketch studies (opposite) of various wall, window and porch configurations were created during an early design session. These helped Windsor's planning team to better understand the region's vernacular style and its possible adaptation to homes in the village.

Traditional materials and techniques for roofing, cladding and glazing were examined. The village's comprehensive codes (pages 76 and 77) were a result of these and other studies.

Various Florida architects were commissioned to design houses for specific village lots as a preliminary test of Windsor's codes.

These examples are by Armando Montero (below left), Rolando Llanes and Thomas Spain (bottom left and center), Denis Hector, Jorge Hernandez and Joanna Lombard (bottom right) and Andres Duany and Elizabeth Plater-Zyberk (below right).

Several of these designs have been built as models to demonstrate the spaciousness and privacy that Windsor's courtyard and sideyard homes provide.

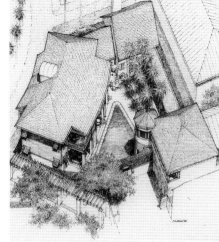

The village center building, occupying Windsor's most prominent site, has been the focus of extensive design exploration. An early plan (bottom) features a horse-shoe-shaped building (left) lined on its interior with an arcade (bottom left).

A later scheme by Hugh Newell Jacobsen (below) follows a similar footprint. This building's more nearly circular plan is continued in the layout of surrounding village streets.

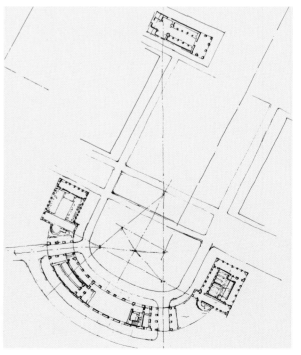

A third plan for the village center inverts the horseshoe (below) to face the entry, partially enclosing a series of smaller buildings. The Windsor design team felt that this scheme's spatial sequence more closely approximates the experience of entering a real village.

This third scheme brings one into Windsor through a carefully orchestrated progression of spaces. A colonnaded forecourt (left) is where entering guests are greeted by security staff.

Visitors then proceed down a narrow street (below) into a semicircular "arrival court." The village proper is finally entered through one of three arched openings in the town center building (bottom), which leads either north, south or west.

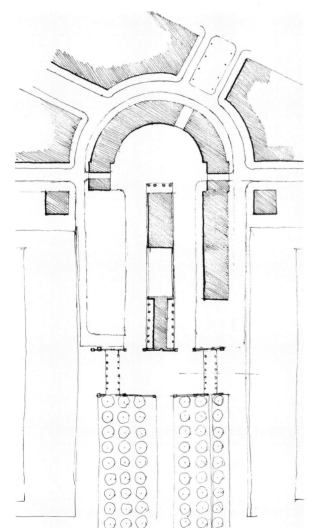

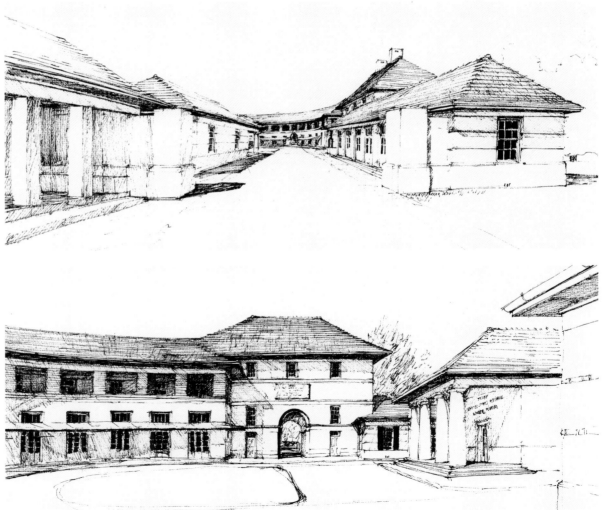

The most recent design for Windsor's village center is by Charles Barrett (entire spread). This scheme defines a single building of a simpler, more rectilinear form than previous versions.

Imposing, when seen from outside, this building's mass is scaled down through a series of roof setbacks on the village side.

Several early studies (right) explore the relationship of different building forms to the geometry of Windsor's street grid. The semicircular loggia shown in the more developed site plan (bottom right) mirrors the shape of the village commons.

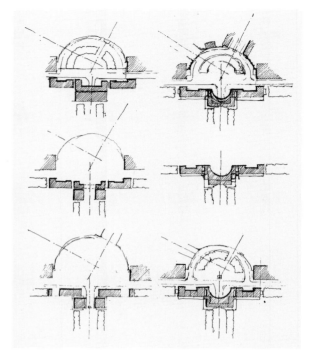

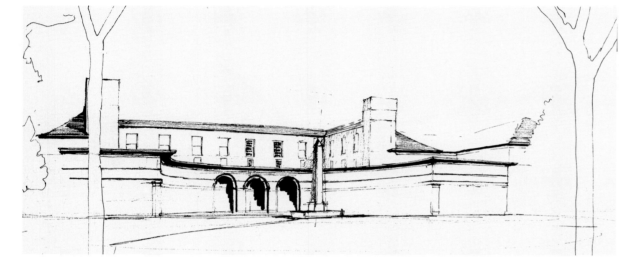

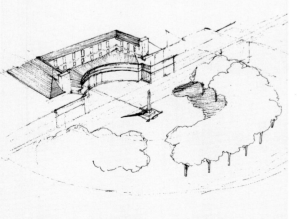

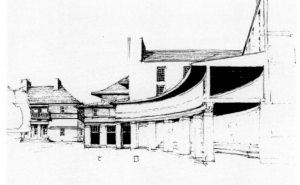

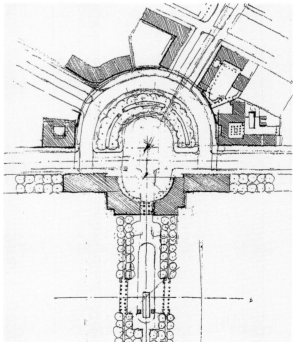

Barrett's classically inspired scheme for the village center and its flanking buildings defines a formal entrance to Windsor that is reminiscent of a traditional European village gate.

Terminating an allee of oak trees, the building's three arched entry portals create a secure entry point for the community. Inside, the expansive village commons serves as a transition to the residential blocks beyond.

Windsor's unique "entrance as building" helps to distinguish the community from other resort developments in the Vero Beach area.

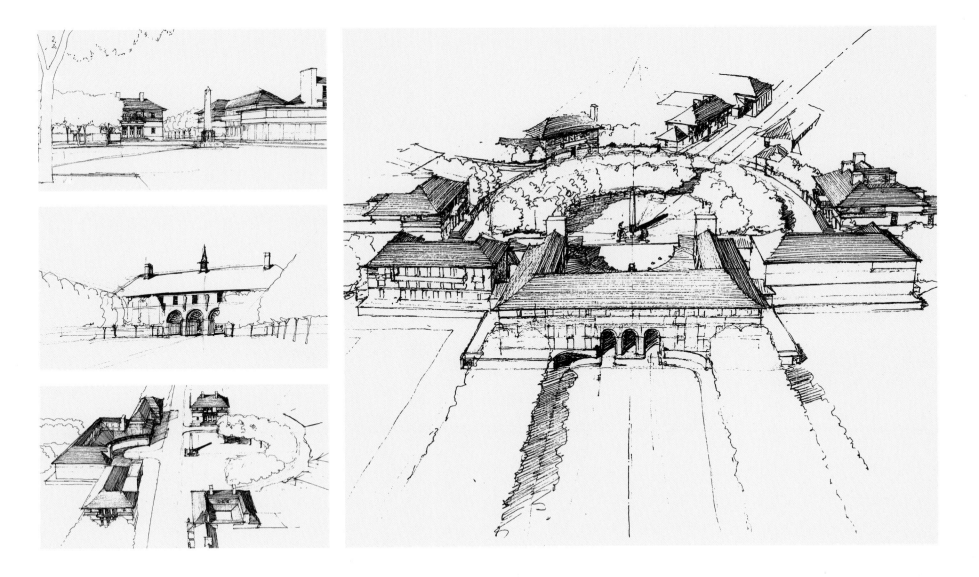

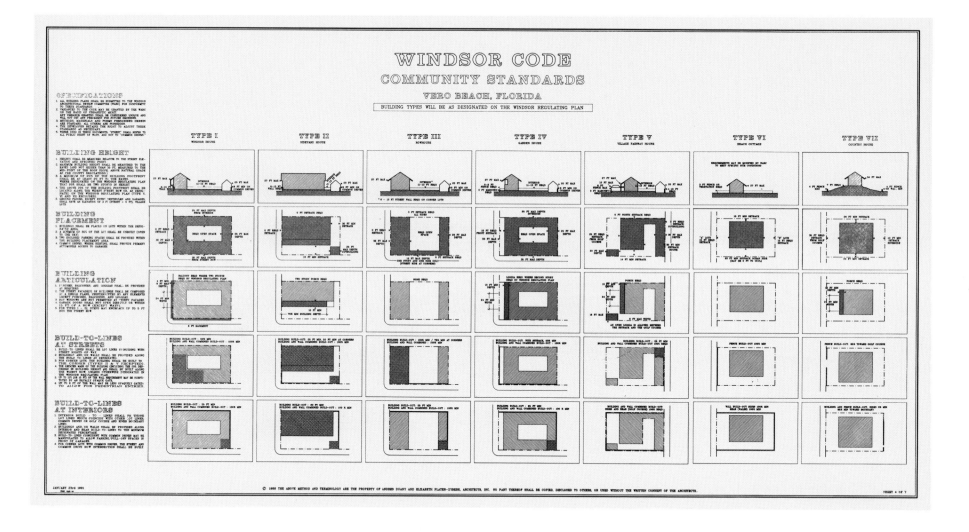

WINDSOR CODE
ARCHITECTURAL STANDARDS
VERO BEACH, FLORIDA

1. ALL BUILDING PLANS SHALL BE SUBMITTED TO THE WINDSOR ARCHITECTURAL REVIEW COMMITTEE (WARC) FOR CONFORMITY TO THESE STANDARDS.
2. VARIANCES TO THE CODE MAY BE GRANTED BY THE WARC ON THE BASIS OF ARCHITECTURAL MERIT. ANY VARIANCE GRANTED SHALL BE CONSIDERED UNIQUE AND WILL NOT SET ANY PRECEDENCE FOR THE FUTURE.
3. METHODS, MATERIALS AND FORMS PRESCRIBED HEREIN ARE STANDARD. ALL OTHERS ARE FORBIDDEN.
4. THE DEVELOPER RETAINS THE RIGHT TO ADJUST THESE STANDARDS AS NECESSARY.
5. WHERE USED IN THESE DOCUMENTS, "STREET" SHALL REFER TO ALL PUBLIC RIGHT OF WAYS, AND NOT TO COMMON DRIVES.

	MATERIALS	CONFIGURATIONS	OPERATIONS	GENERAL
EXTERNAL BUILDING WALLS	The following are permitted: - stucco, with a smooth sand finish or bag finish - wood clapboard 3.5" to 6" to the weather - German dropsiding no more than 8.0" to the weather - board and batten, 1 x 4 batten max. (not rough sawn) - keystone - Beach Cottages (TYPE VI) only; may also be wood shingles	The following are permitted: - openings no more squat than square, no more vertical than a triple square - trim boards between 2" & 6" at openings - visible lintels shall bear beyond the opening a dimension equal to their heights - stone or ersatz stone shall be laid in a true bonding pattern (no stack bond) - arches and lintels configured as true bearing elements (no solder courses supported on metal angles) - all stucco structures - all wood structures - a wooden second story above a stucco ground story		Chimneys may encroach up to 16" into the street Right-of-Way. Chimneys shall be whitewashed brick or stucco with a stone or cast stone coping Interior chimneys may be stucco on metal lath backed with paper on wood frame. Where visible from the street, facade materials shall be consistent horizontally and subject to review by the WARC. Visible foundations shall be stone, cast stone or parged block only. Stucco shall be finished with a steel trowel. The finish should be neither an applied texture nor a mirror smooth surface - but should show the hand of the workmen and general irregularities in the wall
GARDEN WALLS & FENCES	The following are permitted: - stucco and stone (matching principal structure) - fence on masonry base for types IV on the street side and V on the golf course side - wood pickets for Beach Cottage (Type VI) - wrought iron or blackened aluminum in combination with stone or stucco - ventilating panels of barrel tile or "basket weave" brick	The following are permitted: - wall surface with a minimum overall opacity of 85% - gated openings with a minimum overall opacity of 75% - ventilating panels less than 10 sq ft each and no more squat than a triple square (horizontally) and with a minimum overall opacity of 50% - asymmetric foundations on adjoining property lines (to facilitate future building) - ventilating panels between interior lot lines shall be no lower than 9' above the street elevation - walls on common property lines that present a simple planar surface to the adjoining property (i.e. no pilasters)		For Type IV, a wood or wrought iron picket fence atop a 3' masonry base is required toward the street on the street right-of-way line For type V, a 3' masonry knee wall is required on the property line Beach Cottage (type VI) a wood picket fence along property boundary is required on some lots as indicated on the regulating plan and optional on others
BALCONIES & PORCHES	The following are permitted: - stone, cast stone or stucco for piers - wood posts and piers - wood ballustrades for porches	Where visible from the street, only the following are permitted: - masonry arches no less than 16" in depth - piers no less than 12"x18" - posts no less than 6" x 6" and chamfer to begin no higher than 42" - round columns are reserved for public buildings and are not permitted on the facades of private buildings - balusters no more than 2" x 2.5" and 4.5" o.c. pattern to be approved by WARC - porch openings no more squat than square - balconies cantilevered no more than 8ft	Balconies, porches and loggias shall not open toward an adjacent private lot that is less than 15 ft away measured at right angles	Cantilevered structures may not be enclosed
ROOFS & GUTTERS	The following are permitted: - "Galvalume" 5 crimp heavy gauge metal - wood shingles (selected from WARC Master List) - interlocking tiles (selected from WARC Master List) - thatch - Beach Cottage (Type VI) only; metal shingles are additionally permitted. Gutters and roof flashing are copper for wood roofs.	The following are permitted: - simple symmetrical hipped roofs with a pitch between 8:12 and 10:12 and simple symmetrical gabled roofs with a pitch between 6:12 and 10:12 - simple shed with a pitch between 4:12 & 8:12 against a principal building or perimeter wall only - dormers shall sit no closer than 3' to gable end of building - overhangs shall be a minimum of 24" for principal buildings, 18" for shedroofs and outbuildings (where shed or outbuilding roofs abut the adjacent lot lines, the size of that side overhang may be reduced to less than the minimum noted or 0"), overhangs should be proportioned to the mass of the building. - rafters left open exposing rafter end no less than 2".		The following are permitted: - skylights, ventstacks and solar panels (not visible from streets) - skylights to be flat and flush with roof line and no greater than 9 sq ft - half-round gutters
WINDOWS & DOORS	The following are permitted: - clear glass with no more than 10% reduction light transmission - painted wood - paint color to be approved by WARC	Where visible from the street, only the following are permitted: - facades with fenestration less than 30% of their surface area - openings for doors not larger than 6 ft horizontally x 10 ft vertically, 4 ft horizontally x 8 ft vertically for windows - panes of glass not larger than 1 ft horizontally x 2 ft vertically (horizontal and vertical mullions only) - windows with sills which project between 1" and 4" - architraves of a simple section and a constant dimension from the opening (no keystones) - circular, semi-circular and octagonal windows are permitted but only one per building - garage doors shall be 10 ft. max width with pattern approved by WARC - doors shall be recessed wood panel and/or louvered	Where visible from the street only the following are permitted: - single and double hung windows - wood garage doors with exterior swing and hinged at jambs, minimum thickness 2 1/4" (on Common Drives doors may open upwards)	Windows facing and within 25 ft of common property lines shall have a minimum sill height of 6 feet above finished floor level and fixed louver shutters adjusted for air circulation and light while obstructing view of neighboring yard. Windows whose line of sight is held within the lot (i.e. by a Garden Wall) are exempted from this requirement. The following are permitted: - operable wood shutters sized to match openings - operable wood bahamas shutters sized to match openings - operable wood storm shutters sized to match openings - wood or Terra Cotta window boxes, French metal flower pot holders - canvas awnings to be approved by WARC (no 1 4 cylinder configurations)
OUTBUILDINGS & ACCESSORY STRUCTURES	Materials shall conform to that of the primary structure.	Massing shall conform to that of the primary structure. The following is required: - open space under wood decks or steps to be enclosed by wood lattice (vertical & horizontal pattern only) - garage doors shall be 10 ft max width with pattern approved by WARC	The following uses of outbuildings are permitted: - garden pavilions and green houses - gazebos, trellis structures and arbors - garages and workshops - guest houses and artist studios - saunas - pool cabanas and equipment enclosures - barbecues	
LANDSCAPE	All trees and shrubs shall be selected from the WARC Landscape Standards.	There shall be a tree (species from the WARC Landscape Plan) of not less than 3.5" caliper planted no further than every 35 ft along the street frontage, 7.5 ft into the street Right-of-Way and no closer than 15 ft to street lights (except on the Windsor Boulevard, all Ways and Common Drives).		Trees over 6" caliper may not be removed without the approval of the WARC (except for citrus trees). Additional requirements may be made for larger homesites outside the Village.
MISCELLANEOUS	All external building and garden wall colors shall be from the WARC Master List. Doors, shutters and trim colors shall be approved by the WARC Stucco shall be hand finished with a steel trowel. The finish shall be neither an applied texture nor a mirror smooth surface - but should show the hand of the workmen and general irregularities in the wall.	The following items shall be selected from the WARC Master List: - lettering & house numbering	Exterior Hardware to be solid brass, bronze or brushed chrome The following shall be located at Common Drives or within the Auto court - electrical meters & gas meters - waste bins - utility and telephone company boxes	Please refer to the Community Association's Declaration of Covenants, Conditions and Restrictions. The following shall not be visible from the street: - clothes lines - waste bins, above ground storage bins, artificial vegetation - basketball hoops, equipment - air conditioning compressors, electric meters & gas meters utility and telephone company boxes or meters must be accessible from alley, or in auto court if there is no alley

JANUARY 23rd, 1991 © 1989 THE ABOVE FORMAT AND TERMINOLOGY ARE THE PROPERTY OF ANDRES DUANY AND ELIZABETH PLATER-ZYBERK, ARCHITECTS. NO PART THEREOF SHALL BE COPIED, DISCLOSED TO OTHERS, OR USED WITHOUT THE WRITTEN CONSENT OF THE ARCHITECTS. Sheet 5 of 7

Communications Hill

San Jose, California, 1991

An island within a varied patchwork of industrial, commercial and residential areas, Communications Hill (below) is the largest undeveloped property within the city of San Jose.

Only a ten-minute commute from downtown and within walking distance of the city's new light-rail line, the proposed community (opposite) was designed for much higher densities than surrounding areas.

Though its challenging topography makes building more difficult and costly, sweeping views from the site will add considerable value to housing units within Communications Hill.

Gridiron town planning, traced as far back as the 7th century B.C., seemed ideal for the flat landscape covering much of the American west. Such plans were the pattern for hundreds of small prairie towns established during the westward expansion of the United States. Many hilly cities like San Francisco and Seattle also used grid plans with great success.

It was to such models that the designers turned when faced with the topographically challenging Communications Hill, a prominent 500-acre site that rises to a height of 400 feet in the midst of San Jose's low-density sprawl. Architects Daniel Solomon and Kathryn Clarke opted for a compact, traditional grid plan rather than the curved streets commonly used for hillside development in the region.

Though attracted by the charm of places like San Francisco, the designers selected the grid more for its functional benefits. These include higher densities, greater parking efficiency—a must in a city requiring 2.5 parking spaces per unit—and reduced grading since buildings step gradually to follow the slope of the hills.

Important too, the grid provides a network of walkable streets that foster social interaction discouraged in more auto-oriented plans. Small neighborhood centers and a mixed-use village center add to the hoped-for sense of community, defined by a citizens' task force as a major goal of the Communications Hill Specific Plan.

The hilly site (contour map below) influenced the design of Communications Hill's street layout. The plan (bottom and right) seeks to minimize grading, yet it allows for intensive development in defined areas.

Neighborhood streets have been laid out in a traditional gridiron pattern. A single curvilinear arterial follows the contours of the hill, connecting neighborhoods and defining a clear edge between residential areas and the grassy slopes below.

Communications Hill will differ markedly from most hillside developments in California which use extensive grading to flatten hilltops and form terraces for large footprint buildings.

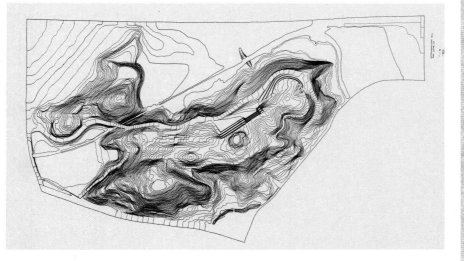

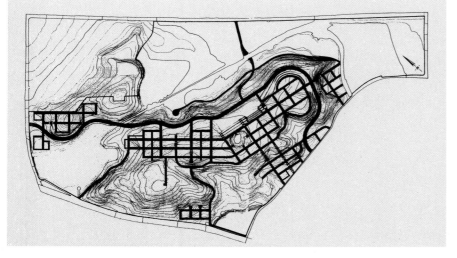

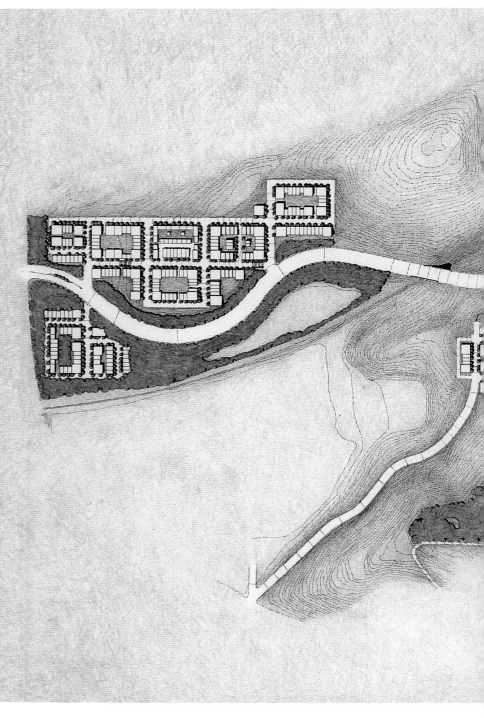

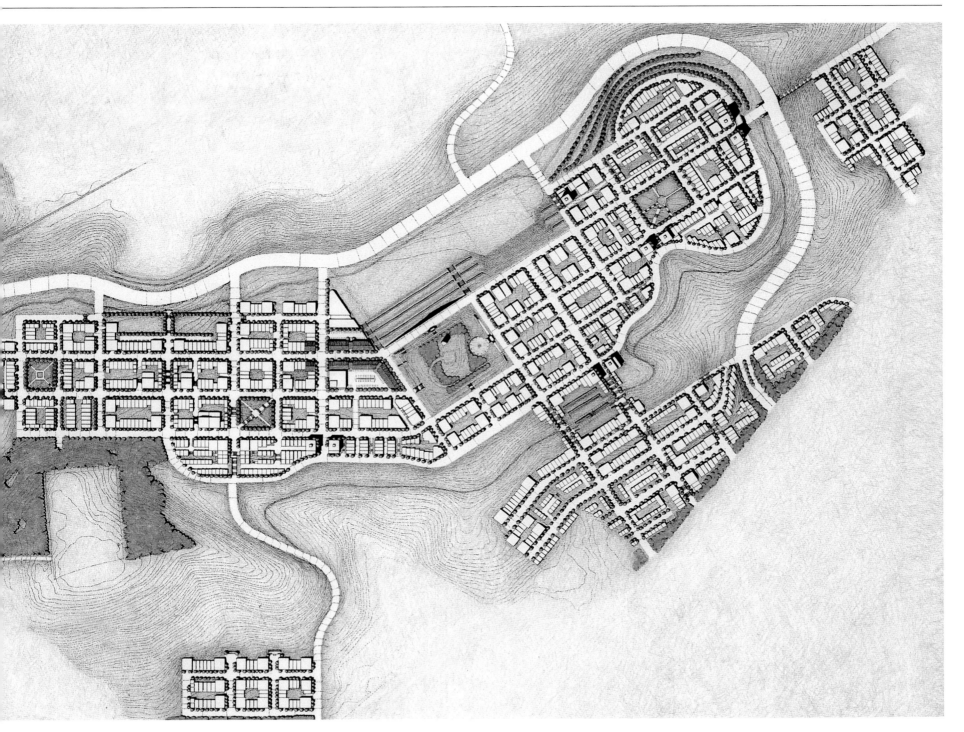

Blocks within Communications Hill respond to a variety of gradient changes (below). These include a simple uphill-downhill slope (top), a cross slope (middle) and a compound slope (bottom).

The design team created a series of prototypical blocks combining different building types and parking layouts. These studies (below) helped to determine which configuration would be best suited to a given slope and location within the plan.

In each case several building types combine to form the block. Conventional units such as townhouses and stacked flats predominate. Several blocks have internal cottages which front on alleys or parking drives.

Small-scale apartment buildings provide the block's highest-density housing and typically occur at corners or along streets of greater slope. The larger footprints of these buildings enable a greater number of parking spaces to be accessed through fewer curb-cuts.

Several innovative building types (opposite) were developed for the block corners. Each demonstrates a different unit combination and parking layout.

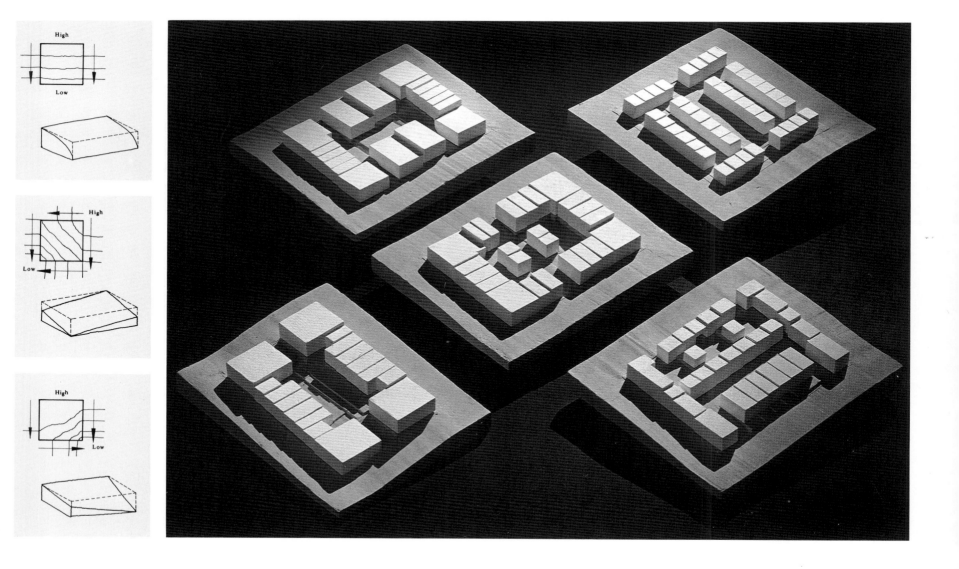

This block corner (below left) works well on an uphill site. The corner building is shown connected to a small townhouse building. Both are shallower than adjacent structures so that light and air can reach into the back of each building.

Three parking spaces are located on the ground floor of the corner building. All are entered through a single garage door. The townhouse has two single-car garages, each with direct street access.

This block corner (below center) combines direct off-street parking with a "walk-in-drive." This entry con-figuration enables several parking spaces to share a common turning area. The walk-in-drive also provides the primary public access to a mid-block garden.

Apartment units above are reached by stairs located in a separate opening on the other face of the block corner. This opening mirrors the form of the walk-in-drive.

All of the six parking spaces in this block corner (below right) share a single walk-in-drive. This configuration creates fewer breaks in the sidewalk than would indivi-dual off-street garages. This corner type works best on a downhill site.

The units shown here have bridging decks connecting their upper levels. While full site coverage above the walk-in-drive is possible, the reduced bulk of this split corner building respects the scale of nearby townhouses.

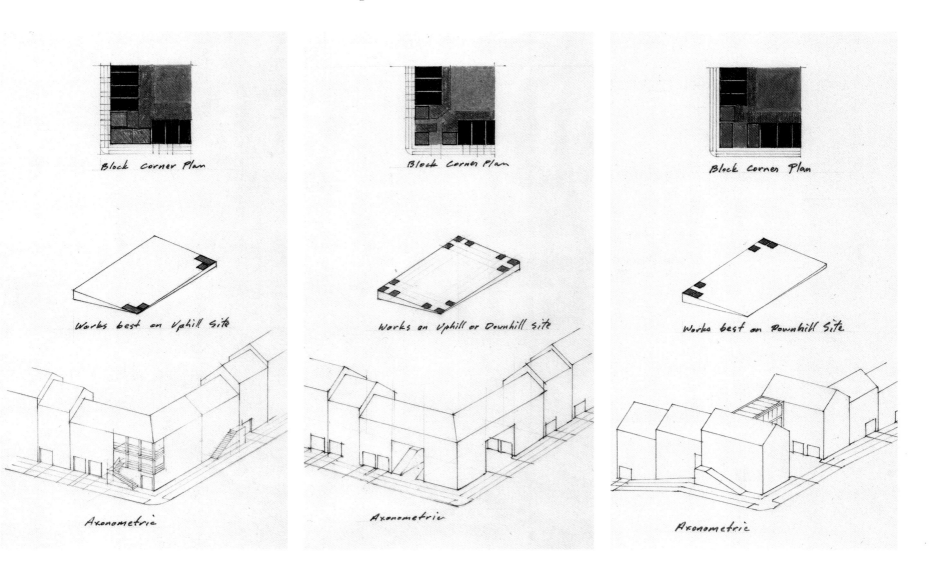

Block Corner Plan

Block Corner Plan

Block Corner Plan

Works best on Uphill Site

Works on Uphill or Downhill Site

Works best on Downhill Site

Axonometric

Axonometric

Axonometric

The Curtner neighborhood (plan, below) is located on a 60-acre parcel at the north end of the Communications Hill site. Planned as a complete neighborhood, it will be one of the first phases of the project to be built.

Comprising 300 to 450 dwellings, the neighborhood's population should be able to support several small stores and services. Four retail store locations (shown in red) have been identified. All are centrally placed near the highest part of the site

A large grove of oak and eucalyptus trees is planned for the lower portion of the site and along the boulevard that defines the north end of this neighborhood. A small cluster of residences is located within the grove.

Recreational facilities for swimming, basketball and tennis are placed at various locations in and around this part of the site. A large elliptical playing field carved out of the south end of the grove is bordered by a ring of poplar trees.

A pedestrian passage under Vistapark Drive links the upper and lower portions of the Curtner neighborhood near the community's main pool and fitness center.

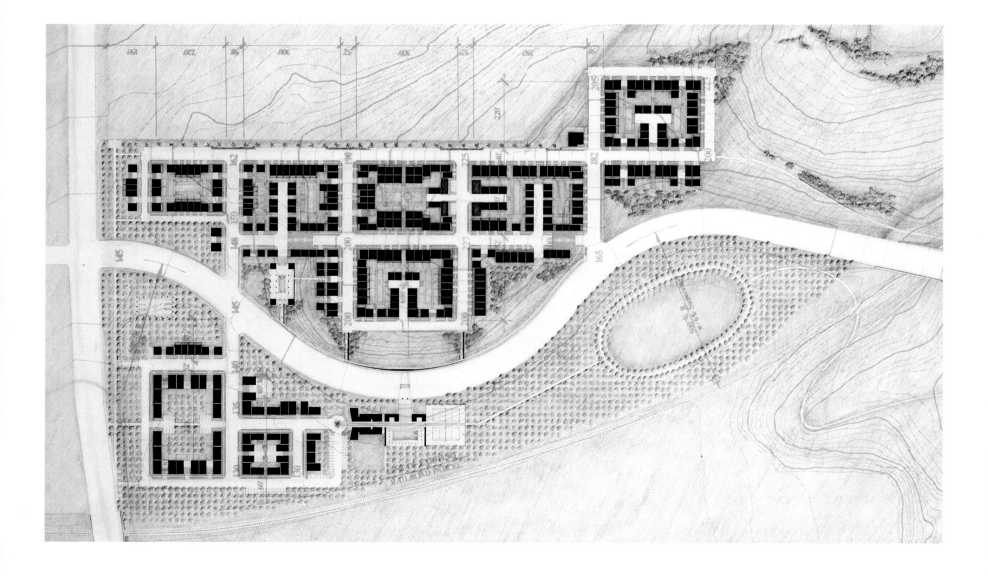

A four-block-long row of palm trees along Avenue K (left) creates a distinguishing landscape element that is visible from a great distance. The trees also reinforce the edge between neighborhood blocks and the open-space areas beyond.

Blocks within the Curtner neighborhood (below) accommodate a range of density between 25 and 40 units per acre. Buildings step with the slope, providing views of nearby hills and downtown San Jose.

AT&T Park (right and below) surrounds the existing landmark communications tower from which the community derives its name. A new water tower is also planned for this site which is bounded on three sides by urban blocks.

A system of walkways and grand stairs (bottom right) establishes a formal character for this park. A large stair, at one corner of the park, terminates the view from a nearby street.

A relatively flat site for a high school, playing fields and community center is located beneath a series of terraces (lower part of plan). This portion of the site has been reclaimed from a pre-existing gravel quarry.

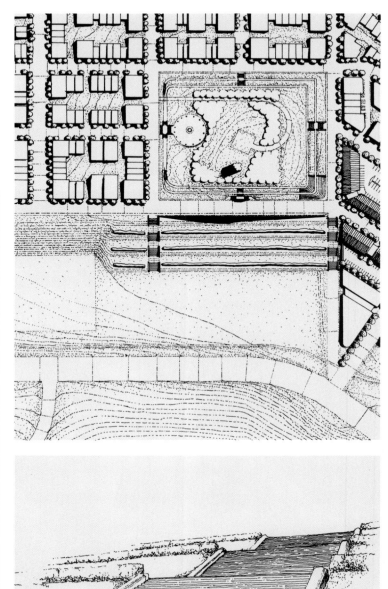

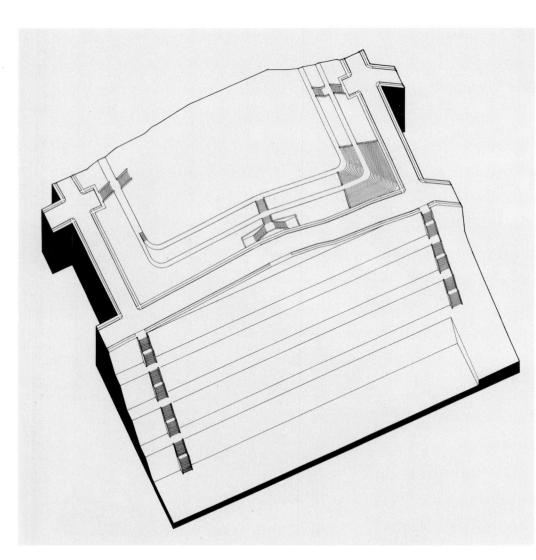

The street network within the Communications Hill plan provides multiple routes for the dispersion of local traffic. When slopes become too steep for auto use, stairs and ramps (below and bottom left) enable pedestrian circulation to remain continuous.

These interruptions create unique places within the street grid (below right) that give vitality and charm to surrounding neighborhoods. Hilly cities like Seattle, San Francisco and Berkeley have many such places.

Despite the seeming conflict between the community's rectilinear grid of streets and the natural topography of the site, this plan has a far greater density and more parking spaces than would a similar development laid out with curvilinear streets.

Further, because buildings step gradually with the slope and view corridors align to straight streets rather than curved ones, many more units offer the prime views that are a compelling feature of Communications Hill.

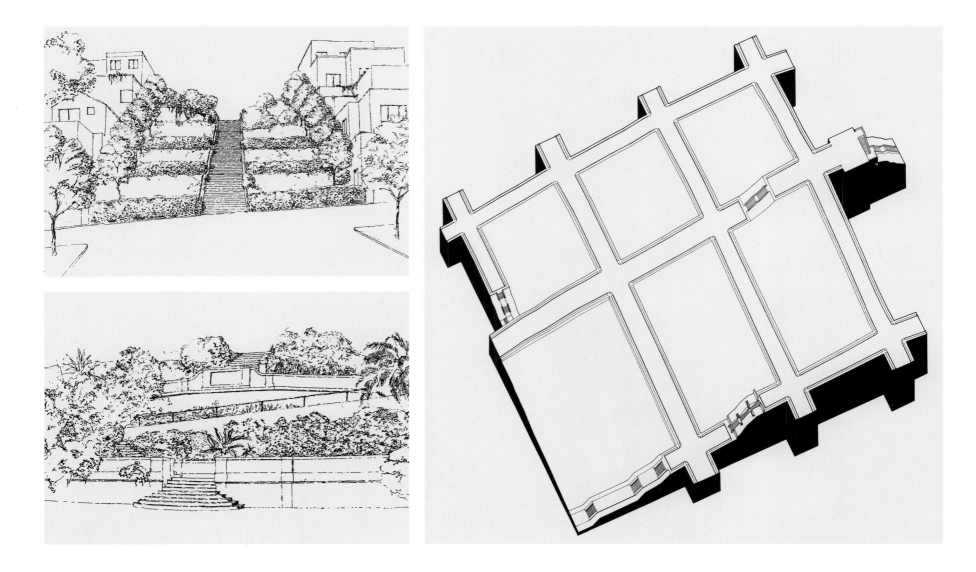

Rosa Vista

Mesa, Arizona, 1991

The developers of Rosa Vista, a mobile home village near Phoenix, believe that better design will change deeply rooted negative perceptions about manufactured housing. Long the choice of retirees in many sunbelt states, this form of dwelling is now being considered by an increasing number of younger families as well.

Because it costs about 35 percent less than conventionally constructed housing, manufactured housing is an affordable alternative. It currently accounts for one-third of all new single-family homes sold in the U.S. Often confused with trailers (which are actually a *form* of manufactured housing), most factory-built houses are quite similar to standard site-built construction in terms of materials and techniques. They follow standards set by HUD and, though shipped on wheeled frames, most are ususally attached to a foundation where they remain for decades.

Despite these advantages, many barriers to building this form of housing exist. Developers of mobile home communities often face zoning policies seeking to limit or exclude them. This results from a perception of cheapness that surrounds such communities and a concern that their presence will harm nearby property values.

The village of Rosa Vista was the result of an intensive planning effort that addressed both overall community layout and the design of the individual units. One goal of the planners was to set an example of "what could be done" with

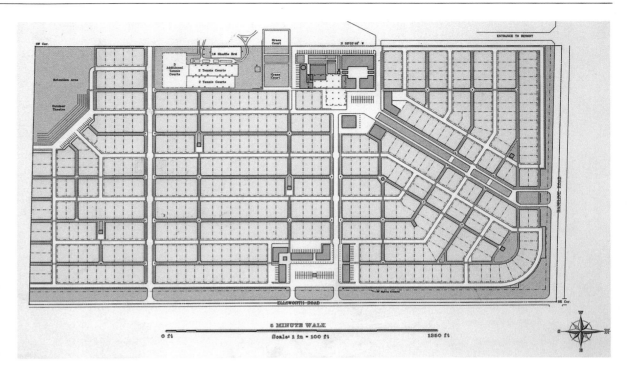

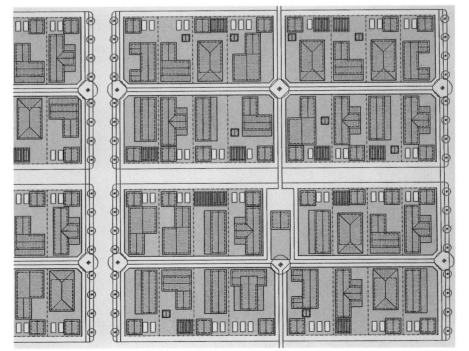

The plan of Rosa Vista (above) incorporates a wide range of street types (pages 94-95). Most houses front narrow paseos (opposite), intended mainly for pedestrian circulation. Small outbuildings and carports line the larger rear lanes. This design inverts the more typical relationship between streets and alleys.

Rosa Vista's blocks (left) are platted into lots of two widths—30' and 45'. These sizes accommodate a broad range of unit types that have been designed for the community.

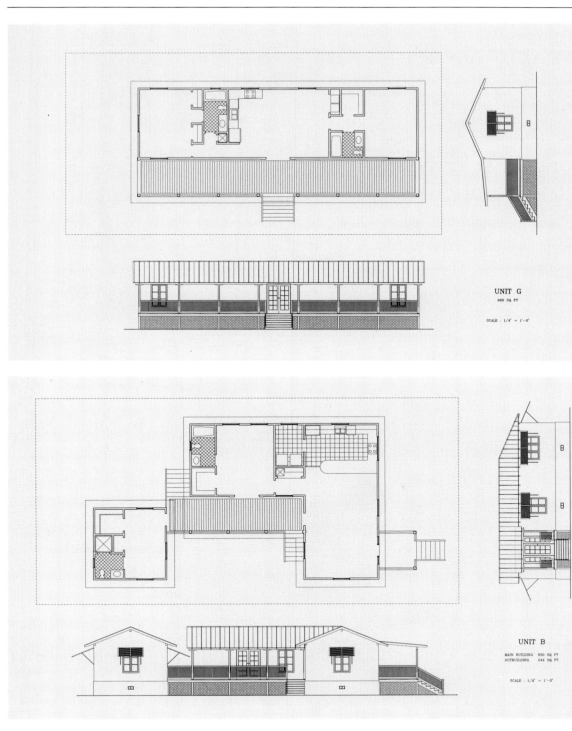

Over 15 different house designs (examples, left) were developed for Rosa Vista based on the standard width modules commonly used in manufactured housing.

UNIT G
960 SQ FT

SCALE : 1/4" = 1'-0"

UNIT B

MAIN BUILDING   930 SQ FT
OUTBUILDING   244 SQ FT

SCALE : 1/4" = 1'-0"

manufactured housing. Instead of simply simulating site-built construction, they sought to understand the inherent limitations and opportunities unique to this form of housing.

Rosa Vista's design team, headed by Andres Duany and Elizabeth Plater-Zyberk, first researched successful mobile home communities elsewhere in the U.S. In the process, they learned that many of their features—close placement of units; extensive common facilities, such as a clubhouse; and a well defined perimeter—actually contributed to a greater sense of community than that found in surrounding, conventionally constructed neighborhoods.

Rosa Vista's plan reflects their findings: Fronts of units are kept close to the small paseos that serve as the primary means of pedestrian circulation between units. Large streets that mobile home communities require to deliver and install units are kept at the rear and left unpaved. Many new and innovative floor plans were created for the housing units—several of which have roof decks and "parasols."

The village of Rosa Vista was recently cited by *Progressive Architecture* Magazine in its annual design awards. While such recognition probably won't affect broad public perception of manufactured housing, it shows that architects and other design professionals are starting to take an interest in a widely used form of housing that they have long shunned.

Rosa Vista's planning team looked carefully at the design of the individual housing units. After researching the area's vernacular architecture, they decided to emulate the best prototypes of the region.

Many small deviations from industry norms were suggested so houses would more closely match the character of local models. For example, the height of a unit above grade was found to significantly affect its sense of scale and presence on the site.

Because units are trucked to their lots, most manufactured housing sits either at 3'-4" above grade (just higher than their wheels) or at grade (if placed on an excavated foundation).

The comparative studies (this page) show units at two different heights above grade. A minimal 1'-0" plinth seems to work best for the courtyard house (below right). A higher 3'-0" base is suggested for the bungalow unit (bottom left).

Various site-applied detail and finishing options have also been recommended. These include eaves with exposed rafters, porches, operable shutters and stucco exterior surfacing.

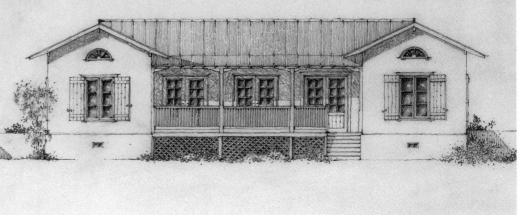

Factory-constructed units attach to a site-built arcade to form Rosa Vista's commercial center (below). Various shops and services required in the community are available here.

The timber arcade, a common feature of southwest architecture, provides shade from the intense Arizona sun. The center's parking area (right in illustation) has been designed in the form of a town square which faces out to the nearby Superstition Mountains.

Most automobile movement at Rosa Vista takes place on the Alameda (opposite, top left) and on two tree-lined east-west streets (opposite, bottom left) that traverse the site.

Visitors are encouraged to park on these streets and continue on foot via the low-walled paseos (opposite, top right) to reach homes within the village. These masonry walkways feature hearty native shade trees at each intersecting corner.

The lanes behind homes (opposite, bottom right) provide parking and service access for residents. Their greater width allows maneuvering room for equipment used to deliver and install houses.

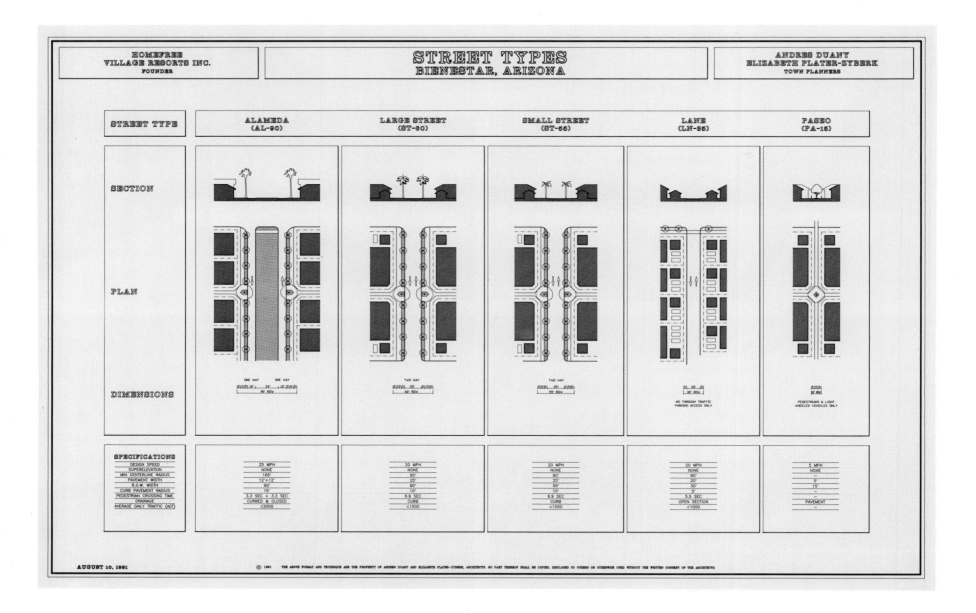

AUGUST 10, 1991   © 1991   THE ABOVE FORMAT AND TECHNIQUE ARE THE PROPERTY OF ANDRES DUANY AND ELIZABETH PLATER-ZYBERK, ARCHITECTS. NO PART THEREOF SHALL BE COPIED, DISCLOSED TO OTHERS OR OTHERWISE USED WITHOUT THE WRITTEN CONSENT OF THE ARCHITECTS.

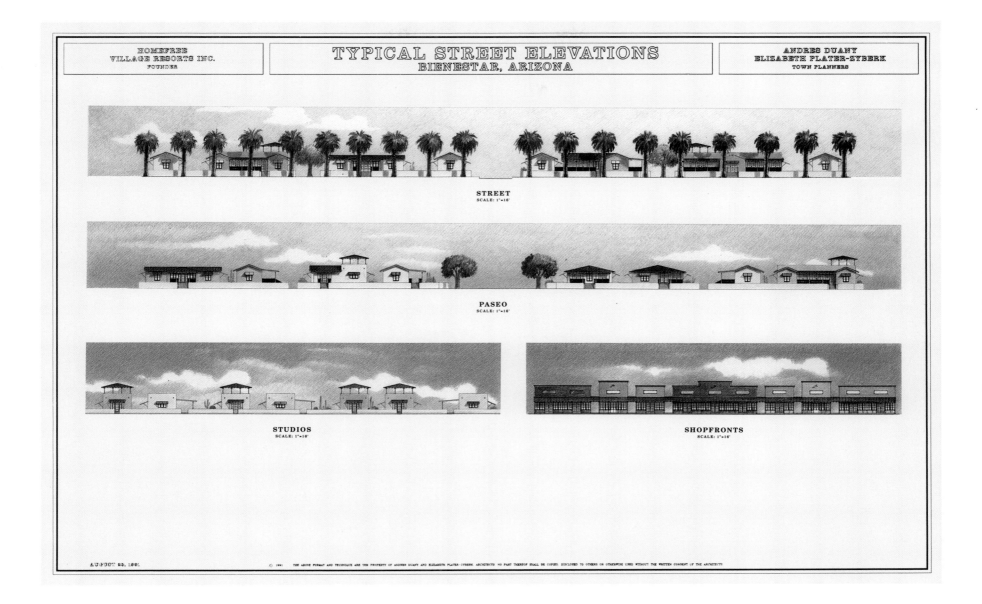

HOMEFREE
VILLAGE RESORTS INC.
FOUNDER

TYPICAL STREET ELEVATIONS
BIENESTAR, ARIZONA

ANDRES DUANY
ELIZABETH PLATER-ZYBERK
TOWN PLANNERS

STREET
SCALE: 1"=16'

PASEO
SCALE: 1"=16'

STUDIOS
SCALE: 1"=16'

SHOPFRONTS
SCALE: 1"=16'

AUGUST 29, 1991   © 1991   THE ABOVE FORMAT AND TECHNIQUE ARE THE PROPERTY OF ANDRES DUANY AND ELIZABETH PLATER-ZYBERK ARCHITECTS. NO PART THEREOF SHALL BE COPIED, DISCLOSED TO OTHERS OR OTHERWISE USED WITHOUT THE WRITTEN CONSENT OF THE ARCHITECTS.

A New Village in the Suburbs

Dade County, Florida, 1992

Developed primarily in the 1970s and 1980s, Kendall, Florida (left), is typical of many of the "edge cities" that have come to symbolize the anonymity of American suburban life.

The plan (below) of the New Village focuses on a center square (opposite) combining civic, commercial and residential uses. This multi-use district injects a key element of public life into the project's largely suburban surroundings.

This New Village, as yet unnamed, will be built in Kendall, one of South Florida's fastest growing areas, just 16 miles southwest of downtown Miami. Its strategically located 100-acre site is near major highways and a busy local airport.

The Village will be the first development to be built in conformance with Dade County's new Traditional Neighborhood Development Ordinance (TND). An alternative to the standard Dade County Zoning Code, the TND allows greater intensity of land use and reduced parking requirements in exchange for design features that make a community more affordable, diverse and pedestrian-friendly.

The project, designed by Dover, Kohl & Partners, includes a mix of housing (890 units), shopping, workplace, entertainment and civic uses—all within a few minutes' walk. A broad range of building types and sizes will meet the needs of a diverse citizenry including both renters and home owners. The plan is organized around a series of inviting, functional public spaces: arcaded shopping streets, a main street leading to a large central square and a scattering of smaller neighborhood parks.

Intended as an oasis of walkability within one of Dade County's most auto-dominated areas, this first test of the TND is seen by many as an important, precedent setting project. Its successes and failures will, no doubt, affect future planning within the county and the region.

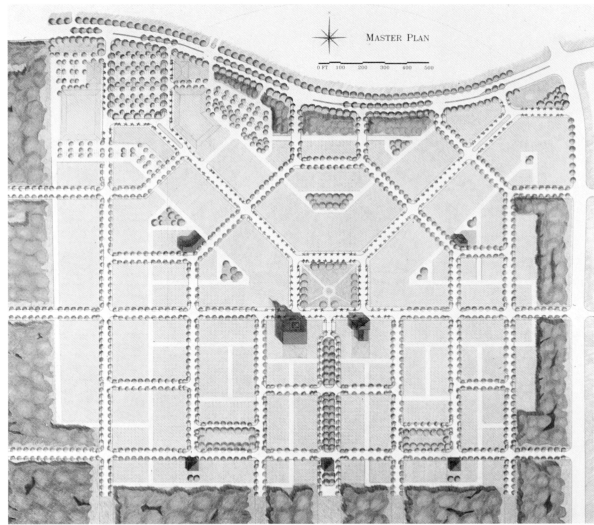

MASTER PLAN

0 FT 100 200 300 400 500

Shopfront buildings in the village (left) are required by the TND code to hold a consistent street line and provide arcades over the sidewalk. The result is a more clearly defined public realm that still allows for considerable diversity of architectural expression.

A full range of housing options are provided within the New Village. Included among these are garden and courtyard apartments (below and bottom, respectively), and apartments located above shops (left and opposite, right).

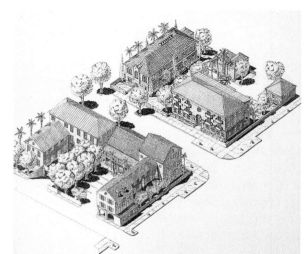

The community also offers detached homes (below) and rowhouses (bottom). Both of these housing types are shown with accessory units in the rear yards of the principal residences.

Such units are encouraged by the TND code, since they provide a further source of affordable housing within the community.

The New Village represents a return to planning for smaller increments of growth. Unlike most large-scale suburban development, lots here have been subdivided into the smallest practical units.

In this way many more individuals of modest means can participate in building the community. Since small lots may still be combined to accommodate larger structures, this approach assures a mix of building sizes that responds to market needs as the village grows.

This incremental strategy has obvious advantages for developers, such as increased flexibility and decreased financial risk. It also results in a more human-scaled environment that benefits the entire community.

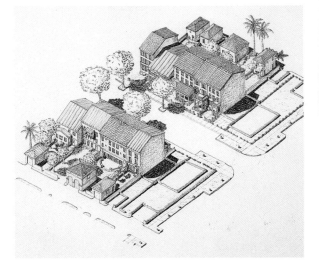

Wellington

Palm Beach County, Florida, 1989

An early plan for the Town of Wellington (below) was the result of a one-week design charette. During that session, the layout of each neighborhood was assigned to a different designer.

Though given a common set of rules to follow, all of the contributors' plans were unique. After the individual neighborhoods were first pieced together, some overall adjustments were required to achieve proper street connections between each.

This working method brings a sense of authentic variety to the larger composition that would not be possible with only one designer.

Planners of the new Town of Wellington proposed this 1,500-acre development as a way for Palm Beach County to "build its way out" of the acute growth-related problems it was experiencing. Approval required a controversial westward extension of the county's urban limit line. It was granted, ironically, because officials felt that this dense mixed-use project would help to both contain further sprawl and reverse a serious jobs/housing imbalance in the area.

Like much of Florida, Palm Beach County has seen tremendous low-density suburban growth in recent years. Residential subdivisions have pushed steadily inland from the desirable island community of Palm Beach and its "downtown" of West Palm Beach. Most of these new developments made little or no provision for shopping or workplaces. Offices and large stores then located on nearby arterials, turning those roads into congested "strips." As a result, east-west commuters who live in the newly developed areas suffer increasing traffic delays despite several recent road widenings.

The new Town of Wellington, at the western edge of the existing Wellington planned unit development (PUD), aims to ease the area's congestion by creating a community with a large workplace element to balance an abundance of housing in the adjacent PUD. Its planners, Andres Duany and Elizabeth Plater-Zyberk, proposed a town composed of nine

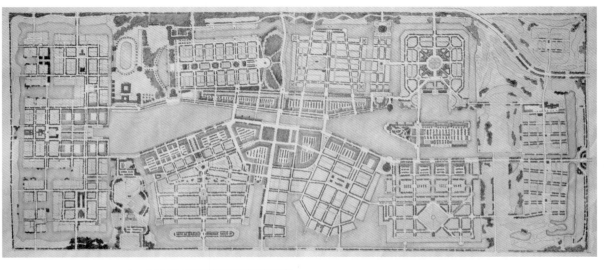

Like many Florida developments, a large percentage of the Town of Wellington's land area is required to be water for drainage purposes. Many such developments, like this one (left) in the present Wellington subdivision, completely surround bodies of water with private houses. While this strategy yields more waterfront homesites, it removes a key civic amenity from public use and enjoyment.

The proposed Town of Wellington (opposite) provides water views and public access to the lakefront from many points. Careful planning preserves the value of prime waterfront homesites and increases the appeal of properties in other parts of the development. The enhanced public realm thus creates a tangible benefit for the entire community.

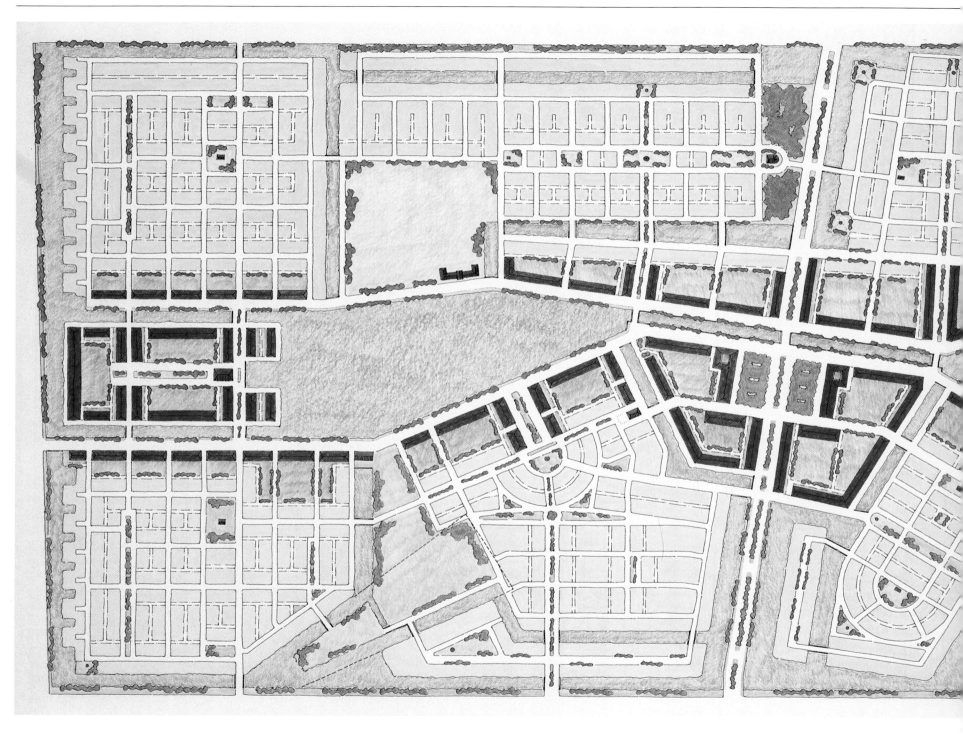

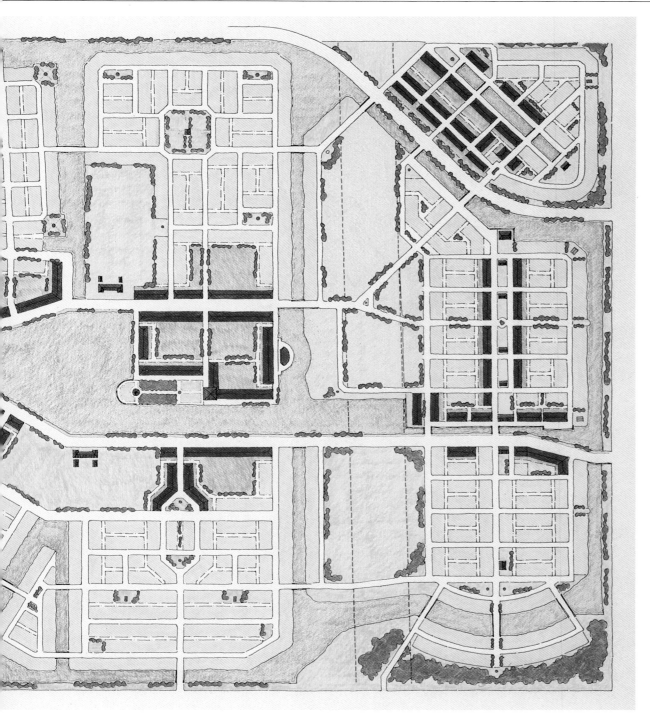

The plan of the Town of Wellington (left) locates the densest part of each neighborhood around a bow-tie shaped central lake. Bordered by two boulevards, the lake narrows in the middle to define the town center (center of plan).

At each end, the lake broadens, providing long views from surrounding neighborhoods. Sites for the town's most important public buildings are located at key inflection points around the lake's perimeter.

distinct neighborhoods that converge across a central lake to form a dense commercial core. A continuous lakefront boulevard connects the densest part of each neighborhood while another boulevard links their central squares, providing a convenient bus loop for the town.

Within the Town of Wellington, large amounts of commercial and retail space are provided. In addition, a wide range of housing options are offered in proximity to the community's jobs. Density in each neighborhood gradates from three- and four-story office, retail and apartment buildings at the lakefront to the freestanding single-family homes lining the perimeter canals. Dwelling types in between include courtyard apartments, several kinds of townhouses, sideyard houses and rear yard accessory units.

Housing affordability was a key concern of the town's planning team. Rental units above stores and in the backyards of principal residences—two forms of housing rarely seen in the suburbs—are included among the community's mix of residential types.

More conventional multi-unit affordable housing follows guidelines set by the design team to ensure compatibility with nearby homes. Such housing is placed only in small groups (never more than 12 units in a row) and always among residences of a higher economic range. Also, the architecture and massing of

This neighborhood (opposite) is situated between Wellington's Town Center and a large regional park. The physical design of all of the town's neighborhoods conforms to Palm Beach County's recently adopted TND ordinance.

This ordinance together with the town's regulating plan, urban code and street sections (pages 110-116) establish a precise urban structure with clearly defined building, street and open-space types.

A series of diagrams (below) indicates the locations of various components within the neighborhood. These include public open spaces (below left), civic buildings (middle left) and places of work (bottom left).

Shops with upper-level apartment units front the commercial boulevard at the lake's edge (below right); medium-density residences such as townhouses and small apartment buildings radiate out from the central green (middle right).

Single-family housing (bottom right) gradates in density from compact sideyard residences on the internal blocks to large detached houses lining the canals.

buildings containing affordable units reflect that of adjacent dwellings.

One of the town's neighborhoods is designed as a college campus. Its mix of academic, residential and commercial activities is meant to evoke the character of a typical "college town."

The community's Town Center, similar in form to a conventional large shopping center, is carefully woven into the small-scale grain of the town. It provides for residents' shopping needs not met in other smaller neighborhood stores.

Several kinds of public open spaces occur within the Town of Wellington. Formal neighborhood squares provide a focus at the center of neighborhoods while smaller playgrounds for active uses are more widely distributed. A large regional park evokes the natural landscape of the region. The extensive lake and waterway system required for drainage completes the plan's generous open-space network.

Though the Town of Wellington's approvals have been secured, recent downturns in real estate have made financing difficult, causing the project to be put on hold. Despite this, low-density sprawl growth continues in Palm Beach County–further adding to the area's severe congestion. If innovative towns like this could proceed, it would enable us to test its basic premise: that problems of existing poorly planned areas can indeed be fixed by the building of new places designed to compensate for old ills.

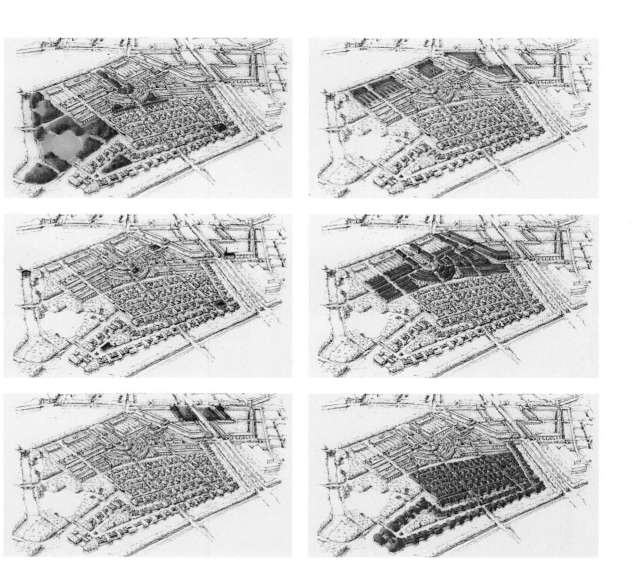

A typical neighborhood center in the Town of Wellington (below) consists of a small public square surrounded by community buildings such as a post office, meeting hall or child-care center. Apartment housing may also be suitable in this location.

While uses can be flexible, it is important for these buildings to have a physical presence and formality that give dignity and spatial definition to the adjacent public square.

Architectural and urban codes for the Town of Wellington call for simple, well-proportioned buildings constructed in the most basic local style—in this case stucco over concrete block with pitched tile roofs.

An extensive network of canals and waterways is required for storm water retention in Wellington. The design team used this combination of water and architecture to define a distinctly picturesque image for the town (opposite).

Waterfront edges alternate between masonry walls and landscaped banks. The use of overhanging balconies and hybrid construction (wood and masonry) is reminiscent of traditional Caribbean architecture.

An early plan of the Town of Wellington included a generic college campus (below) among its neighborhoods. A more recent design (right and opposite) follows a specific program set by a local university.

A conference center forms the heart of this university's campus, intended to feel like a typical "college town." Seminar participants live on campus within easy walking distance of this neighborhood's restaurants, shops and other amenities.

The historic ambiance of such South Florida communities as Palm Beach and Coral Gables is reflected in the architecture and site planning of this mixed-use campus/neighborhood.

Framed by the university's public buildings, a landscaped mall (below) is terminated at one end by a large auditorium and campanile (opposite). Classrooms, labs and faculty offices flank the mall above street level, while shops line it below.

Full-block courtyard buildings provide student housing (bottom) near the campus center. The housing options in this neighborhood range from dorms and apartments to single-family houses.

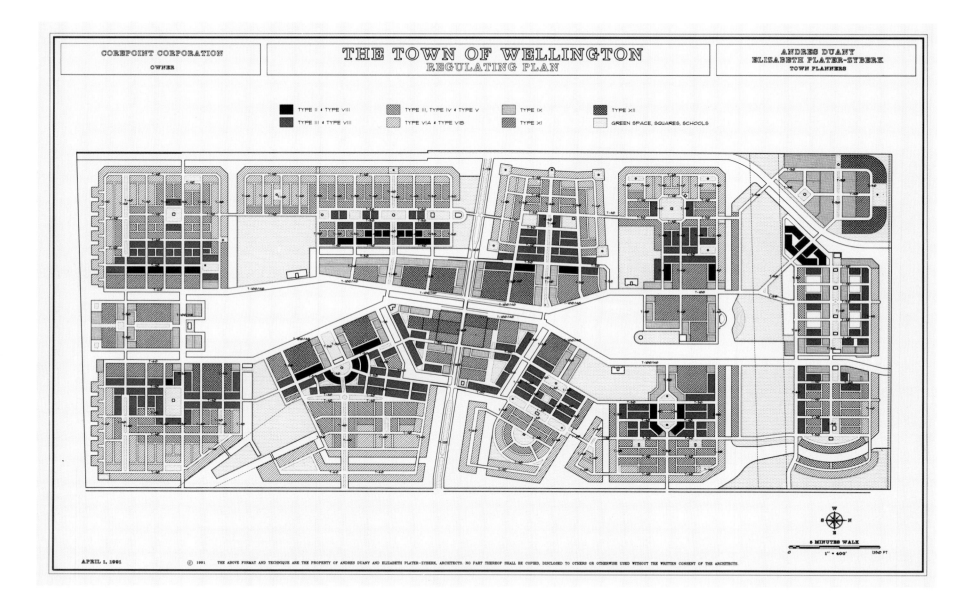

APRIL 1, 1991   © 1991   THE ABOVE FORMAT AND TECHNIQUE ARE THE PROPERTY OF ANDRES DUANY AND ELIZABETH PLATER-ZYBERK, ARCHITECTS. NO PART THEREOF SHALL BE COPIED, DISCLOSED TO OTHERS OR OTHERWISE USED WITHOUT THE WRITTEN CONSENT OF THE ARCHITECTS.

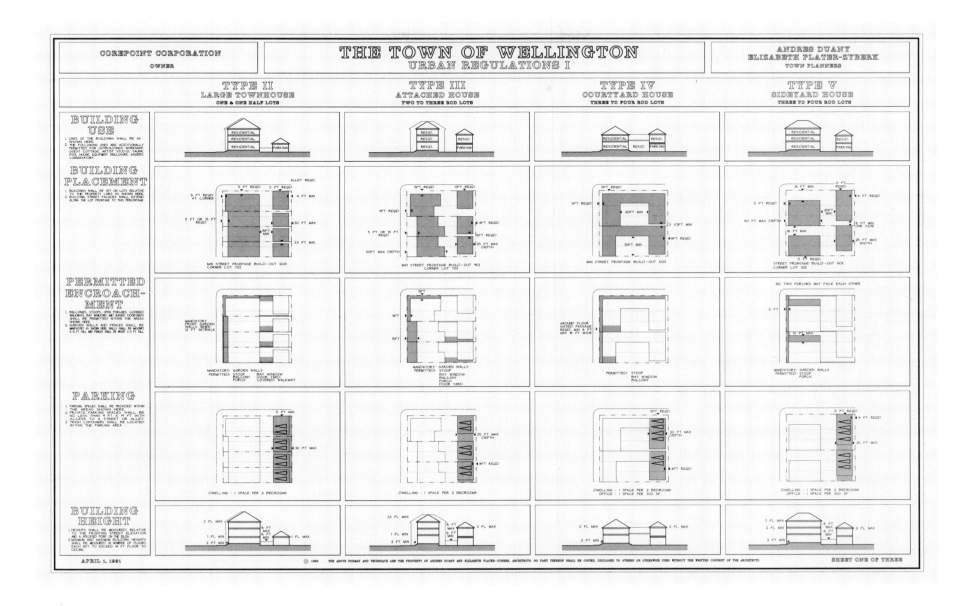

THE TOWN OF WELLINGTON
URBAN REGULATIONS I

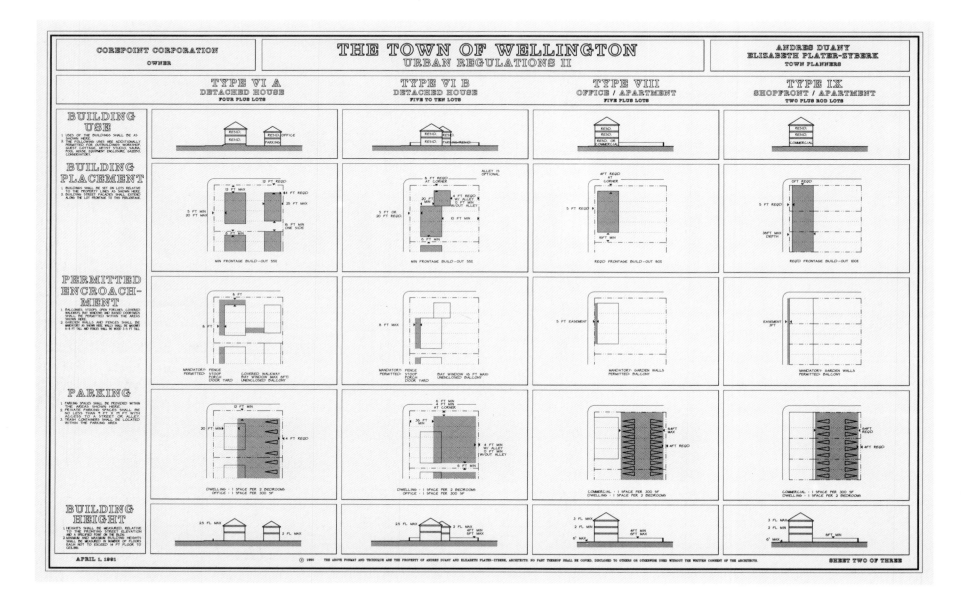

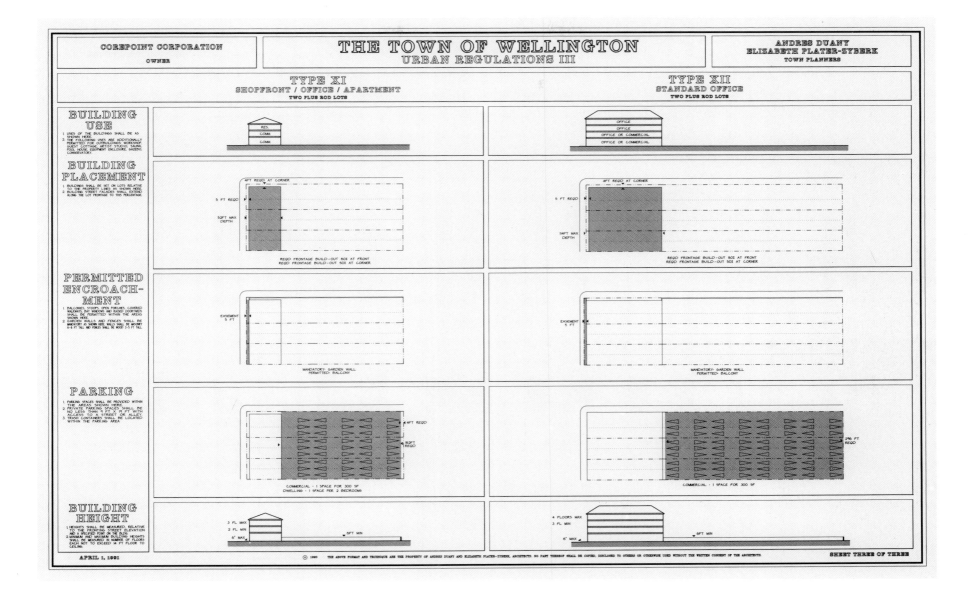

THE TOWN OF WELLINGTON
URBAN REGULATIONS III

COREPOINT CORPORATION — OWNER

ANDRES DUANY
ELIZABETH PLATER-ZYBERK — TOWN PLANNERS

TYPE XI — SHOPFRONT / OFFICE / APARTMENT — TWO PLUS ROD LOTS

TYPE XII — STANDARD OFFICE — TWO PLUS ROD LOTS

BUILDING USE · BUILDING PLACEMENT · PERMITTED ENCROACHMENT · PARKING · BUILDING HEIGHT

APRIL 1, 1991

SHEET THREE OF THREE

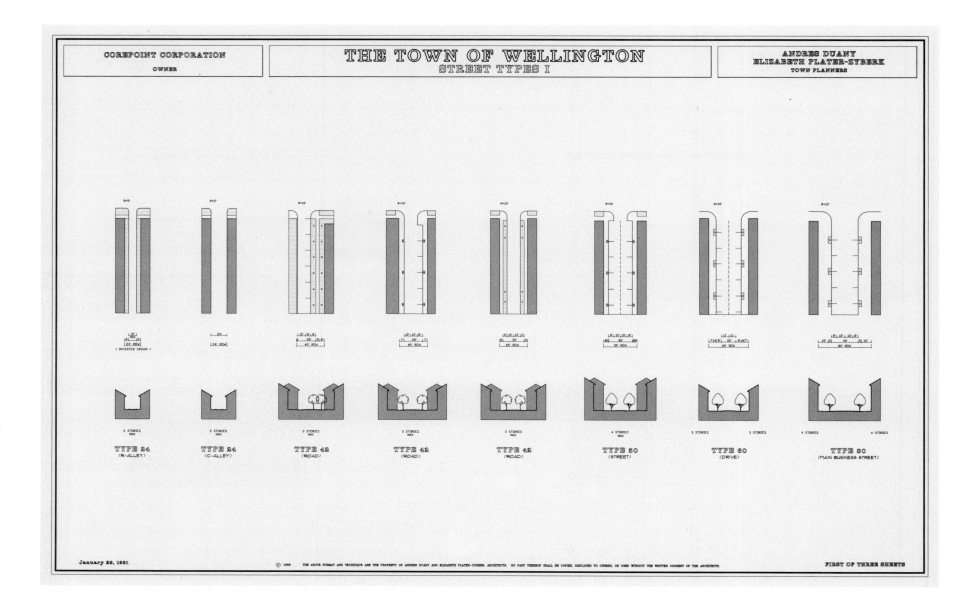

© 1989 THE ABOVE FORMAT AND TECHNIQUE ARE THE PROPERTY OF ANDRES DUANY AND ELIZABETH PLATER-ZYBERK ARCHITECTS. NO PART THEREOF SHALL BE COPIED, DISCLOSED TO OTHERS, OR USED WITHOUT THE WRITTEN CONSENT OF THE ARCHITECTS.

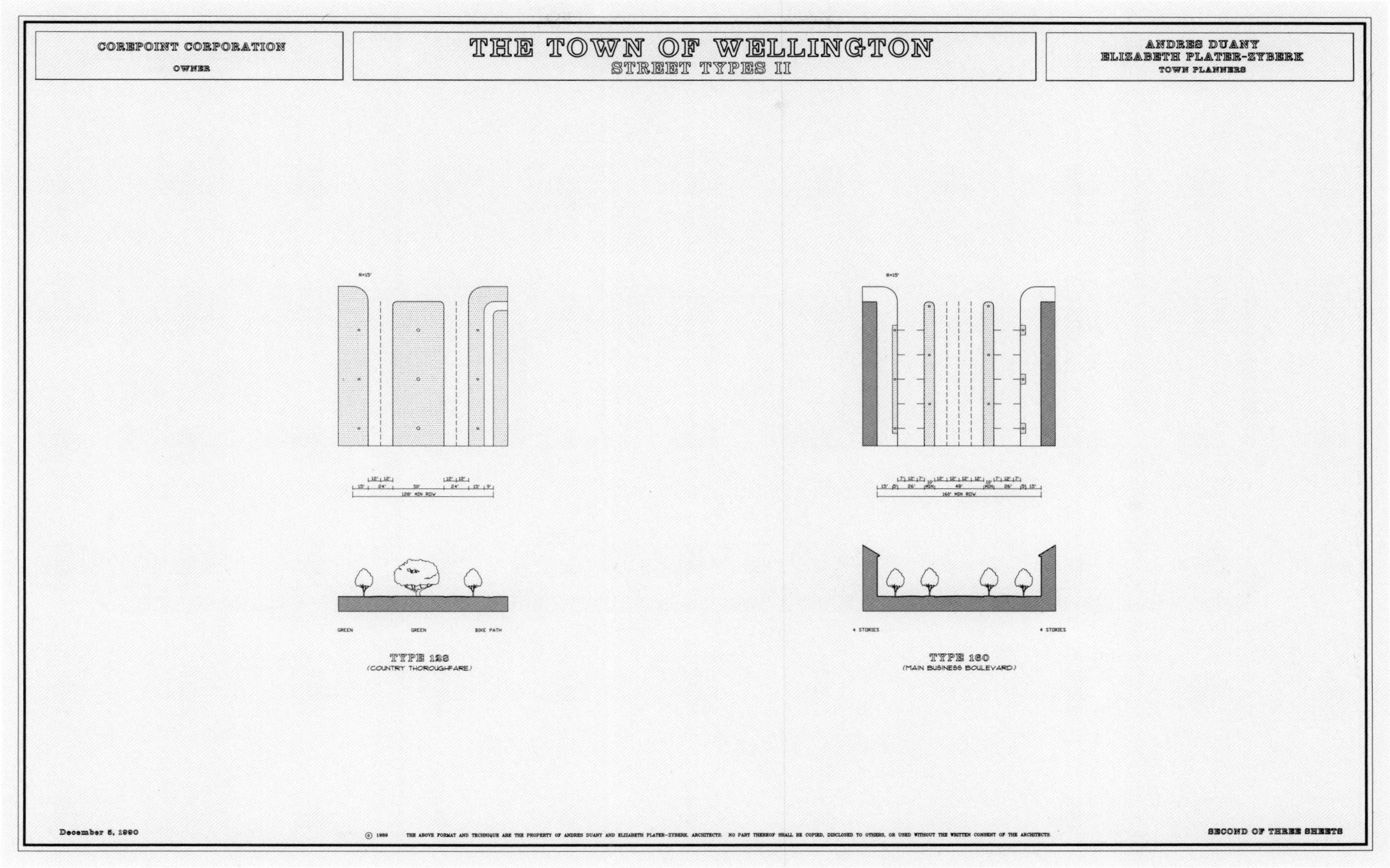
COREPOINT CORPORATION
OWNER
THE TOWN OF WELLINGTON
STREET TYPES II
ANDRES DUANY
ELIZABETH PLATER-ZYBERK
TOWN PLANNERS
R=15'
12' 12' 12' 12'
15' 24' 50' 24' 15' 9'
128' MIN ROW
GREEN
GREEN
BIKE PATH
TYPE 128
(COUNTRY THOROUGHFARE)
R=15'
7' 12' 7' 12' 12' 12' 12' 7' 12' 7'
15' (5') 26' 10' MIN 48' 10' MIN 26' (5') 15'
160' MIN ROW
4 STORIES
4 STORIES
TYPE 160
(MAIN BUSINESS BOULEVARD)
December 5, 1990
© 1989 THE ABOVE FORMAT AND TECHNIQUE ARE THE PROPERTY OF ANDRES DUANY AND ELIZABETH PLATER-ZYBERK. ARCHITECTS. NO PART THEREOF SHALL BE COPIED, DISCLOSED TO OTHERS, OR USED WITHOUT THE WRITTEN CONSENT OF THE ARCHITECTS.
SECOND OF THREE SHEETS

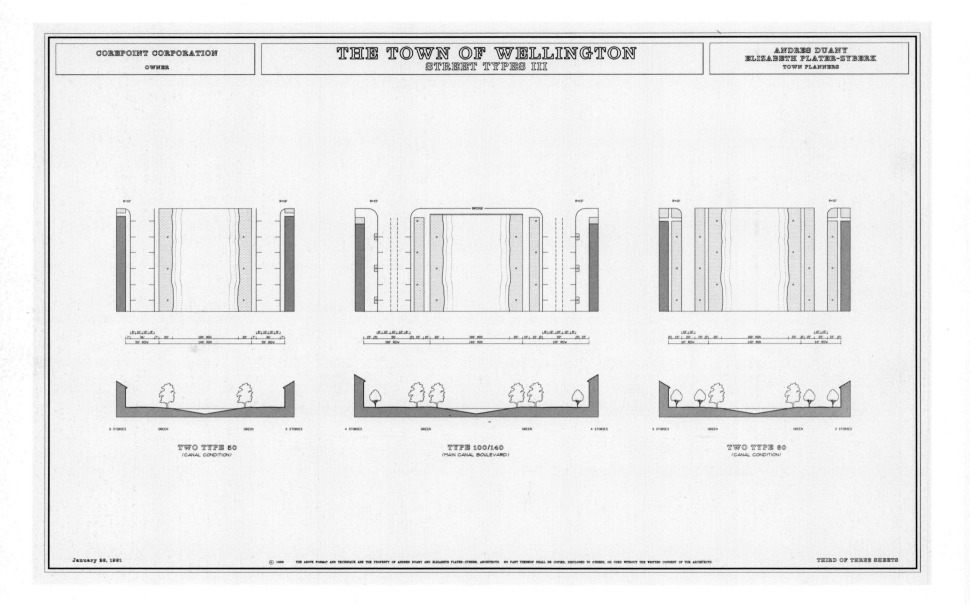

TWO TYPE 50
(CANAL CONDITION)

TYPE 100/140
(MAIN CANAL BOULEVARD)

TWO TYPE 60
(CANAL CONDITION)

Reconstructing the Urban Fabric

Decisions made in the past impose powerful restraints on the future. The location of buildings, of streets, and of highway systems imposes a measure of permanence on the form of community. Quite simply, the investment costs of building are so great that no generation can afford to replace old fabric with new; adaptation of the old has always been dominant.

Kenneth T. Jackson,
Crabgrass Frontier, 1985

Cité Internationale

Montréal, Canada, 1990

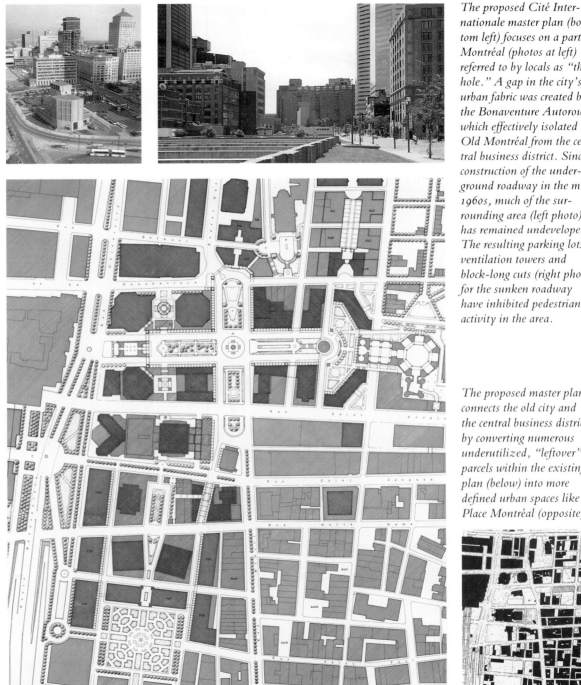

The proposed Cité Internationale master plan (bottom left) focuses on a part of Montréal (photos at left) referred to by locals as "the hole." A gap in the city's urban fabric was created by the Bonaventure Autoroute which effectively isolated Old Montréal from the central business district. Since construction of the underground roadway in the mid-1960s, much of the surrounding area (left photo) has remained undeveloped. The resulting parking lots, ventilation towers and block-long cuts (right photo) for the sunken roadway have inhibited pedestrian activity in the area.

Montréal's Cité Internationale plan aims, in the jargon of real estate, to create "location" within its 100-acre site. Like New York's Park Avenue or San Francisco's Union Square, the memorable public spaces defined in this new commercial and retail district are meant to give identity to surrounding neighborhoods. This, its planners contend, will create added value in an area now known for parking lots, expressways and isolated buildings.

Architects Peterson and Littenberg's master plan for a new international quarter between Montréal's old city and its financial district was chosen over 93 other entries in a competition sponsored by the city and 20 private developers. Their scheme seeks to restore and enhance the urban fabric in an area scarred by the insertion of two expressways in the 1960s. Three major "public rooms"–a cruciform space called Place Montréal, a three-acre park named Parc Square and a formal tree-lined boulevard dubbed the Champs d' Entrée–give new structure to a place which previously lacked a defined urban grid.

Combining new large floorplate buildings with older historic ones, the scheme's innovative lot assembly and setback guidelines enable its new civic spaces to be created without any public purchase of private land. Further, the proposed Cité Internationale master plan will retain, and in many cases increase, the buildable potential of each owner's property.

The proposed master plan connects the old city and the central business district by converting numerous underutilized, "leftover" parcels within the existing plan (below) into more defined urban spaces like the Place Montréal (opposite).

An international conference center (below) provides office space and meeting facilities for 2,000 people. It is the focus of a new international quarter, meant to complement the city's adjacent historic and financial districts.

The conference complex anchors one end of the east-west axis of Place Montréal, the new district's principal public space. An existing mixed-use building housing the city's train station, Place Bonaventure, terminates the other end of Avenue Viger.

A raised terrace forms a spacious entry court for the conference facility. Two large office buildings frame the "civic stage" that serves as the public face for this internally oriented building.

The Champs d'Entrée (below), at the edge of the project site near an existing rail viaduct, functions as an arrival court for the city. This large space, at the confluence of a major highway and several local streets, is organized in the manner of a public garden.

The Cité Internationale plan (opposite) incorporates adjacent streets, squares and landmarks into a larger network of civic spaces (bottom), each with its own defined physical form and symbolic character.

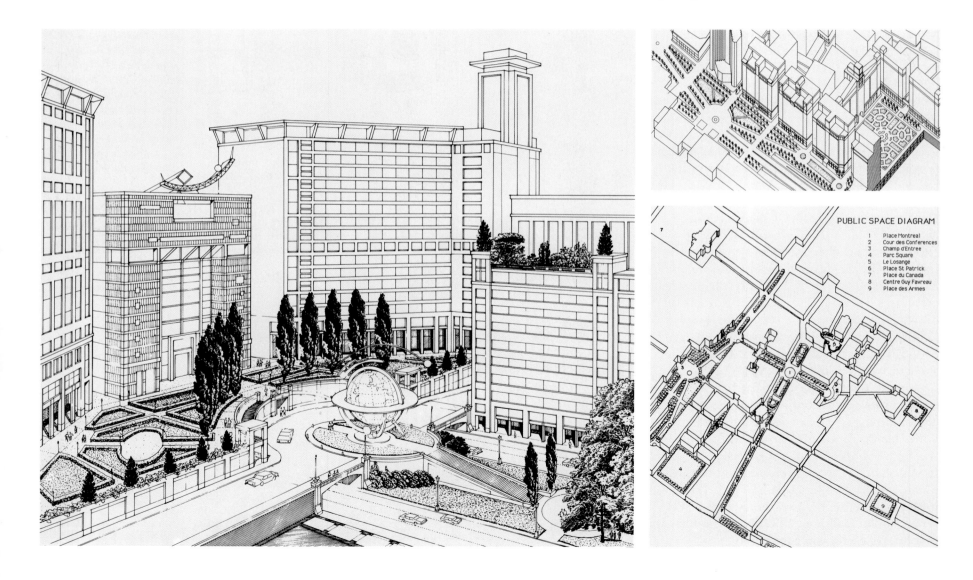

PUBLIC SPACE DIAGRAM

1 Place Montreal
2 Cour des Conferences
3 Champ d'Entree
4 Parc Square
5 Le Losange
6 Place St Patrick
7 Place du Canada
8 Centre Guy Favreau
9 Place des Armes

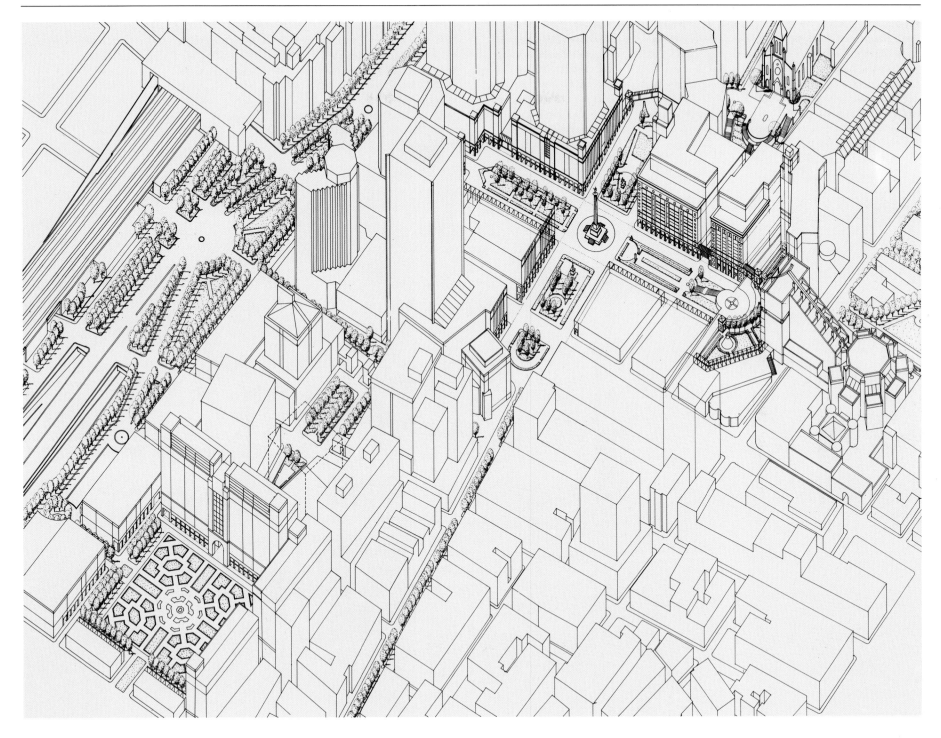

A continuous street-level retail arcade lines the entire perimeter of the new Place Montréal (below). A two-story base added to several existing towers at the east end forms a consistent streetwall. A grove of trees extends across each arm of the cruciform plan.

Conceived as a "grand crossroads," Place Montréal organizes a patchwork of disconnected sites into a dignified, spatially defined public garden—an oasis of calm amidst the activity of the city.

The underground expressway which had previously inhibited development in this area lies beneath one leg of Place Montréal's cruciform plan. An oversized pyramidal garden pavilion (at center of illustration below) serves as a ventilation shaft for the roadway.

This transformation demonstrates how modern large-scale infrastructure elements can be successfully integrated into the fabric of the city. In this project, a previously undesirable intervention became the catalyst for positive change.

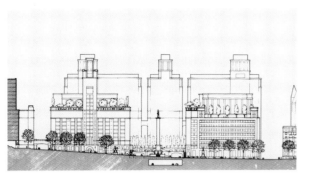

Multiple levels of vehicular
and pedestrian circulation
interconnect within Place
Montréal. This section view
(left) through the Cote du
Beaver Hall shows how
the slope of the site relates to
a second-level system of
bridges, terraces and walks.

The section through Avenue
Viger (below) shows the
conference center's semi-
circular vehicular entry court
which connects at the same
level to the Rue de la
Gauchetiere (left in section
at left).

The stepped ramp (below)
provides a gracious, axial
pedestrian approach to the
complex. While this design
accommodates the functional
needs of automobile access,
it also contributes to the
making of a prominent civic
space within the district.

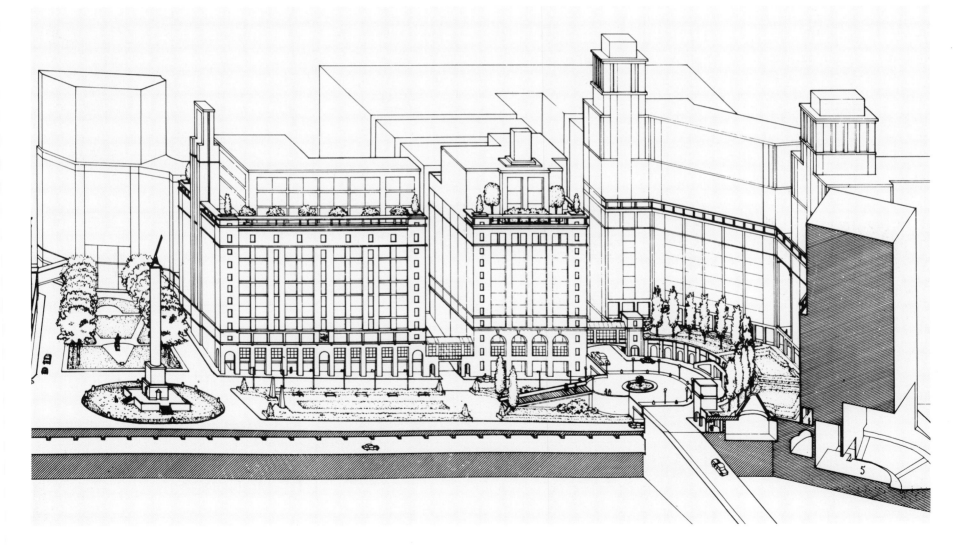

This summary of typological elements (below) can be thought of as a "kit of parts" for the design of the Cité Internationale district.

These design elements are relatively few in number and are individually simple. They are used to resolve problems of both function and composition and impart a sense of place to various locations within the plan.

Implementation of the Cité Internationale plan is described in a set of detailed guidelines (opposite) that illustrate specific lot assembly and urban design strategies for each block and parcel in the district.

Two levels of compliance with the master plan are described. The "preferred" scheme rewards full-block and cooperating property owners by enabling them to realize the cumulative development potential of the entire block.

A "contingent" scheme shows how the plan's public spaces can still be formed by piecemeal development of smaller, individually owned parcels within the block.

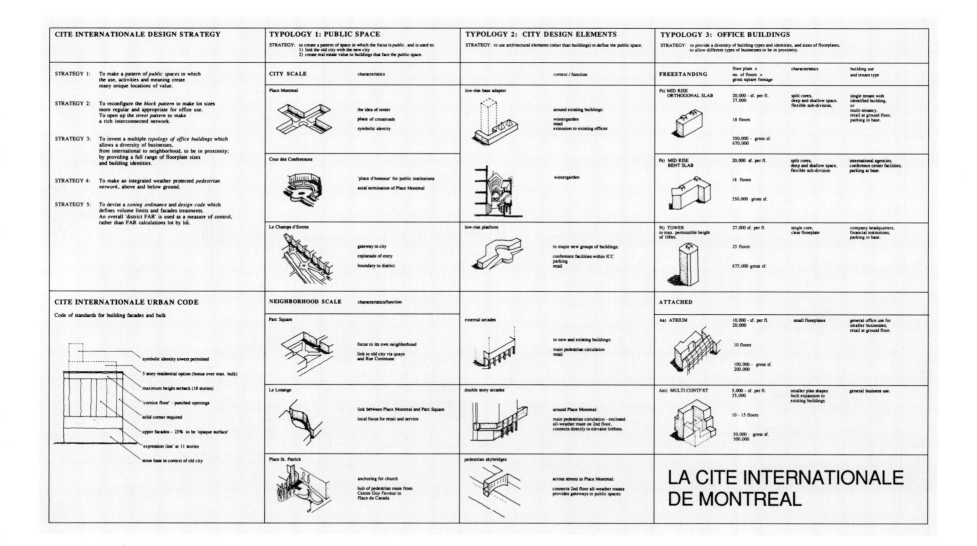

CITE INTERNATIONALE DESIGN STRATEGY

STRATEGY 1: To make a pattern of *public spaces* in which the use, activities and meaning create many unique locations of value.

STRATEGY 2: To reconfigure the *block pattern* to make lot sizes more regular and appropriate for office use. To open up the *street pattern* to make a rich interconnected network.

STRATEGY 3: To invent a multiple *typology of office buildings* which allows a diversity of businesses, from international to neighborhood, to be in proximity; by providing a full range of floorplate sizes and building identities.

STRATEGY 4: To make an integrated weather protected *pedestrian network*, above and below ground.

STRATEGY 5: To devise a *zoning ordinance* and *design code* which defines volume limits and facades treatments. An overall 'district FAR' is used as a measure of control, rather than FAR calculations lot by lot.

CITE INTERNATIONALE URBAN CODE

Code of standards for building facades and bulk

- symbolic identity towers permitted
- 3 story residential option (bonus over max. bulk)
- maximum height setback (18 stories)
- 'cornice floor' - punched openings
- solid corner required
- upper facades - 25% to be 'opaque surface'
- 'expression line' at 11 stories
- stone base in context of old city

TYPOLOGY 1: PUBLIC SPACE

STRATEGY: to create a pattern of space in which the focus is *public*, and is used to:
1) link the old city with the new city
2) create real estate value to buildings that face the public space.

CITY SCALE	characteristics
Place Montreal	the idea of center / place of crossroads / symbolic identity
Cour des Conferences	'place d'honneur' for public institutions / axial termination of Place Montreal
Le Champs d'Entree	gateway to city / esplanade of entry / boundary to district

NEIGHBORHOOD SCALE	characteristics/function
Parc Square	focus to its own neighborhood / link to old city via quays and Rue Commune
Le Losange	link between Place Montreal and Parc Square / local focus for retail and service
Place St. Patrick	anchoring for church / hub of pedestrian route from Centre Guy Favreur to Place du Canada

TYPOLOGY 2: CITY DESIGN ELEMENTS

STRATEGY: to use architectural elements (other than buildings) to define the public space.

	context / function
low-rise base adapter	around existing buildings: wintergarden / retail / extension to existing offices
	wintergarden
low-rise platform	to major new groups of buildings: conference facilities within ICC / parking / retail
external arcades	to new and existing buildings: main pedestrian circulation / retail
double story arcades	around Place Montreal: main pedestrian circulation - enclosed all-weather route on 2nd floor, connects directly to elevator lobbies.
pedestrian skybridges	across streets in Place Montreal: connects 2nd floor all-weather routes provides gateways to public spaces

TYPOLOGY 3: OFFICE BUILDINGS

STRATEGY: to provide a diversity of building types and identities, and sizes of floorplates, to allow different types of businesses to be in proximity.

FREESTANDING	floor plate x no. of floors = gross square footage	characteristics	building use and tenant type
Fs) MID RISE ORTHOGONAL SLAB	20,000 - sf. per fl. / 37,000 / 18 floors / 350,000 - gross sf. / 670,000	split cores, deep and shallow space, flexible sub-division	single tenant with identified building, or multi-tenancy, retail at ground floor, parking in base.
Fs) MID RISE BENT SLAB	20,000 sf. per fl. / 18 floors / 350,000 gross sf.	split cores, deep and shallow space, flexible sub-division	international agencies, conference center facilities, parking at base.
Ft) TOWER to max. permissible height of 100m.	27,000 sf. per fl. / 25 floors / 675,000 gross sf.	single core, clear floorplate	company headquarters, financial institutions, parking in base.

ATTACHED			
Aa) ATRIUM	10,000 - sf. per fl. / 20,000 / 10 floors / 100,000 - gross sf. / 200,000	small floorplates	general office use for smaller businesses, retail at ground floor.
Am) MULTI CONTEXT	5,000 - sf. per fl. / 35,000 / 10 - 15 floors / 50,000 - gross sf. / 500,000	smaller plan shapes built expansion to existing buildings	general business use.

LA CITE INTERNATIONALE DE MONTREAL

Block II (below left and key plan, right) fronts the new Champs d' Entrée. The easement creating that civic space eliminated a small street and block fragment to the west. Compensatory credits for greater building mass are transferred to other parcels within the block.

The low building in the contingent plan maintains a four-story wall at the edge of the public space. The large building in the preferred scenario represents the type currently desired in the international office market.

Block X (below right and key plan, right) defines part of the new Place Montréal. In the contingent scheme, individual buildings hold a nearly continuous street-wall. One large floorplate building is the intended result of the preferred plan.

In both scenarios the Rue Saint Alexandre has been bridged at the second-story level for enhanced pedestrian circulation. Importantly, it has been preserved as a public thoroughfare at grade.

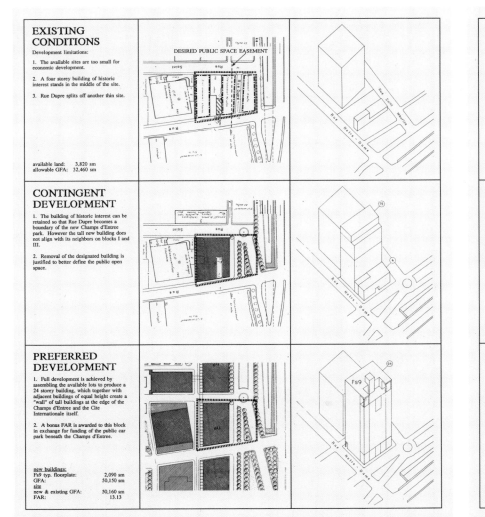

EXISTING CONDITIONS

Development limitations:

1. The available sites are too small for economic development.

2. A four storey building of historic interest stands in the middle of the site.

3. Rue Dupre splits off another thin site.

available land: 3,820 sm
allowable GFA: 32,460 sm

CONTINGENT DEVELOPMENT

1. The building of historic interest can be retained so that Rue Dupre becomes a boundary of the new Champs d'Entree park. However the tall new building does not align with its neighbors on blocks I and III.

2. Removal of the designated building is justified to better define the public open space.

PREFERRED DEVELOPMENT

1. Full development is achieved by assembling the available lots to produce a 24 storey building, which together with adjacent buildings of equal height create a "wall" of tall buildings at the edge of the Champs d'Entree and the Cite Internationale itself.

2. A bonus FAR is awarded to this block in exchange for funding of the public car park beneath the Champs d'Entree.

new buildings:
Fs9 typ. floorplate: 2,090 sm
GFA: 50,150 sm
site
new & existing GFA: 50,160 sm
FAR: 13.13

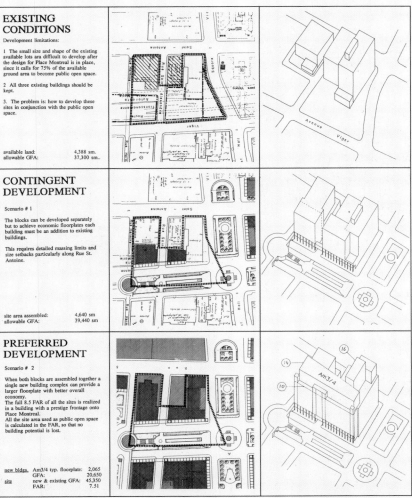

EXISTING CONDITIONS

Development limitations:

1 The small size and shape of the existing available lots are difficult to develop after the design for Place Montreal is in place, since it calls for 75% of the available ground area to become public open space.

2 All three existing buildings should be kept.

3. The problem is: how to develop these sites in conjunction with the public open space.

available land: 4,388 sm.
allowable GFA: 37,300 sm..

CONTINGENT DEVELOPMENT

Scenario # 1

The blocks can be developed separately but to achieve economic floorplates each building must be an addition to existing buildings.

This requires detailed massing limits and size setbacks particularly along Rue St. Antoine.

site area assembled: 4,640 sm
allowable GFA: 39,440 sm

PREFERRED DEVELOPMENT

Scenario # 2

When both blocks are assembled together a single new building complex can provide a larger floorplate with better overall economy.
The full 8.5 FAR of all the sites is realized in a building with a prestige frontage onto Place Montreal.
All the site area used as public open space is calculated in the FAR, so that no building potential is lost.

new bldgs. Am3/4 typ. floorplate: 2,065
                   GFA: 20,650
site   new & existing GFA: 45,350
                   FAR: 7.51

Downtown Hayward

Hayward, California, 1992

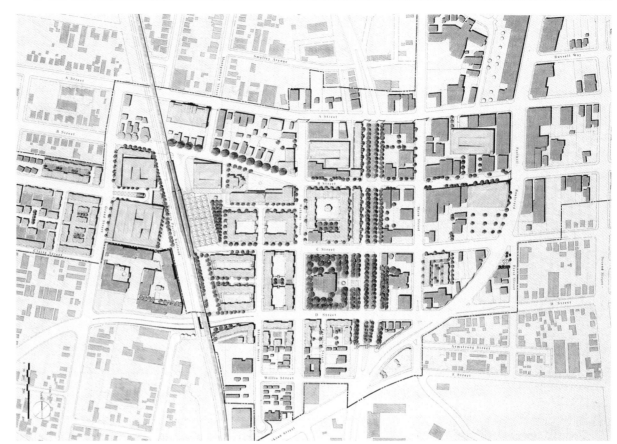

The city of Hayward is known to area motorists as the "missing link" in the San Francisco Bay region's elaborate network of bridges and freeways. In the 1960s and early 1970s environmental and citizens' groups opposed a planned connection between a newly completed bay bridge crossing and freeway, each at opposite ends of town. Foothill Boulevard, a major surface road, was forced to play that role instead.

Today, regional traffic between the bridge and the freeway is choking Foothill Boulevard. Much of the vitality of its once healthy retail businesses and those of nearby downtown Hayward has been lost to several malls outside the area. Large office complexes, accessed mainly by car, have replaced Foothill's stores. Though close in distance, these workplaces have little physical connection to downtown.

Compounding these problems, several blocks at the opposite end of downtown were demolished in the 1960s to build parking for BART (Bay Area Rapid Transit), a commuter rail system. In yet another part of downtown, a 50-foot setback zone for new construction was declared along an active fault in the wake of the devastating 1989 Loma Prieta earthquake. Hayward's historic "old city hall," main fire station and a major street, Mission Boulevard, are all located over the fault.

By the early 1990s, the combined effects of these and other assaults on the physical fabric of

The scheme for downtown Hayward (opposite and plan, above) includes a number of proposals aimed at mitigating various large, poorly integrated transportation elements. The city's urban fabric was badly compromised by the demolition of several downtown blocks for commuter parking in the 1960s (left). A new civic and transit center has been proposed for this area.

One major element of the Hayward master plan is a downtown plaza and civic center near the historic heart of the city (plan, below). Previously used as a parking lot for commuters, the complex is intended to serve as a hub for the newly revitalized downtown.

Several schemes have been proposed for the civic center area. In each, a prominent public building (such as a new city hall) terminates the view from B Street, creating a focal point for downtown's principal shopping street.

A large parking garage and second public building (a library or a recreation center) are shown in this scheme. A phased build-out for the site is suggested whereby part of the property can continue to be used for parking until needed.

The optimal form of the downtown plaza and focal point building required a landswap between the city and the commuter rail line. The previous parcel layout (below right) splits the frontage of each property along both B and C Streets.

The reparcelized site (bottom right) permits development of the entire block frontage along B Street. A public plaza is carved out of the streetwall (below left) creating a foreground for the focal point building.

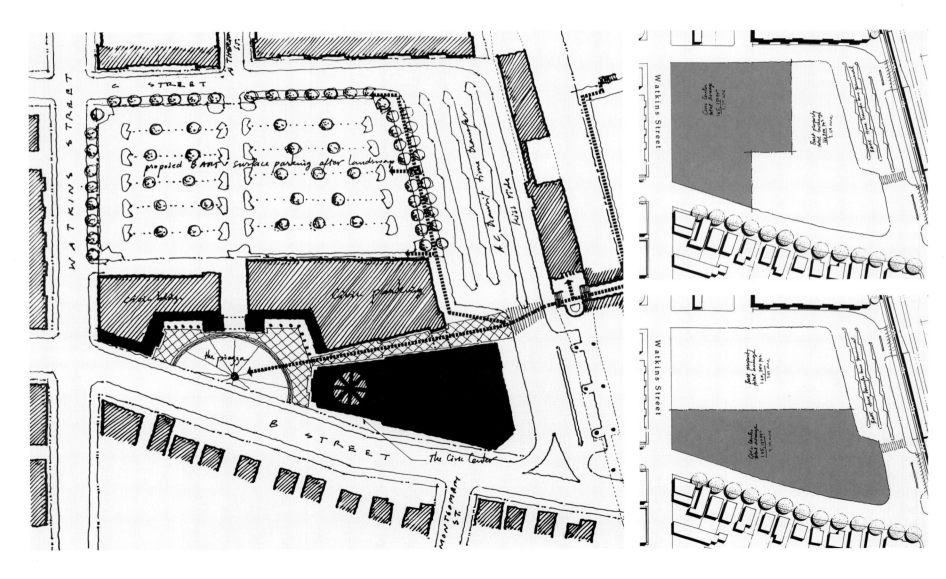

Another scheme for the civic center area (right) includes an additional group of office buildings fronting on C Street. Upper level bridges (bottom left) connect various buildings with each other and parking.

The dome of the focal point building is intended to be a prominent element when viewed from B Street (bottom right).

downtown suggested a bleak future for what remained of this once vital district. Seeking to reverse the seemingly inevitable decline of its historic core, the city of Hayward launched an ambitious downtown revitalization effort.

A lengthy public process led by architect Daniel Solomon resulted in a master plan to restore the economic vitality and pedestrian character of downtown. Proposals include a new civic center complex with a public plaza and prominent civic building as its focal point. A transit center for bus and BART riders is planned, along with parking garages and an improved undercrossing beneath the rail line.

Large portions of downtown are slated for housing, all within close proximity of BART and shopping. B Street, downtown's main retail corridor, is the focus of an effort to enhance the viability of area businesses. Several new streets and the realignment of others are intended to reverse the effects of several poorly planned interventions that have eroded the integrity of Hayward's historic gridiron plan.

A park for billboards and a prominent tower on Foothill Boulevard show that the Hayward plan is more than just a return to the past. These innovative proposals are meant to harness and redirect the negative attributes of Foothill, now a blighted strip. The result, its planners believe, will help restore the vitality and positive identity of Hayward and its downtown core.

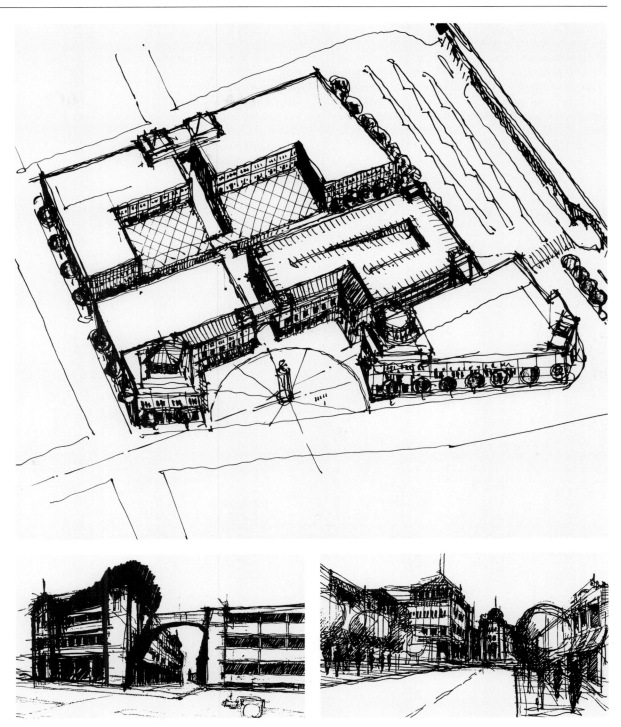

One goal of the Hayward plan was to repair the split in downtown caused by the commuter rail line. A large parking garage to be built next to the tracks on the station's west side (plan, right) is realigned with Grand Street (plan, below).

This allows a more direct pedestrian route through the train station (bottom right and opposite) that continues the axis of C Street from the west. It also creates a narrow building site along Grand Street.

A thin "liner building" on this site (partially visible at right in sketch, bottom right) hides the garage from the view of new residences across Grand Street. Ideally this building will be residential also, reflecting the use and character of the adjacent neighborhood.

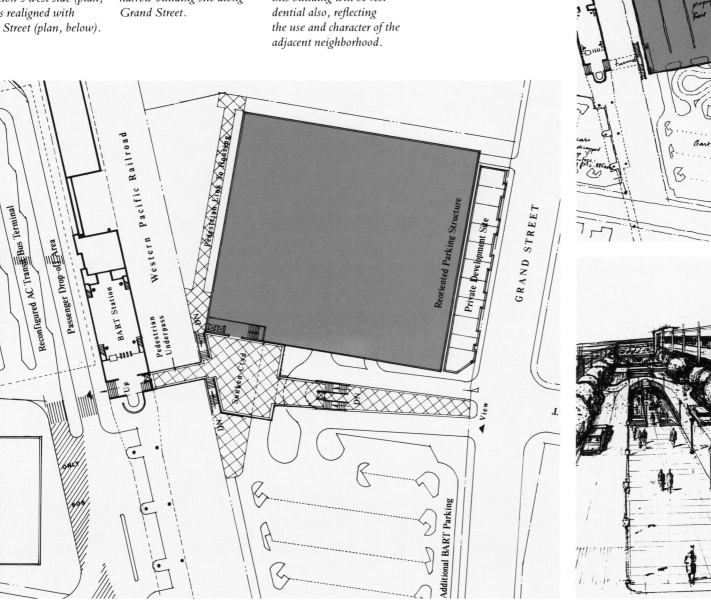

A new and enlarged pedestrian connection to the train station from the west (below and plan sketch, right) replaces a narrow, enclosed stairway which led to an underground passageway.

The reconfigured entry sequence includes a small kiosk (with elevator for disabled persons), multiple open stairs and a sunken courtyard. All of these elements are arranged to avoid intersecting the path of automobiles.

A section view through several downtown blocks (bottom) shows the relationship between the proposed civic center and plaza, pedestrian undercrossing and neighborhood west of Grand Street.

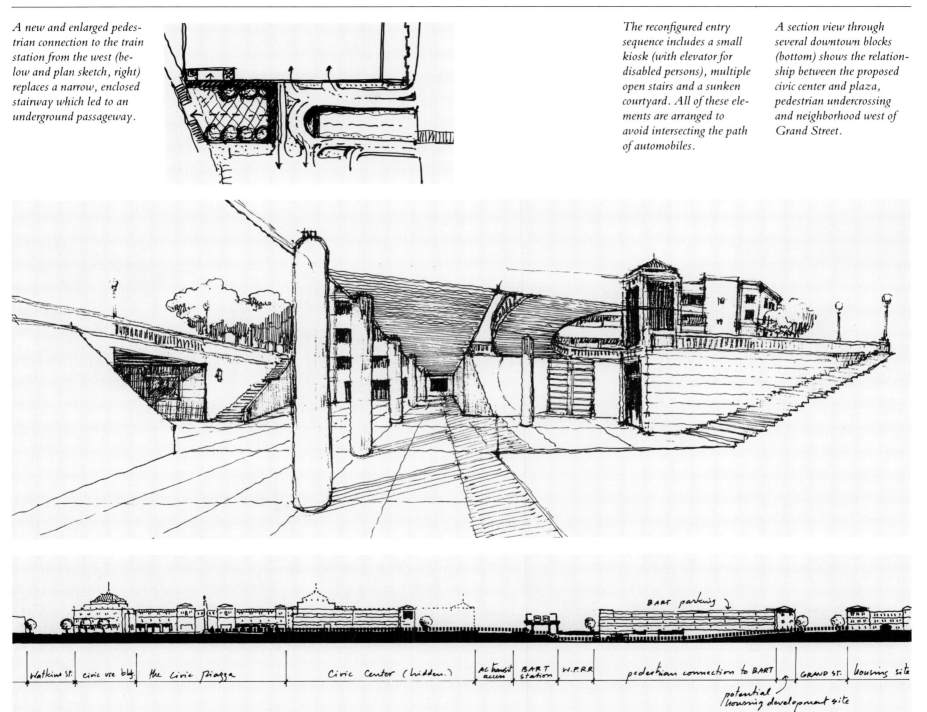

Watkins St. | civic use bldg. | the Civic Piazza | Civic Center (hidden.) | AC transit access | BART station | W.P.R.R. | pedestrian connection to BART | Grand St. | housing site

BART parking

potential housing development site

Housing has been identified as a critical component of the downtown revitalization. It is seen as the only way to repopulate the city center and reverse the present pattern of disinvestment in downtown real estate.

Several key sites are targeted for residential development. Library Square (below) includes parts of six downtown blocks surrounding Hayward's existing main library and post office.

Building types that bring vitality to the street such as townhouses and podium apartments (with garages no more than one-half level above grade) are encouraged. Internally oriented housing types and those with off-street parking at grade are prohibited by code.

Streets in Hayward's downtown vary in character. A generous tree-lined median at the center of Mission Boulevard (bottom left) occupies a newly created setback zone over the city's active earthquake fault. A pushcart marketplace has been proposed for this site.

Tree-lined B Street (bottom right) will continue as downtown's principal retail corridor. Guidelines concerning its storefront design, signage and pedestrian amenities are covered within the downtown plan.

Billboard Park (below and middle; plan, bottom) has been suggested for the Foothill Boulevard edge of downtown. This income-generating "urban event" brings all of the city's billboards together in one highly visible location.

An existing supermarket set at the rear of a large parking lot on Foothill Boulevard has been reconfigured to function as a gateway to B Street (below). A series of studies (bottom) explores the form of the tower which marks this key intersection.

While the plan for down-town Hayward seeks to restore a walkable environment within its center, it doesn't ignore the district's vehicular identity as seen from its edges.

Proposals such as Billboard Park and the "marker building" at the corner of B Street are meant to function at the scale and speed of a six-lane arterial. While they reflect the character of the strip, these strong visual elements bring focus to an otherwise chaotic landscape.

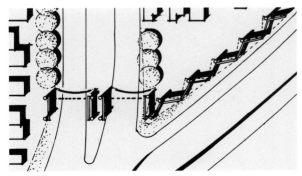

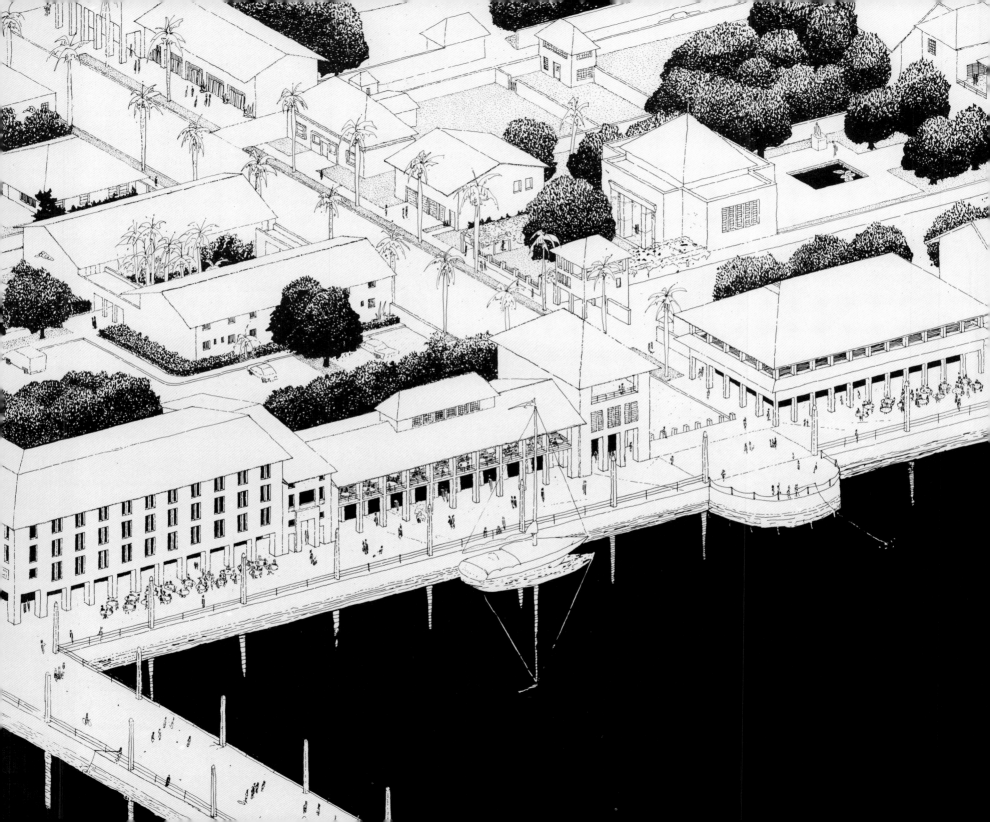

Riviera Beach

Palm Beach County, Florida, 1991

Though blessed with the same natural assets as its wealthier neighbors on all sides, the city of Riviera Beach has long suffered from a negative image. One of the poorest cities in Palm Beach county, it provides for many of the area's utilitarian needs. It is home to the Port of Palm Beach, a regional power plant and a working waterfront with marinas, boat yards and commercial fishing facilities.

Because of its enviable waterfront location and reasonable land prices, Riviera Beach began to interest developers in the late 1980s. However, the kind of high-rise beachfront development they envisioned would effectively "wall off" the waterfront for all but the wealthiest citizens. This was seen by many as destructive to the city's future vitality.

Seeking to improve its image and economic base while still providing broad long-term benefits, Riviera Beach's Community Redevelopment Agency led a citizen-driven planning effort for a 1,600-acre site including the city's 600-acre downtown. The result was a detailed new master plan and zoning codes for the district as well as adjacent neighborhoods.

One key element of the master plan by urban designer Mark Schimmenti and the firm of Dover, Correa, Kohl, Cockshutt, Valle was the rethinking of the city as nine mixed-use neighborhoods. Each has its own identity created by a new neighborhood center and square. These

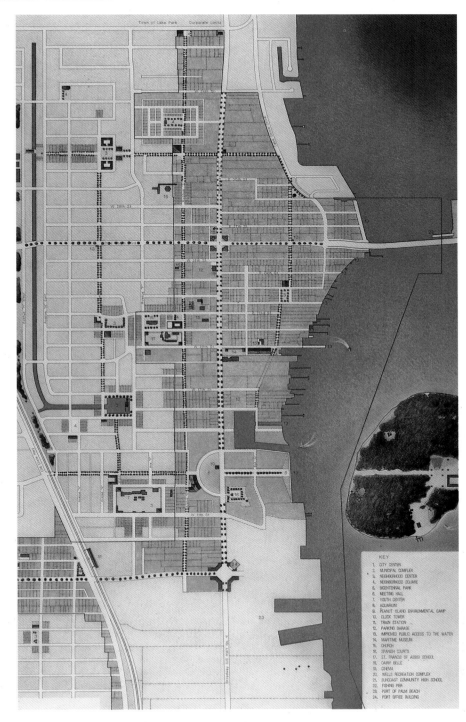

KEY
1. CITY CENTER
2. MUNICIPAL COMPLEX
3. NEIGHBORHOOD CENTER
4. NEIGHBORHOOD SQUARE
5. BICENTENNIAL PARK
6. MEETING HALL
7. YOUTH CENTER
8. AQUARIUM
9. PEANUT ISLAND ENVIRONMENTAL CAMP
10. CLOCK TOWER
11. TRAIN STATION
12. PARKING GARAGE
13. IMPROVED PUBLIC ACCESS TO THE WATER
14. MARITIME MUSEUM
15. CHURCH
16. SPANISH COURTS
17. ST. FRANCIS OF ASSISI SCHOOL
18. DAIRY BELLE
19. CINEMA
20. WELLS RECREATION COMPLEX
21. SUNCOAST COMMUNITY HIGH SCHOOL
22. FISHING PIER
23. PORT OF PALM BEACH
24. PORT OFFICE BUILDING

The city of Riviera Beach is located immediately north of West Palm Beach on Florida's Intracoastal Waterway. Improved view corridors to the water, a proposed maritime museum, several new public piers and a waterfront promenade (opposite) all reinforce the maritime character of this coastal city. The new master plan (left) establishes nine distinct neighborhoods each with its own defined edges and center.

Riviera Beach (below) experienced dramatic growth between 1940 and 1960. Singer Island, an upscale community to the east (background in photo), is a separate part of the city, linked by a bridge across the Intracoastal Waterway.

Broadway (US 1) is Riviera Beach's principal north-south route. Locals blame the state mandated removal of on-street parking for the decline of its businesses. The increased width turned what was once the city's main street into a high-speed arterial "strip."

A series of simulations enabled citizens to compare Broadway today (bottom left) with its likely build-out according to existing zoning (right), versus the result that could be achieved by following the new master plan and codes (bottom right).

centers are planned to meet the daily needs of all of Riviera Beach's residents within a one-quarter-mile walking distance.

Another element of the plan was the restoration of Broadway as the city's "main street." New codes call for a defined streetwall and sidewalk arcades, thus encouraging pedestrian activity. Bicentennial Park, moved from its waterfront location, is the focus of a new city center and downtown shopping district.

Perhaps the most significant aspect of Riviera Beach's new plan was its use of computer imaging as a tool for public participation. The design team transformed video images of the existing city instantaneously into several alternative future scenarios. Though the master plan will ultimately be built-out in small increments, these "snapshot" previews enabled the citizens of Riviera Beach to make informed choices about the destiny of their community.

Sequential diagrams, illustrating the consequences of Riviera Beach's present and proposed codes (this page), show how both of the future scenarios (opposite) would be realized.

Excessive setbacks and parking requirements now force buildings back from the street and away from each other as they increase in size (top series). The resulting large distances between buildings and "sea of parking" create a hostile pedestrian environment.

By contrast (bottom series), Riviera Beach's proposed urban code aligns buildings of varying sizes with the street edge, relocates parking to the rear of each lot and introduces a continuous arcade above the sidewalk.

Accommodating both cars and pedestrians, the former strip again functions as a real main street. Also, since parking can now be shared among several businesses, less of it is needed so buildings can occupy a greater proportion of each lot.

Overleaf: Sets of computer simulations of Riviera Beach (top row, before, and bottom row, after) show how a variety of existing situations in the city can be improved through incremental physical modification.

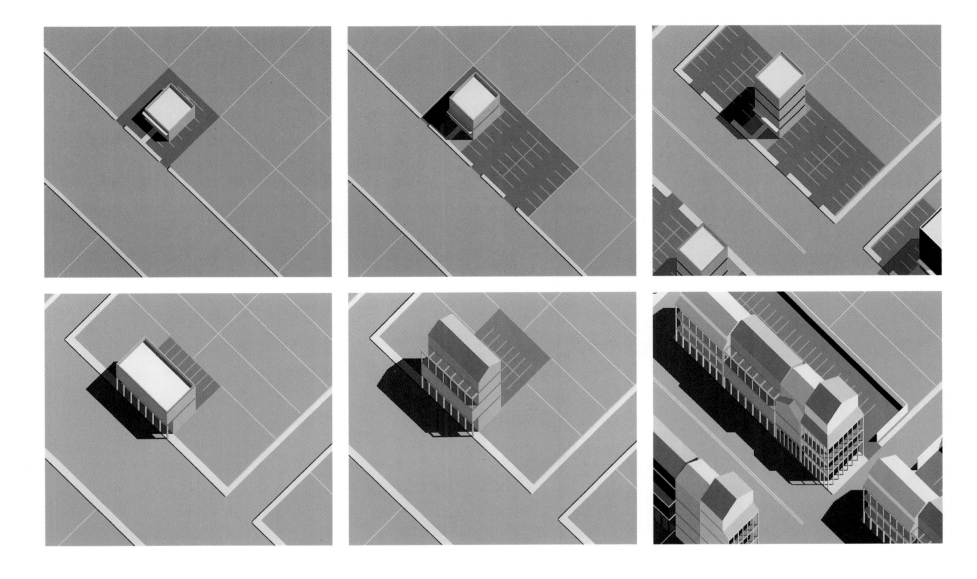

Riviera Beach's proposed master plan identified one strategic district (below), intended to function as the downtown and civic center for the community.

Bicentennial Park, the result of a complex property swap involving a derelict waterfront park, is bordered by a crescent of civic buildings. An arcaded, tree-lined boulevard leads from the park to the water, creating a distinctive retail street.

This grand boulevard, set at a perpendicular to US 1, completes a formal sequence of public spaces that gives Riviera Beach a strong, new regional identity.

Each of Riviera Beach's neighborhoods has a center that includes some form of public open space as well as the commercial and civic buildings essential to the daily life of the community.

The waterfront neighborhood (below), like several others in the master plan, has a small tree-lined central square. The southwest neighborhood (bottom) is configured around an existing church and school and a proposed day-care center.

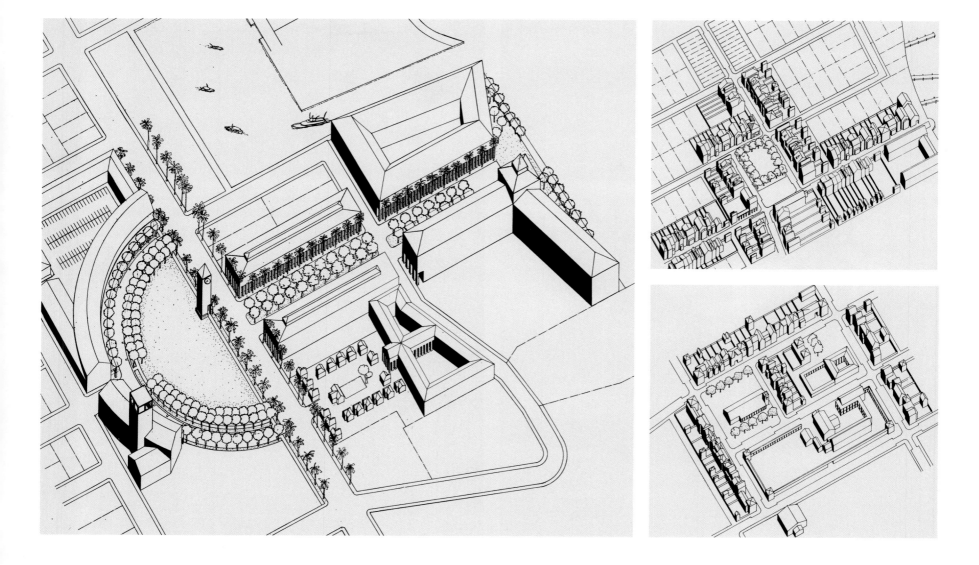

Unlike the city's previous complicated zoning documents, the proposed code by Geoffrey Ferrell is concise enough to fit on one large sheet (reduced at right). Organized by a hierarchy of street types, the code references an accompanying plan (below).

This plan shows property owners which part of the urban code applies to them. Riviera Beach's street-based code is unique among zoning guidelines; most are structured by block, lot or building type.

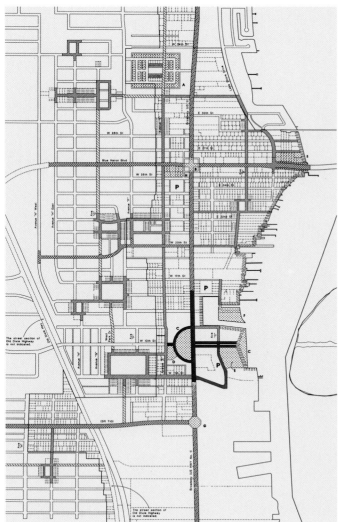

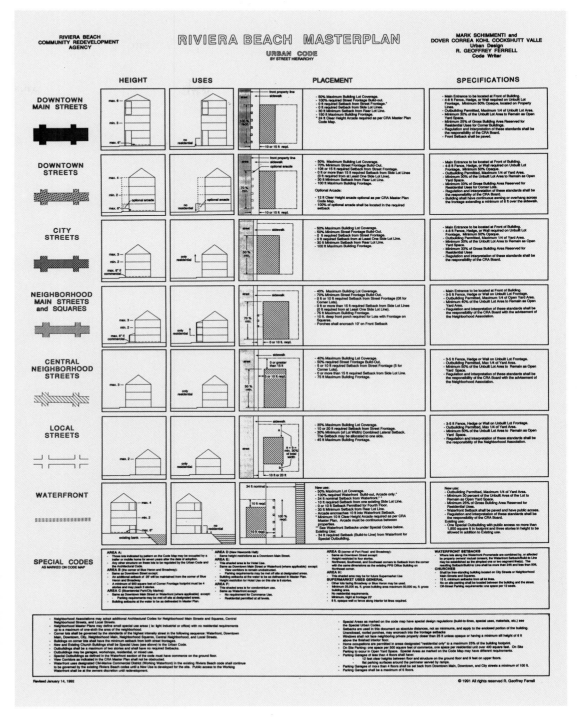

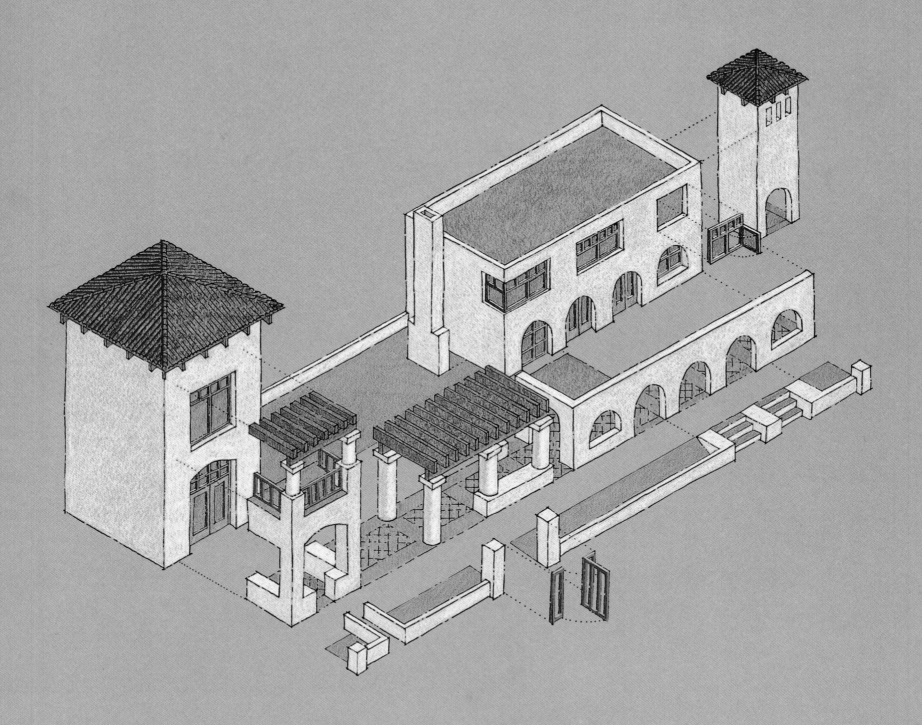

Rio Vista West

San Diego, California, 1992

Architectural guidelines for Rio Vista West emphasize simple, distinct forms that reflect the traditions of the region. Historic buildings by San Diego architect Irving Gill, such as the La Jolla Women's Club (left), influenced the design team's recommendations.

An exploded axonometric diagram (opposite) identifies the various elements and details that form the basis of these guidelines.

Automobile-oriented retailing seems to be a fact of suburban life. As roads have become larger, so have the "big-box" stores and "power centers" that flank them. Few can resist their apparent benefits of price and convenience.

The character of these places with their large expanses of pavement and billboard-like architecture seems at odds, however, with the kind of walkable neighborhoods envisioned in San Diego's new Transit-Oriented Development (TOD) Guidelines. These opposites are precisely what the neighborhood of Rio Vista West in Mission Valley seeks to marry in its 95-acre site.

As one of the first tests of San Diego's newly adopted TOD guidelines, this plan by Calthorpe Associates transforms a former sand and gravel quarry into a pedestrian-friendly mixed-use community with 1,070 housing units. The site is served by a planned trolley line linked to downtown and other regional destinations.

A mixed-use core adjacent to the trolley station includes specialty stores, restaurants, a multi-screen cinema, office buildings and housing over shops. These uses are adjacent to Rio Vista West's principal civic space, a block-long commons. A community building such as a day-care center, meeting hall or amphitheater is planned for a site within this park.

Residential blocks in Rio Vista West provide a range of multi-family housing types for both rental and sale. Its residential design guidelines

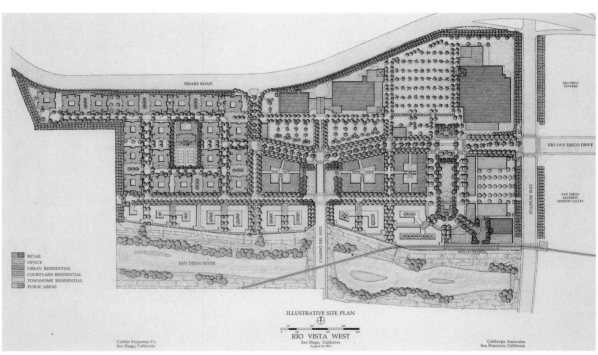

ILLUSTRATIVE SITE PLAN

RIO VISTA WEST
San Diego, California

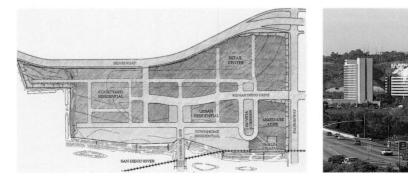

The Rio Vista West master plan (above) adds significant residential, retail and public land uses (plan, far left) to an existing high-rise office and hotel development just east of the site (near left).

An auto-oriented regional retail center (partial view, below left) is included within Rio Vista West's plan. Traffic lanes and walkways in the center continue the grid of local streets. This helps to make its large areas of parking more manageable for pedestrians.

A prominent architectural element (bottom left) terminates the view from Camino del Este, the shopping center's main entry road; arcades provide continuous shelter for pedestrians.

The mixed-use core (below right) combines residential, retail and office uses in the project's most "urban" area. Its composite blocks are to be developed in two phases, starting with the arcaded retail and residential portion fronting on the Commons.

Several short paseos (bottom right) provide access to the second-phase office buildings and decked parking behind. These mid-rise structures define the project's edge at Stadium Way, a busy six-lane arterial.

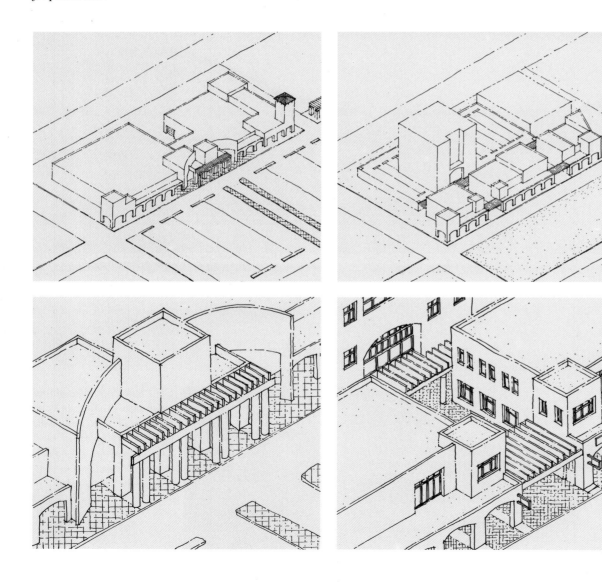

consciously emulate an architectural tradition appropriate to the history and climate of the San Diego region.

Narrow tree-lined streets within the development connect the site's various land uses. A riverfront promenade is linked to the street grid by a series of pedestrian-only paseos between the community's townhouse blocks.

One corner of the project near the intersection of two heavily traveled arterials is the site of a regional retail center. It includes a 120,000-square-foot discount superstore, supermarket and drugstore. Though clearly out of scale to the community, this key component was critical to the economic feasibility of the project.

The Rio Vista West master plan employs several design strategies aimed at integrating this seemingly incompatible element into the fabric of the community. The center's driving lanes and walkways continue the grid of local streets. Stores and parking lots are placed to shorten walking distances for pedestrians. Design guidelines call for frequent store entries, tree-shaded parking areas and human-scaled features.

The challenge of taming the retail center—a ubiquitous suburban land use—has led to Rio Vista West's unique hybrid strategy. The project's arterial face orients out to passing motorists, while its internal layout, tree-lined streets and vital public areas cater primarily to the needs of residents and those arriving by trolley.

Several residential types are found within the Rio Vista West plan. Apartments of three and four stories are located near the center of the project area (below). They frame the Camino del Este entrance to the project site and provide round-the-clock activity near the Commons.

To achieve higher densities (25 to 55 units per acre), apartments are built above podium parking. Primary entrances occur one-half level above the street (bottom left) with secondary entrances from semi-public interior courtyards.

Another residential type within Rio Vista West (below center) is medium-density housing (20 to 30 units per acre) in three-story buildings. Covered parking is accessed from rear courtyards while primary entries occur on streets or public pathways (bottom center).

Architectural guidelines for these and other apartments in the community call for an active street edge. Porches, porticos, bay windows and separate entries for ground-floor units are required.

Two-story townhouses (below right) are the lowest-density housing (15 to 25 units per acre) within the development. Individual units (bottom right) face either streets, walkways or a riverfront promenade.

Planned for sale rather than rental occupancy, these residences offer private rear parking accessed from within each unit.

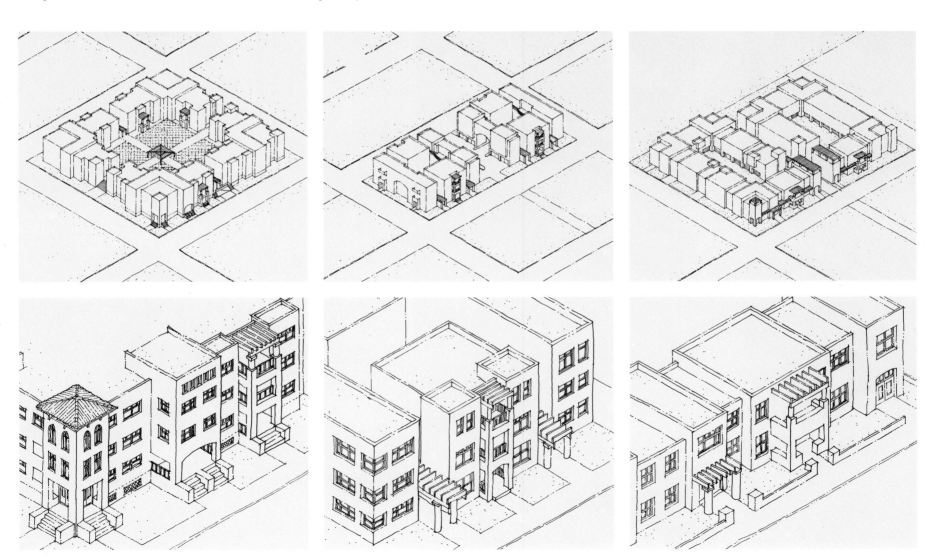

Lake West

Dallas, Texas, 1981

Like so many inner-city urban renewal projects of the 1950s and 1960s, the West Dallas Housing Projects ultimately became a far worse place than the slums it replaced. The new Lake West master plan proposes a comprehensive transformation of these barracks-like projects into a functioning mixed-use community.

A one-square-mile area adjacent to downtown Dallas, the site contains 3,500 nearly identical rowhouse apartment units—the largest concentration of low-rise public housing in the country. The new plan by architects Peterson and Littenberg creates a "normal" grid pattern of blocks and neighborhoods. The resulting physical fabric provides a clearer definition of both public and private space and a greater overall sense of community "ownership."

To accomplish this change, the plan adds new streets, moves some existing buildings and provides private backyards and garages. Extensive modifications to the units themselves further improve Lake West's residential image.

The plan introduces a new town center at the lakefront with workplaces and offices, retail and civic uses. A community campus, large town green, community meeting center, amphitheater and senior housing are located nearby.

At a time when so many of America's inner cities are in dire need of rebuilding, Lake West's example shows that it may be feasible to "recycle," rather than demolish our past mistakes.

The curvilinear network of streets within the existing West Dallas Housing Projects (left) interrupts the surrounding grid of city streets and blocks (top of photo). Most through streets from nearby neighborhoods end abruptly at the edge of the project.

The master plan of Lake West (above) defines a new urban structure of small-scale streets, blocks and residential squares. A proposed lakefront town center (opposite) has been integrated into this fabric.

The existing 550-acre West Dallas Housing Projects (plan, below left) are almost entirely comprised of one building type–flat-roofed rowhouse structures containing six to eight apartment units in each.

This basic building is replicated with little variation throughout the project area. Large undefined open areas exist near Fishtrap Lake and at the center of the site.

The proposed Lake West redevelopment plan (below right) modifies and fills in around existing rowhouse buildings to structure normal town blocks. In some locations adjacent buildings are moved to form blocks of differing shapes and size.

Individual single-family homes are moved (a common practice in some parts of Dallas) from nearby neighborhoods to fill in several underutilized areas within the project site.

A new town center focuses on a reshaped Fishtrap Lake (bottom center of plan). An existing drainage pond has been reconfigured into a series of waterways that weave in and around several large public open spaces.

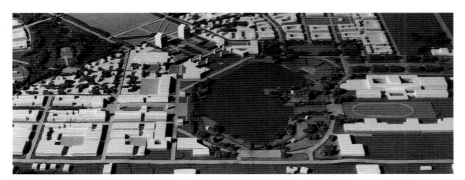

The proposed town center (left and plan, below left) organizes workplace, civic and retail uses around a new town square and an existing north-south road. Warehouse and light manufacturing facilities (foreground in photo, left) are at the project's outer edge.

Within Lake West's new plan, a series of small squares occur at regular intervals among its residential blocks. In one part of the development (plan, below right) five such squares can be found.

Small modules of about 450 housing units (example highlighted at lower right in plan) cluster around a single neighborhood square. A small service building, pavilion and playground are among the facilities provided within each.

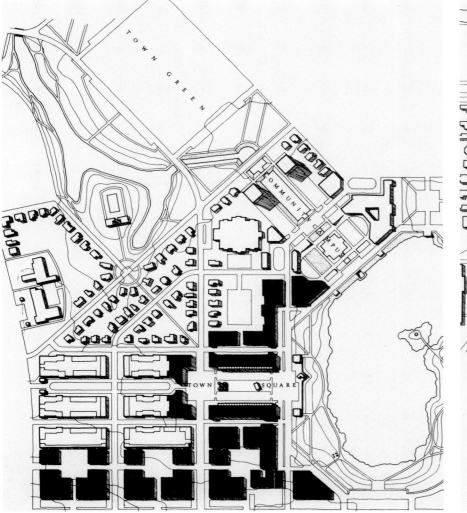

The existing barracks-style housing units (this page) within the West Dallas Housing Projects are similar to those found in countless other urban slum clearance projects of the 1950s.

Blank windowless ends of building units front the street and parking areas. Some residents must walk a full block to reach their units. Because of the weak visual connection between apartments and nearby streets, vandalism and auto theft are rampant.

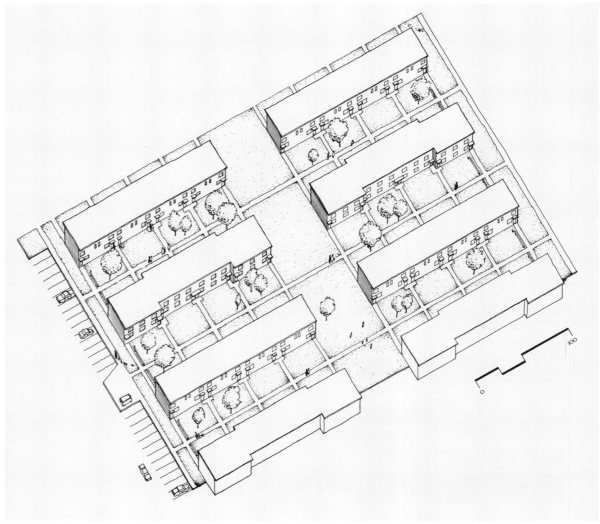

The reconfigured rowhouse blocks (left and below left) provide a more defined street connection and residential image for the units. New streets are located between pairs of rowhouses; rear yards fill the blocks' center.

Proposed infill buildings and projecting wings at the ends of blocks help to contain the perimeter that separates public (street) and private (rear yard) spaces.

Lake West's planning team used only four block types (below right). Each results from a different modification of the existing building pattern. They include a short block, long block, "L" block and "H" block.

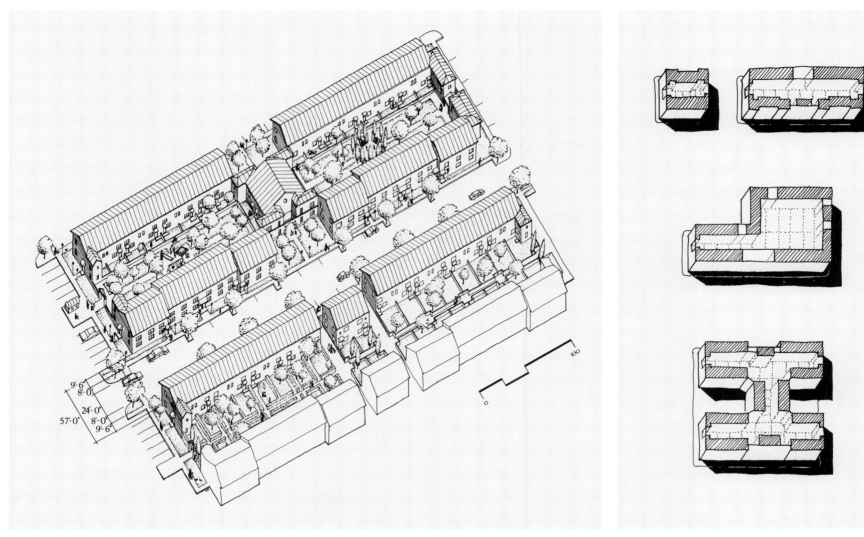

Each of Lake West's four block types plays a role within the larger geometry of the neighborhood fabric. Differences in shape and dimension allow certain unit types and programmatic elements to be incorporated within the block structure.

The "L" blocks (below left) are located at the eastern edge of the site near a park and an established residential neighborhood. The upgraded rowhouses in these blocks are meant to be sold rather than rented.

The greater depth of these blocks allows the use of rear alleys. All units in these special blocks have enclosed, off-street parking—a highly desired amenity among residents. Some of the units have private garages and extra large backyards.

Several variations of Lake West's short blocks (below right) are planned. The typical block (top) is just a shorter version of the standard long block. Since alleys are not feasible here, small sheds are provided at the end of the block for garbage storage and collection.

A few special blocks integrate existing one-story housing units (bottom). In such cases, garages are inserted between units and added at the end of blocks, forming parking courts.

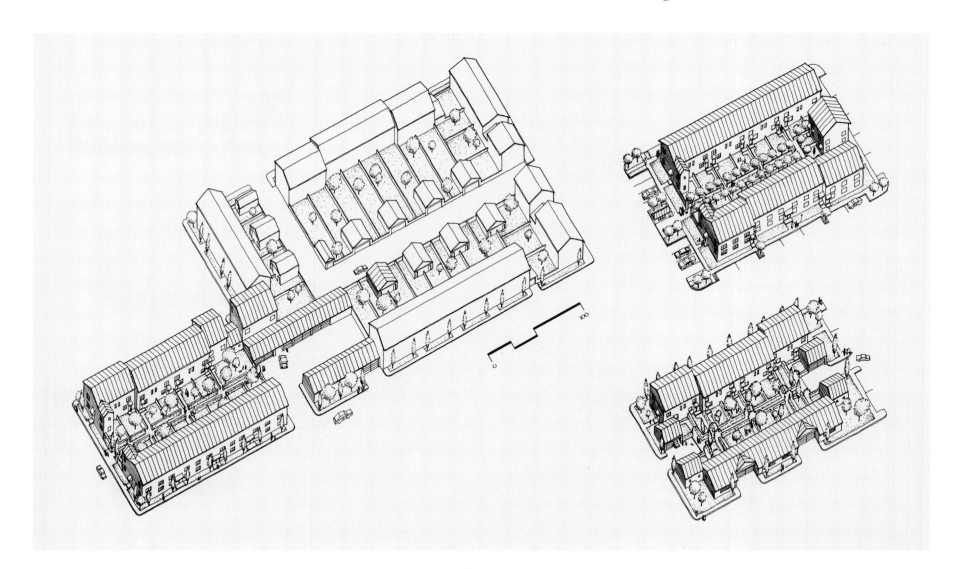

One unusual feature of the Lake West plan is the method used in its rebuilding. Because HUD funding was available only for renovation, rather than building anew, the planning team adopted an innovative strategy of moving existing units to form new blocks.

The regular geometry of the existing building layout (below left) made it easy to establish a new urban grid. Neighborhood squares (bottom left) are created by the repositioning of just four buildings (below right).

Interestingly, this approach was not the first choice of the planning team. It was, however, the most economical way to realize the goals of the master plan, and it could be accomplished in a manner that fell within the narrow guidelines of government funding sources.

One result of HUD's prohibition on demolition of existing units was that not a single building or apartment would be lost in the transformation of the West Dallas Housing Projects.

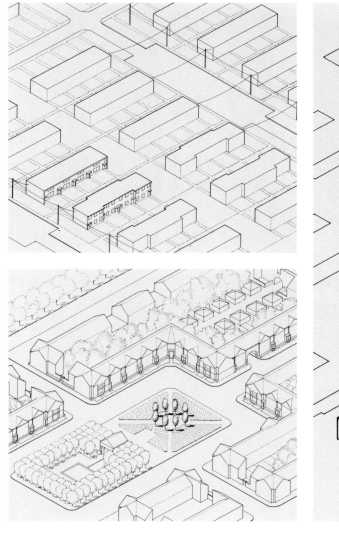

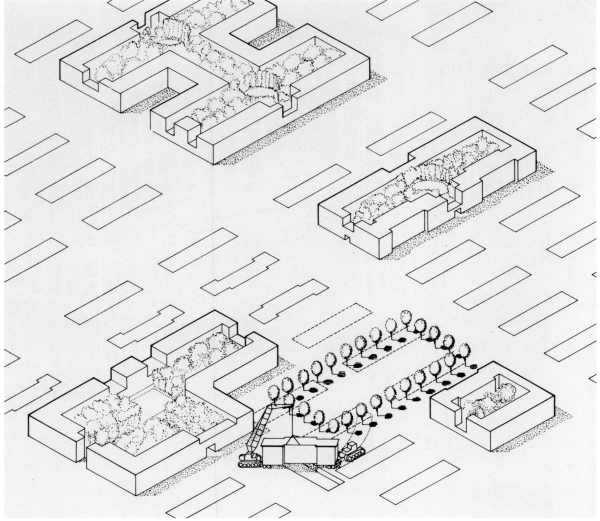

Downcity Providence

Providence, Rhode Island, 1992

The new Grace Square (opposite) is one of several special projects proposed in the Downcity plan. This intimate public space located across from the newly renovated Grace Church replaces four small buildings (left) of marginal quality.

The square is defined by new "liner buildings" on two sides, ideally tenanted on the ground floor with a bookstore and cafe.

The leaders of the Downcity Providence planning team contrast their multiple, interrelated, small-scale projects with the large, single-purpose "dinosaurs" that have been proposed, and in some cases built, in Providence over the past 40 years. Unlike those costly redevelopment and public works projects, this plan's incremental strategy requires relatively little government or private funding.

The Downcity Providence master plan took shape in a series of public charettes sponsored by a coalition of local businesses, institutions and individuals as well as city government. The planning team, led by Andres Duany and Elizabeth Plater-Zyberk, included experts in housing, retail, marketing and management. The team adopted the name "Downcity"as that was the term used by locals to refer to downtown when it was at its zenith in the 1940s.

To its credit, downtown Providence has managed to retain a relatively intact urban fabric of blocks, streets and older buildings of quality. As a result, the Downcity plan focuses most of its recommendations in areas of use, operations, administration and marketing. The plan also builds on several of the large-scale projects recently (or about to be) completed in and around downtown. These include a new convention center, the rerouting of train tracks, the opening up and rechanneling of a river and the relocation of a deteriorating highway.

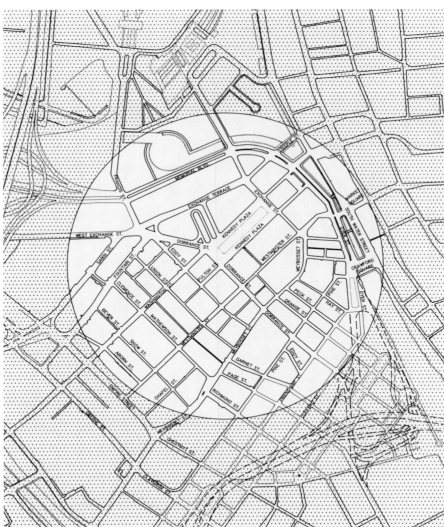

Narrow streets in downtown Providence are lined with an impressive collection of 19th and early 20th century buildings (above). The resulting urban fabric is one of exceptional architectural and spatial quality.

The focus of this revitalization effort (left) is an area circumscribed by the radius of a five-minute walk from the southwest corner of Kennedy Plaza. An expanded campus for Johnson & Wales University (page 158) overlays the lower portion of this plan (immediately above the present Interstate 195, shown with dotted lines).

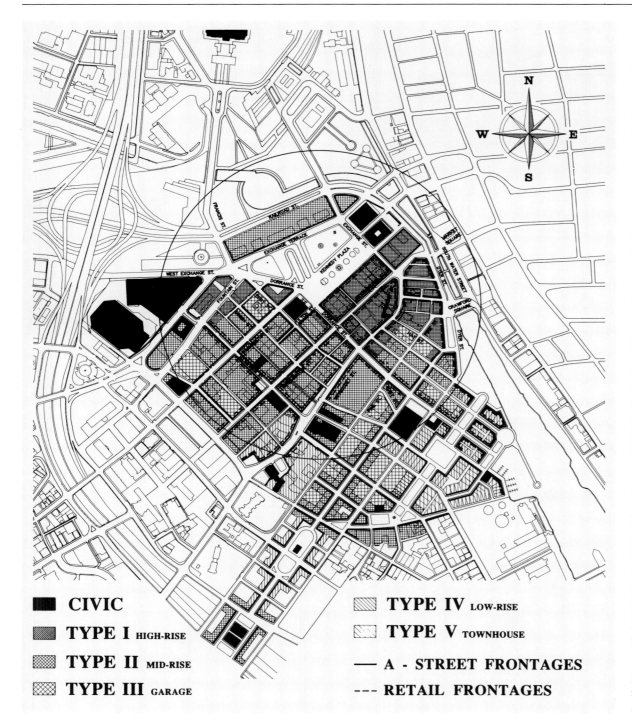

CIVIC

TYPE I HIGH-RISE

TYPE II MID-RISE

TYPE III GARAGE

TYPE IV LOW-RISE

TYPE V TOWNHOUSE

— A - STREET FRONTAGES

--- RETAIL FRONTAGES

The Downcity Providence regulating plan (left) defines a hierarchy of five different building types in addition to civic facilities. The plan is referenced to a simple code that specifies the allowable uses and physical characteristics for each type.

The initial Downcity charette, which focused on a circular area around City Hall in downtown Providence, led to a later charette for the downtown campus of an expanding local university. The team also looked at the design of a new neighborhood at the edge of the project area created by the relocation of the highway.

Downtown retail was a major focus for the planning team. Though most of Providence's large downtown merchants have disappeared, research showed that upscale residents of nearby neighborhoods were interested in downtown shopping and would be willing to walk or use public transit to get there. The same resident group also cited an aversion to suburban malls because one needed to drive to reach them.

The plan proposes successful mall management techniques for use in the downtown core. The centralized structure it recommends is seen by the planning team as the best way to coordinate the simultaneous transformation of several blocks of downtown. Such critical mass is considered essential for reestablishing the area as a premier shopping destination. The management entity would also provide direction in matters of tenant mix, merchandising, storefront design, maintenance, security and parking.

Downtown housing was another area explored by the planning team. The plan identifies students, artists and retirees as potential residents of a revitalized downtown. Loft housing, a

A system of A and B streets are designated within the Downcity plan (below left). This strategy recognizes that not all streets are equally well suited for pedestrian activity and enjoyment.

A streets (indicated in solid black), programmed for intensive pedestrian use, are coded to a higher standard. B streets (cross-hatched) provide for the area's vehicular and service needs. These include drive-through uses, parking access and truck loading.

In this way, many of downtown's vehicle intensive activities can be concentrated away from places that are favored by pedestrians.

Large gaps in downtown Providence's urban fabric (cross-hatched areas in plan, below right) have resulted from the demolition of older buildings. Typically used for parking, these expanses of unbuilt land are destructive to nearby retail and pedestrian activity.

Thin "liner buildings" (solid black areas in plan) are proposed to restore gaps in the streetwall. These buildings (historic example, right) provide continuous retail street frontage while keeping most of a site in parking use.

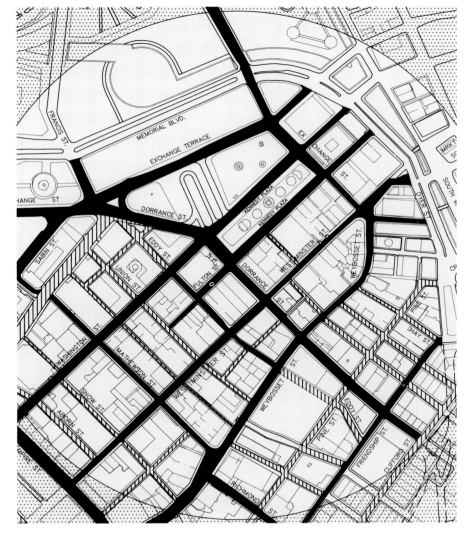

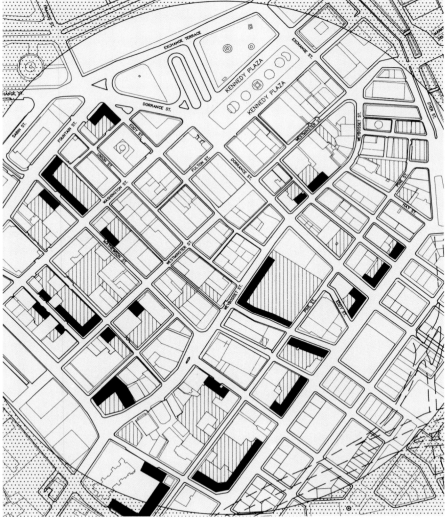

A proposed library building for Johnson & Wales University (left in illustration, below) by architect Charles Barrett is one of several projects in the first phase of an expanded downtown campus for that institution.

The library's classical portico (center of illustration, right) faces across Weybosset Street to a similar element of the Beneficent Church (below), a familiar Providence landmark. Like matched bookends, this composition creates a formal gateway to the city's downtown.

An existing green (right) adjacent to the church and library anchors one leg of the university's Weybosset Street spine. It is one of a network of existing and proposed public open spaces that give identity to the new downtown campus.

A master plan (right) of the proposed Johnson & Wales campus identifies important sites for future acquisition and development.

A multi-purpose classroom and dormitory facility (bottom right) on Weybosset Street by architects Charles Barrett and Randall Imai is the largest building envisioned within the plan.

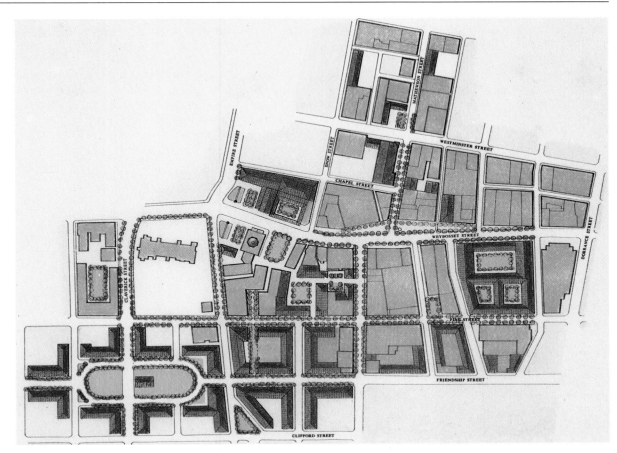

popular form of dwelling in some U.S. cities, is proposed as a less expensive way to convert many of downtown's large footprint buildings to housing use.

The plan emphasizes the importance of weaving culture into the fabric of downtown life. The presence of several nearby educational institutions and an expanding downtown campus for Johnson & Wales University is seen as an energizing force for retail, housing and street life within the city core. Studies showed that the perception of downtown as a "college town" was considered appealing to a variety of potential resident groups, most notably retirees.

A few key physical modifications are proposed in the plan. These include the creation of Grace Square across from a prominent downtown church, the addition of "liner buildings" to fill gaps in blocks eroded by parking lots and several important new buildings for Johnson & Wales. Operational changes include revisions to existing street directions, improved signage for parking areas, better lighting of buildings, the expansion of a Saturday farmers' market and a fare-free downtown bus loop.

The Downcity plan lacks any one single "big move." It is hoped, however, that the collective impact of its many modest proposals will ultimately enable Providence to, in the words of one planning team member, "fulfill its destiny" as a truly great American city.

Orange Tree Courts

Riverside, California, 1988

Riverside's historic Mission Inn (left), built between 1902 and 1932, is located one block to the south of the project site. The hotel's annex, a group of existing low-rise buildings (visible in photo below right), is integrated into the proposed development (opposite).

The relationship between preservation and redevelopment has sometimes been an uneasy one. Efforts to save and reuse historic buildings have often been single-mindedly focused on one or a few notable structures without regard for the surrounding urban context.

Orange Tree Courts in Riverside, California, attempts to fix one such planning mistake through the careful reconstruction of a single block in that city's downtown.

In the 1980s, a block of small-scale commercial buildings behind Riverside's Mission Inn was partially destroyed to build a new parking garage to serve that historic hotel and nearby businesses. Unfortunately, the large gap created by the garage isolated one side of the hotel and hurt pedestrian activity in the area.

Recognizing the problem, the City of Riverside held a competition to develop over the garage. The winning design, Orange Tree Courts, by deBretteville & Polyzoides (modified version shown here by Moule & Polyzoides) combines retail, office and entrances to parking at street level with 74 living units and office space above.

The proposed scheme renders the large parking garage less visible, helping to restore the urban character of downtown Riverside. As the first housing built in the area in over 30 years, it will also begin to reestablish the city core as a viable neighborhood, instead of a place to come only for working, shopping or banking.

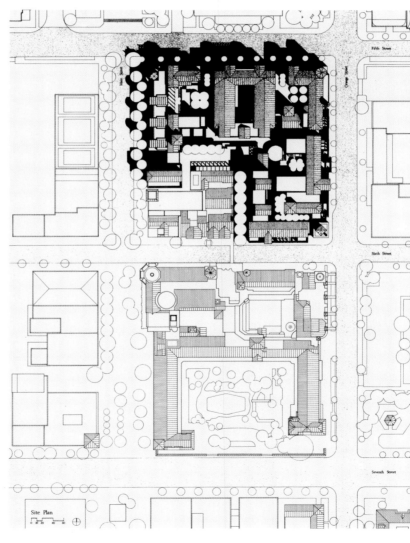

Site Plan

The project site (plan, left) spans a large parking structure (above) built in the mid-1980s by the City of Riverside. While the concrete deck planned to cover the garage could support almost any type of low-rise, wood-frame structure, Orange Tree Courts distributes the project's program among five separate buildings. This approach continues the fine-grained scale and massing of the adjacent hotel annex.

The existing 350-car parking garage beneath the complex (plan, below) is a concrete structure with sloped floors. The project conceals the garage and establishes a new "ground" at the second level.

Multiple stairs and ramps around the perimeter of the block connect to several public courtyards through which one can reach second-story residential and office units. A ground-level retail paseo connects the garage entrance to Main Street and the rear of the Mission Inn.

A continuous network of public courtyards and private patios on the second level (plan, below) defines five distinct buildings within the project. The Main Street building has retail at street level and offices above. A total of 74 housing units are in the other buildings.

Every one of the project's five courtyards is named for and features a different kind of tree—olive, grapefruit, orange, lemon and pomegranate. Each is significant to the historic agriculture of the Riverside region.

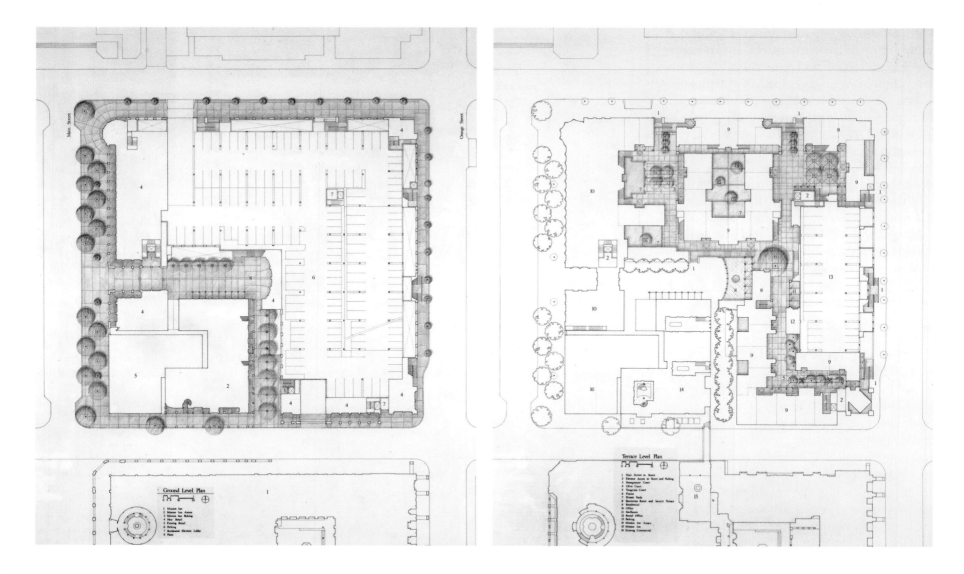

Orange Tree Plaza's paseo (right and below), private patios (left in illustration, below) and public courtyards (bottom right) provide a wide range of outdoor spaces within a relatively dense urban block structure.

The low-rise building type used in the development has been adapted from successful examples in Santa Barbara and other Southern California cities and towns.

Based on historic models, these walk-up residences are well suited to the climate and lifestyle of the region. They also accommodate present-day parking requirements in a manner that preserves a walkable street environment.

Atlantic Center

Brooklyn, New York, 1986

Atlantic Center's master plan (below) ties together several tracts of derelict land stretching across two-thirds of a mile within downtown Brooklyn. The site centers on the corner of Atlantic and Flatbush Avenues (bottom left), one of the borough's busiest intersections.

The main entrance to the Long Island Railroad station and a 10-line subway stop (bottom right) is located at the corner. Once housed in a grand, Neo-Renaissance terminal, the present rail station is now entirely underground.

Phase I locates two 25-story office towers (opposite and center of plan, below) above the station. These large floorplate towers and several low-rise buildings define a small square green. Atlantic Commons, a new residential neighborhood is situated just to the east.

Phase II, occupying the westernmost parcel (far left in plan), is planned as a location for commercial tenants needing exceptionally large floor areas. A total of 1.3 million square feet is provided on 12 floors.

In the late 1980s the rising cost of Manhattan real estate forced many New York City businesses to relocate their less critical "back-office" facilities to outlying suburban areas. Hoping to stem the loss of jobs and tax revenue, then mayor Ed Koch launched a program of financial and development incentives aimed at retaining back-office activities within the city limits.

One result of the program was the master plan for downtown Brooklyn's new Atlantic Center, an office, retail and residential development for a vacant 24-acre urban renewal site over a commuter rail terminal. Ten subway lines and numerous bus routes converge at the location, providing unparalleled transit access.

The scheme by architects Peter Calthorpe and Skidmore Owings & Merrill includes 3 million square feet of office space—half in two large towers directly over the terminal. A skylit retail concourse with restaurants, shops and a 10-screen cinema is near the center of the complex. A 641-unit neighborhood to the east accommodates low- to medium-income renters along with several street-level retail businesses.

After gaining local approvals, Atlantic Center was stopped by an environmental group concerned with congestion from the project. Their legal challenge, unfortunately, didn't take into account the true ecological costs of diverting the region's growth to more sensitive rural and agricultural lands outside the city.

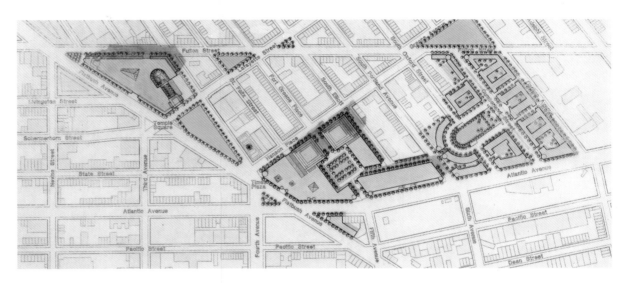

Three and one-half million square feet of office and retail space are included in Phase I of Atlantic Center (left and center of illustration below).

The project's proximity to rail and subway lines allows it to compete for back-office tenants on a regional basis. Though the development emphasizes transit access, a 1,700-car parking garage on Atlantic Avenue is included in the master plan.

Atlantic Center's 641-unit residential neighborhood was inspired by the intimacy and charm of nearby historic brownstone neighborhoods (left, Adelphi Street).

This part of the development, referred to as Atlantic Commons (below, right in illustration), organizes four-story housing units within existing city streets, a block-long park and a series of semi-public mews. The project's mini-blocks enclose small private courtyards.

Small neighborhood shops and services are planned along the Fulton Street edge of the project, and a large supermarket is located on Atlantic Avenue.

Mashpee Commons

Cape Cod, Massachusetts, 1986

Twenty years ago, *U.S. News and World Report* announced that the shopping mall was replacing "main street" as the core of America's communities. Seeking to reverse that trend, the owners of an existing 1960s era strip mall decided to actually turn their 65,000-square-foot shopping center into a small town main street. Then for good measure, they decided to build a classic New England village around the thriving new retail district they had created.

Buff Chace and Douglas Storrs, the developer/planners of Mashpee Commons, have received national attention for their dramatic transformation of the once tired New Seabury Shopping Center in the town of Mashpee, about 65 miles south of Boston. Two new intersecting streets—Market and Steeple—form the core of a new downtown behind the existing center. The district includes retail stores (some with apartments above), offices, restaurants, banks, a post office and multi-screen movie theater. A library, church, school, police station and fire station are clustered around a nearby town common.

After the initial transformation of the retail area was underway, architects Andres Duany and Elizabeth Plater-Zyberk were brought in to lead a public charette to plan a community surrounding the core commercial district. The resulting master plan adds more retail stores, offices and several residential groupings. In-

THE REGULATING PLAN OF
MASHPEE COMMONS
MASHPEE MASSACHUSETTS
Founded 1995

Fields Point Limited Partnership
Owner

Andres Duany & Elizabeth Plater-Zyberk
Town Planners

Charles Barrett   Stephane Bothwell   Rick Chellman
William Dennis   Andres Duany   Douglas Duany
Tarik El-Naggar   Manuel Fernandez   Scott Hedge
Alex Krieger   Bill Lennertz   John Montague Massengale
Alick McLean   Ann Tate   Elizabeth Plater-Zyberk
                   Douglas Storrs

Prominent in the plan of Mashpee Commons (above) is a traffic circle that connects roads from five directions. The former New Seabury Shopping Center, built in the 1960s (left), is located at 8 o'clock on the circle. While most of what is seen here remains, new buildings added behind existing stores (opposite) define a new, more pedestrian-oriented street network.

The Town Common (below) is located at the western end of Steeple Street. It includes a planned town hall, church (at extreme right in illustration) and public library (not pictured).

This public space will serve as a civic center for the existing town of Mashpee, a highly dispersed 23-square-mile area that presently lacks a defined center.

The planners of Mashpee Commons saw the town's lack of civic facilities as an opportunity to stimulate a more diverse public life in the area. Inclusion of these facilities at the village center was meant to complement nearby commercial and residential activities.

Sites for public buildings in the Town Common were donated by the developers to the community. A favorable land transaction helped to encourage a local church congregation to build in this part of the village.

North Market Street (right, top and bottom) is an expansion of Mashpee Commons' existing retail district. Its large floorplate stores line the main road through town providing critical visibility for retailers.

Unlike most commercial "strips," buildings here sit close to the road, between parking areas screened by trees. In this layout, the physical form of the stores and their easily seen merchandise advertise the nature of the businesses within.

cluded among these are a mix of small-lot single-family homes, townhouses, rear yard accessory units and apartments over shops. Lot and unit sizes vary to accommodate residents of all ages and income levels. Each cluster of houses focuses on a community green, typically the location of one of the town's public buildings.

Mashpee Commons has thus far concentrated on its retail, office and community buildings. Now well established as a commercial center, it offers a range of shops, services and civic amenities within easy walking distance of the planned residential areas.

The village's phasing sequence runs counter to the pattern of most postwar suburban development. In that scenario, large tracts of housing are typically built first, most often on inexpensive land at the edge of town. Large single-use "pods" containing retail and workplace uses then follow when sufficient market demand has been generated.

Mashpee Commons' unconventional "retail-first" strategy recalls a proven model from a much earlier time—that of a country store at the intersection of two well traveled roads. In this traditional pattern, the store is eventually joined by a house, then a blacksmith's shop, an inn, another store, more houses, a bank and so on. In this model, as at Mashpee Commons, growth responds to market forces in a more sensitive, balanced and incremental way.

The village of Mashpee Commons includes four small neighborhoods, each with a central public open space. Community buildings have been planned for several sites within the residential clusters.

Whitings Green (below left), just west of the Town Common, includes mostly small-lot single-family homes. A meeting hall is located in its central square.

Jobs Green (bottom left) is to the south of the village's main commercial district. Mashpee Commons' village hall will be located in this section which combines various types of residences— single-family houses, town-houses and apartments.

Great Neck Circle (below right) is southeast of the village center. It consists of small-scale commercial structures with upper level apartments and office units.

Quashnet Fields (bottom right), located at the western end of the site, is the most rural of the village's residential areas. Its large single-family homesites face out to a generous green.

Manor House   Captain's House   Manor House   Greek Revival

Benefit Street Rowhouse   Nantucket   Benefit Street Rowhouse   Nantucket   Full Cape

Full Cape   Captain's House   Nantucket   Greek Revival   Half Cape

Manor House   Captain's House   Courtyard Apartments

*Mashpee Commons'
residential building types
draw heavily from tradi-
tional Cape Cod village
architecture. The rational,
compact New England
saltbox is a basic component
of this vernacular style.
Several elevations (left) were
drawn by the design team to
illustrate how buildings of
different types and sizes can
coexist on village streets.
The courtyard apartments
(at right in bottom elevation) have projecting wings
that echo the form and scale
of nearby freestanding
houses. This design device
helps to reduce the apparent
size of larger buildings
so they do not overwhelm
nearby houses.*

Mashpee Commons' reconfigured commercial district is centered at the corner of Market and Steeple Streets. Buildings here incorporate many physical and symbolic features that are commonly observed in older New England towns and cities.

The modest village post office (below) by local architect Tony Ferragamo is made more prominent by its placement between flanking symmetrical storefronts. A small public plaza gives even further emphasis.

Across the street, a classical portico (below right) by Bill Dennis defines the entry to a mid-block arcade. A red brick bank and an office building (bottom right and opposite), both by Randall Imai, anchor the corner of Market and Steeple Streets.

Substantial masonry bank buildings have long been a fixture of small town main streets. Before the advent of federal banking insurance, the image and appearance of one's building conveyed an important message about the soundness of the institution within.

Though times (and banking practices) have changed, the developers of Mashpee Commons have continued this tradition by locating a formally designed bank at the village's most prominent intersection.

The village's new retail streets (this spread) provide an intimate, friendly place to shop and stroll. Buildings are close to the street and sidewalk. On-street parking puts shoppers nearer to stores, and it creates a buffer between pedestrians and moving traffic.

Street trees, benches, storefronts, sidewalks and canopies at Mashpee Commons have all been detailed to provide a comfortable and engaging environment for pedestrians.

Because the 40-foot setbacks mandated by local codes would have made it impossible to locate buildings so close to the sidewalk edge, the developer instead chose to retain ownership of all of the village's streets.

For zoning reasons, such streets are considered to be part of the center's own internal circulation and parking system.

Playa Vista

Los Angeles, California, 1989

The master plan for Playa Vista (below) organizes a sequence of neighborhoods within a system of streets, open spaces and parks. The plan's fine-grained mix of uses contrasts with an earlier land-use plan (right) that is more typical of conventional suburban development.

The village center (opposite) is a focal point of the plan. One of the community's more dense areas, it locates residential, retail and civic uses in close proximity.

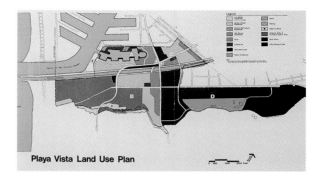

Playa Vista Land Use Plan

Long regarded as a mecca for America's car culture, the Los Angeles area seems an unlikely setting for a new community dedicated to pedestrian independence and ecological sensitivity. Described by its developer as "a singular departure from the more conventional suburban development that has dominated postwar growth in Southern California," Playa Vista represents one of the most ambitious efforts yet toward reversing today's prevalent and destructive pattern of auto-oriented sprawl.

Located on the former site of Howard Hughes' airport and factory between Venice, Marina del Rey, Playa del Rey and Culver City, the proposed community incorporates a broad range of planning and environmental initiatives. Unlike several earlier development schemes, strongly opposed by nearby residents because of their intensive commercial uses, the current master plan for the property sets forth a varied mix of land uses more closely resembling that of an authentic neighborhood.

The design process itself, which led to the current scheme, was also far more responsive to regional growth issues and local concerns than were the previous efforts. At various stages, the developer invited the participation of community groups that had opposed earlier schemes. Each had specific concerns but agreed on certain basics. These included the expansion and restoration of a degraded wetland on the site;

HABITAT AREA
RECREATIONAL OPEN SPACE
RESIDENTIAL
RESIDENTIAL OVER GROUND FLOOR COMMERCIAL
OFFICE SPACE
VILLAGE CENTER - MIXED USE
COMMUNITY SERVING
ENVIRONMENTAL FACILITIES

PLAYA VISTA MASTER PLAN PROJECT

Playa Vista's 1,087-acre site (left) is located just inland from the beach community of Playa del Rey. The property was acquired by Howard Hughes in the 1940s for the original Hughes Aircraft plant and runway. The legendary Spruce Goose was built in a large hangar which still exists on the site.

Now surrounded on all sides by residential, commercial and industrial uses, the property is the largest undeveloped tract in Los Angeles. The Ballona Wetlands at the western end of the site is one of the few remaining tidal marshes in Southern California. Over 260 acres of this unique natural habitat are to be restored and preserved.

The grid pattern of local streets and blocks (below) plays a key role in shaping Playa Vista's urban character. The size and configuration of these elements seek to balance the needs of pedestrians with those of the automobile.

The predominant north-south orientation of the grid was selected to optimize views to the bluffs located at the south end of the site.

Playa Vista's ecological systems (bottom) have been carefully considered. The most advanced technologies for solid-waste treatment, wastewater reclamation, storm water collection and recycling are to be used.

An internal transit system using electric or natural gas vehicles and bicycle paths provide convenient alternatives to auto usage within the community.

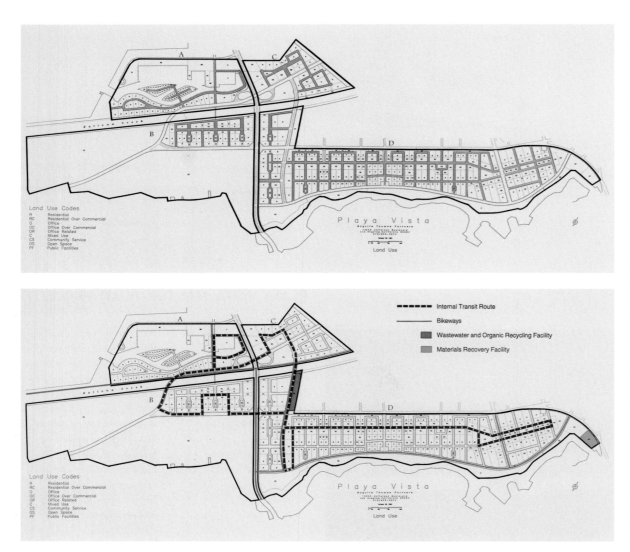

establishment of building height standards consistent with nearby communities; and reduced traffic impacts from the development.

Responding to these concerns, the developer assembled a planning team of individuals who have shown a willingness to work with citizens to achieve innovative results. The group included principals from the architectural firms of Elizabeth Moule and Stefanos Polyzoides, Moore Ruble Yudell, Andres Duany and Elizabeth Plater-Zyberk, Legorreta Architectos and landscape architects Hanna/Olin.

Together with consultants from other disciplines, the planning team conducted a series of workshops involving representatives from the community, local government and environmental groups. These participatory sessions enabled citizen concerns to be tackled directly, at the start of the planning process.

The resulting Playa Vista master plan defines a balanced community of low- to mid-rise buildings with a strong emphasis on the provision of a generous public realm. Like many of the most admired older Southern California towns and cities, Playa Vista uses a defined hierarchy of street and open-space types to shape its neighborhoods. Though predominantly residential in character, they also include a mix of other uses: office, retail, recreational, cultural and civic. Each neighborhood is designed to provide an array of such uses within

*More than half of Playa
Vista's land area has been
set aside for community
open-space and park uses.*

*Regional open-space areas
(below) include the 260-acre
Ballona wetland preserve
and a continuous greenbelt
along the Westchester
Bluffs. More than 40 smaller neighborhood parks
(bottom) are within or adjacent to the community's grid
of streets and blocks.*

*Overleaf: This illustrative
plan establishes the project's
open-space network and
public landscape. The platting of blocks and individual
lots accommodates a range
of development densities.*

a comfortable walking distance. The plan also
includes several special districts, such as an office
campus, village center and marina.

Over half of Playa Vista's site has been set
aside for various forms of open space. These
include major parks and playing fields, smaller
neighborhood parks and squares, cycling and
jogging trails and pedestrian promenades. A
restored bluff, wetland preserve and riparian
corridor serve as greenbelts for the community.

Playa Vista's environmental management
program features state-of-the-art methods for
wastewater and solid-waste reclamation and
natural systems for storm water purification.
The community provides and encourages
alternatives to the private auto both within and
outside the community. Streets are designed for
the comfort and safety of both pedestrians and
cars. The plan also includes a low-emission
internal shuttle service that will be linked to
regional transportation systems. In addition, car
pooling, ride sharing and public transit incentives are to be actively promoted.

Playa Vista has been cited by the Southern
California Association of Governments for its
"potential for making a significant contribution
to the implementation of regional policy." An
environmental impact report has been issued,
and the first phase of the project, representing
25 percent of Playa Vista's ultimate build-out, is
expected to be approved during 1993.

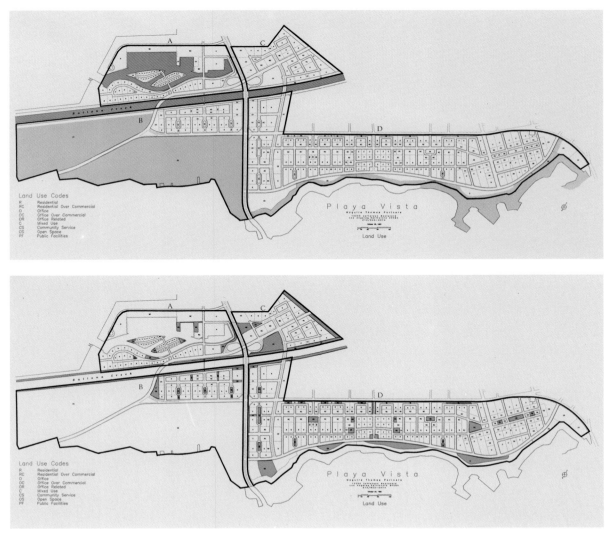

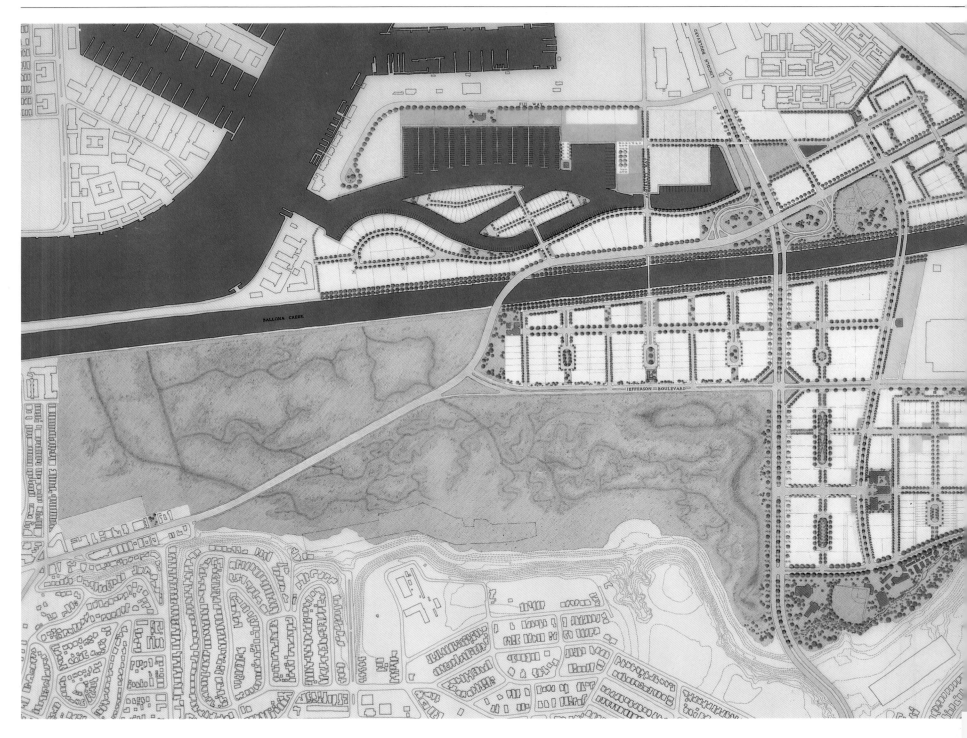

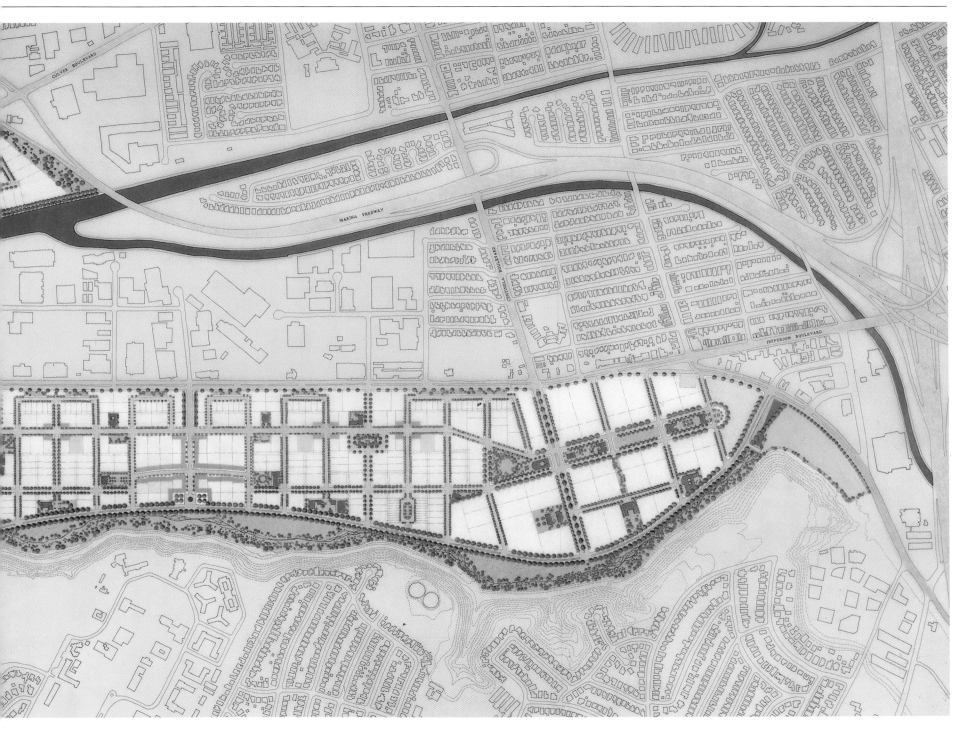

Playa Vista's public realm is defined by several existing and proposed elements. The Ballona Channel (left), originally built by the Army Corps of Engineers, is enhanced with the addition of a recreational esplanade along its edges.

The expanded and restored Ballona Wetlands (bottom left) serves as a greenbelt for the community. A riparian corridor (below) uses natural processes to treat water runoff. Neighborhood parks (bottom right) were carefully designed in relation to the buildings that frame them.

Much attention has been given to the detailing of the community's streets (example, right). Special emphasis was placed on the quality and functionality of the pedestrian environment in order to discourage auto use within the community.

Street design standards for sidewalks, roadways, curbs, lighting and planting (typical intersection plan, below) were formulated with input from many user groups, including the visually and physically impaired.

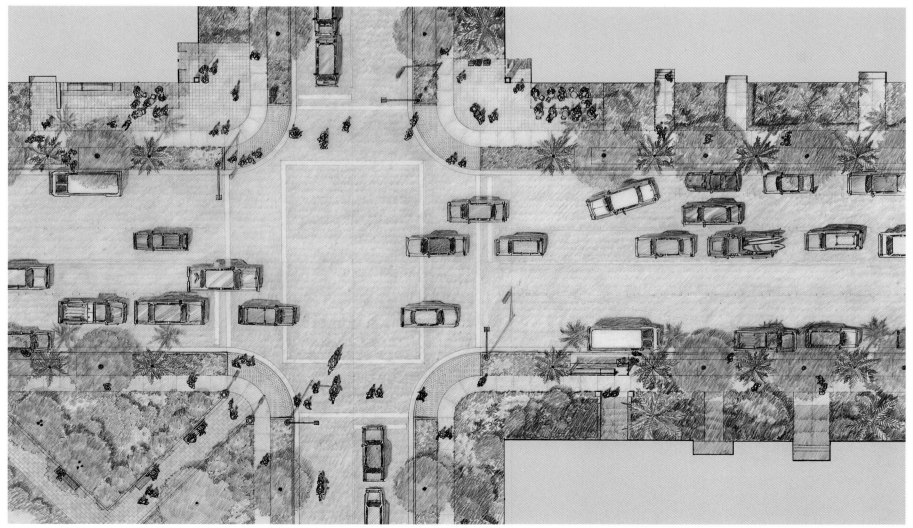

Each of Playa Vista's residential neighborhoods has a distinct identity based on its physical layout and proximity to the major features of the site—the wetlands preserve, marina and Westchester Bluffs.

Small parks surrounded by civic, cultural and retail buildings (below, left and right) are another distinguishing element that lends individual character to each part of the community.

Various types of multi-family housing including courtyard apartments, town-houses, quadruplexes and duplexes are included among Playa Vista's over 13,000 dwellings. Fifteen percent are to be offered as affordable housing.

Several "demonstration blocks" have been designed (bottom right) as a test of the community's proposed mix of residential types and urban design guidelines.

A detailed plan (opposite) of several of Playa Vista's residential neighborhoods illustrates the complex mix of building, street and open-space types that are necessary ingredients of a lively and varied community.

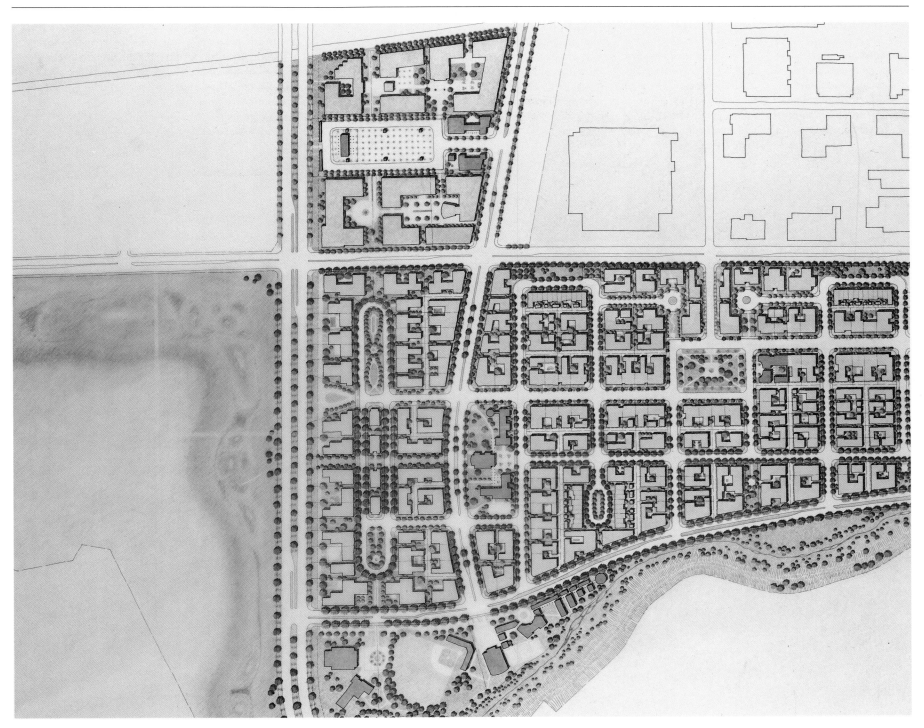

Several special districts are envisioned within the Playa Vista master plan. Both the village center and marina combine residential uses with other activities that define their special character within the community.

Playa Vista's principal shopping areas are found in the village center (plan, below). While experienced as a traditional main street, the retail district takes advantage of many administrative and merchandising methods more typical of malls.

Security, tenant mix, store-front design, parking and store hours are some of the areas that may be coordinated within the centralized management structure proposed for the district.

The streetscape of Runway Boulevard (below), Playa Vista's main artery, reflects the combination of uses found in the village center. Ground-floor commercial frontage predominates, with residential uses above.

Neighborhood retail (bottom) is provided in specific locations throughout the plan, most often adjacent to public parks.

Playa Vista's marina district (this page) combines public boat berthing facilities with residential, hotel and commercial uses. A two-mile-long shoreline promenade (below and right) provides continuous public access to the water's edge.

Two small islands (visible in plan, bottom left) with parks at their centers contain the only detached dwellings to be built within Playa Vista. A major public plaza (bottom right) lined with shops and restaurants opens out to the harbor from the northern edge of the site.

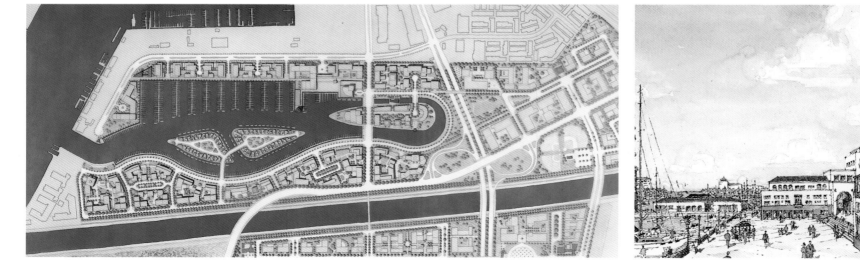

The Playa Vista plan dis-tributes office uses through-out the site. The largest concentration of such uses is at the eastern end of the community, adjacent to the San Diego Freeway.

Planned as a campus, more than 3.5 million square feet of office space is provided in an urban setting of streets and blocks arranged around a central landscaped mall.

Retail stores, restaurants, civic buildings and cultural facilities (indicated in red on plan) are interspersed among the buildings of the office campus. Nearby residential neighborhoods are within easy walking distance.

This district's somewhat larger blocks are better able to accommodate the large floorplate buildings and parking capacities desired by office tenants.

Low- and mid-rise office buildings (this page) define the perimeter of blocks in this district. This configuration creates a courtyard within each block's center.

Like quads in a traditional college campus, these semi-public spaces are designed to facilitate easy pedestrian movement and interaction.

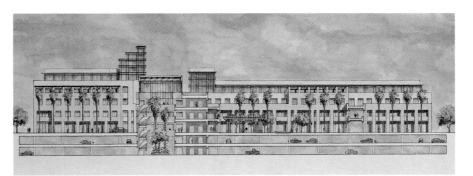

Jackson-Taylor

San Jose, California, 1991

Originally a food processing center serving the San Jose region's once extensive orchards and farms, the Jackson-Taylor neighborhood might now be best described as a place "in between." It includes edges of two ethnic neighborhoods—one Japanese and another predominantly Hispanic—and an historic district with the city's largest concentration of Victorian homes. Industry remains, but it is rapidly giving way to small incubator and professional businesses attracted by the low rents in the district's easily subdivided former industrial buildings.

One element that weaves the neighborhood together is an underutilized rail line that may one day be converted to commuter use. Along with Communications Hill (page 78) and several other neighborhoods near rail lines, the 75-acre Jackson-Taylor area has been targeted by the City of San Jose for intensive development.

Combining up to 1,600 residential units and 550,000 square feet of retail, office and industrial uses, the master plan by Calthorpe Associates reflects the input of a broad coalition of neighborhood groups, property owners and concerned citizens. The scheme, to be implemented gradually, will follow a set of detailed architectural guidelines. Though the project's goal is the creation of an active and vital neighborhood core, its proposed configuration of building types is planned to blend seamlessly into surrounding residential neighborhoods.

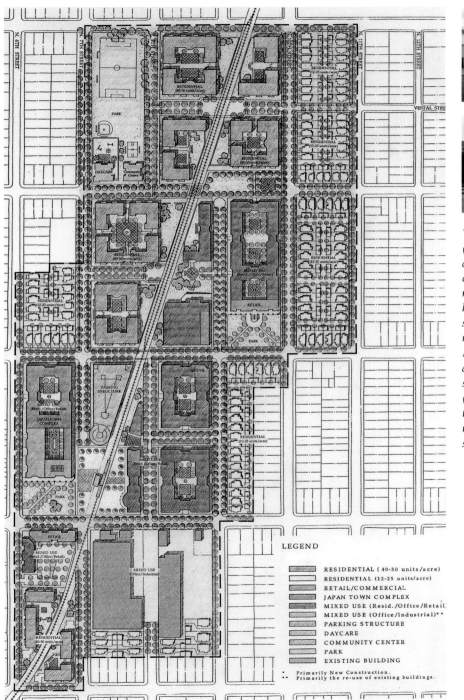

LEGEND

RESIDENTIAL (40-50 units/acre)
RESIDENTIAL (12-25 units/acre)
RETAIL/COMMERCIAL
JAPAN TOWN COMPLEX
MIXED USE (Resid./Office/Retail)
MIXED USE (Office/Industrial)**
PARKING STRUCTURE
DAYCARE
COMMUNITY CENTER
PARK
EXISTING BUILDING

* Primarily New Construction.
** Primarily the re-use of existing buildings.

The Jackson-Taylor plan (left) inserts a mixed-use core of high- and medium-density housing, office and retail uses into an existing light industrial area (top) surrounded by residential neighborhoods (above). Larger buildings close to the center (opposite) gradate to smaller housing elements (center of illustration) near the edges of the plan. These reflect the scale of nearby single-family homes.

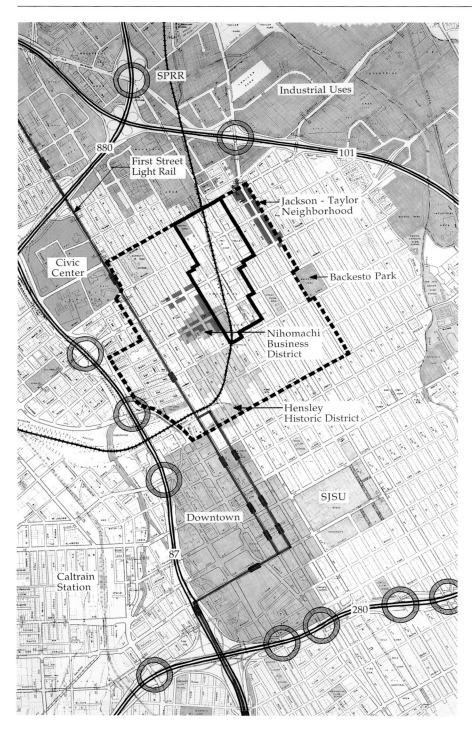

Several of San Jose's established historic and ethnic neighborhoods border the 15-block Jackson-Taylor site (left). An existing rail spur may become part of a future regional commuter train system; light-rail and bus lines now serve the site.

A number of alternative scenarios, each with a different combination of uses and implementation strategy, were proposed for public review and comment. The final neighborhood master plan (previous page) uses elements derived from each of these early studies.

One approach (plan, below) suggested minimal change to existing built areas in the district. It focused primarily on parcels of vacant land that can be easily developed without disrupting the economic and social life of the community.

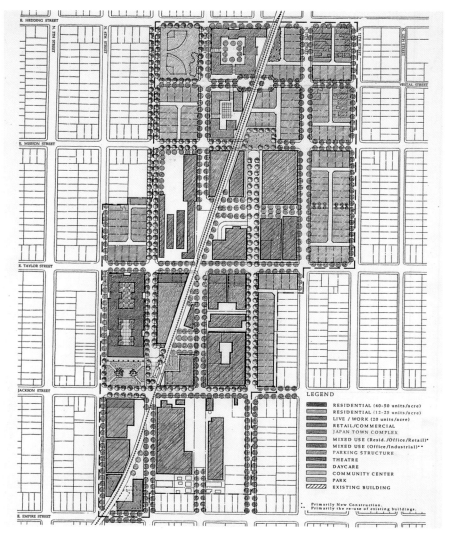

LEGEND

- RESIDENTIAL (40-50 units/acre)
- RESIDENTIAL (12-25 units/acre)
- LIVE / WORK (20 units/acre)
- RETAIL/COMMERCIAL
- JAPAN TOWN COMPLEX
- MIXED USE (Resid./Office/Retail)*
- MIXED USE (Office/Industrial)**
- PARKING STRUCTURE
- THEATRE
- DAYCARE
- COMMUNITY CENTER
- PARK
- EXISTING BUILDING

*Primarily New Construction.
**Primarily the re-use of existing buildings.

A second scheme (plan, below) replaced many of the existing, obsolete industrial buildings on the east side of the train tracks with higher-intensity mixed-use buildings. On the west side, such buildings were replaced with multi-family housing.

One viable business, a fruit processing company near the south end of the site (dark purple blocks at bottom of plan), remains in the two plans shown on this page as well as in the final plan.

A third, predominantly residential approach (plan, below), was organized around several public open spaces. One small, centrally located square was lined on three sides with street-level retail. A more active park at the north end of the site filled an entire city block.

This plan responded to the City of San Jose's strategy of locating large concentrations of housing near existing and planned commuter rail stations.

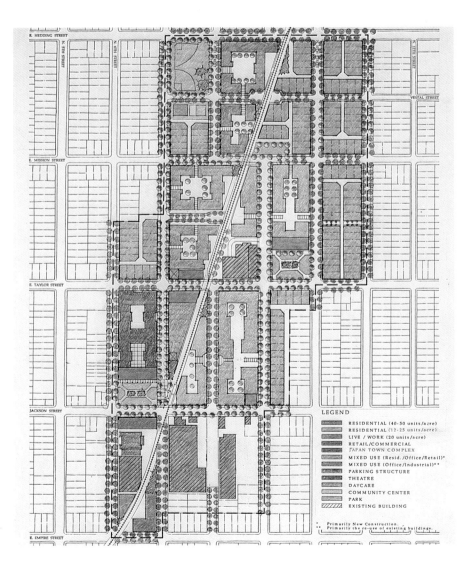

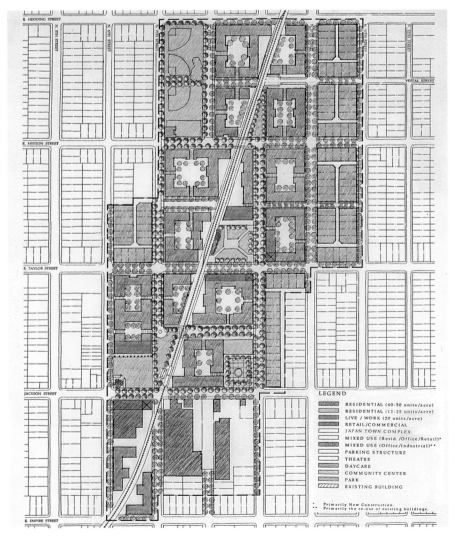

LEGEND

RESIDENTIAL (40-50 units/acre)
RESIDENTIAL (12-25 units/acre)
LIVE / WORK (20 units/acre)
RETAIL/COMMERCIAL
JAPAN TOWN COMPLEX
MIXED USE (Resid./Office/Retail)*
MIXED USE (Office/Industrial)**
PARKING STRUCTURE
THEATRE
DAYCARE
COMMUNITY CENTER
PARK
EXISTING BUILDING

* Primarily New Construction.
** Primarily the re-use of existing buildings.

Three different types of blocks have been proposed within the Jackson-Taylor master plan. Comprehensive design guidelines (this spread) define a clear physical model of each.

The community's mixed-use blocks (below left and detail plan, right) maintain a density of 40 to 50 units per acre. Ground floor uses in these buildings must be commercial. Upper floors are either entirely residential or they may include offices on their second levels.

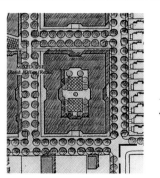

Residential blocks (below right and detail plan, right), also planned for densities of 40 to 50 units per acre, are constructed on a parking podium one-half level above grade. This is necessary to achieve compliance with the area's parking requirement of 2.2 spaces per unit.

The massing and placement of bays and entries within buildings on these blocks reflect the lot increment and scale of surrounding single-family neighborhoods.

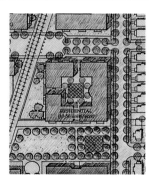

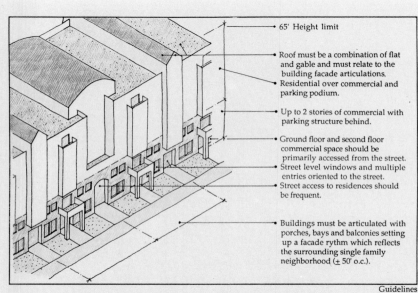

- 65' Height limit
- Roof must be a combination of flat and gable and must relate to the building facade articulations.
- Residential over commercial and parking podium.
- Up to 2 stories of commercial with parking structure behind.
- Ground floor and second floor commercial space should be primarily accessed from the street.
- Street level windows and multiple entries oriented to the street.
- Street access to residences should be frequent.
- Buildings must be articulated with porches, bays and balconies setting up a facade rythm which reflects the surrounding single family neighborhood (± 50' o.c.).

Guidelines

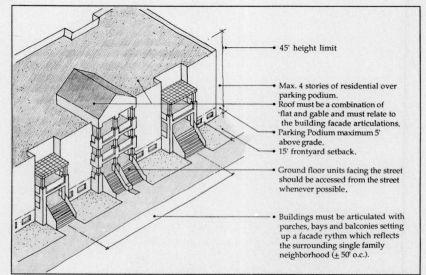

- 45' height limit
- Max. 4 stories of residential over parking podium.
- Roof must be a combination of flat and gable and must relate to the building facade articulations.
- Parking Podium maximum 5' above grade.
- 15' frontyard setback.
- Ground floor units facing the street should be accessed from the street whenever possible.
- Buildings must be articulated with porches, bays and balconies setting up a facade rythm which reflects the surrounding single family neighborhood (± 50' o.c.).

Guidelines

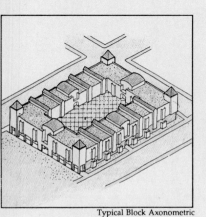

Typical Block Axonometric

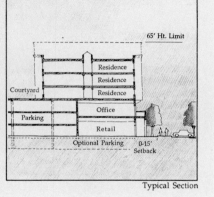

65' Ht. Limit

Courtyard	Residence
	Residence
	Residence
Parking	Office
	Retail
Optional Parking	0-15' Setback

Typical Section

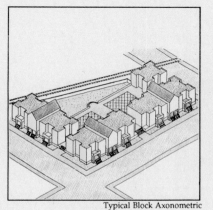

Typical Block Axonometric

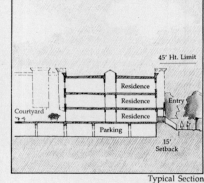

45' Ht. Limit

Courtyard	Residence
	Residence
	Residence
	Parking
	15' Setback	Entry

Typical Section

Lower-density residential areas (below left and detail plan, right) provide between 12 and 25 units per acre. Though buildings resemble the form of adjacent single-family homes, each lot can include up to three residential units plus parking.

A mix of owner-occupied and rental units is planned for this area. This strategy will be implemented in the manner of a traditional neighborhood on a parcel-by-parcel basis.

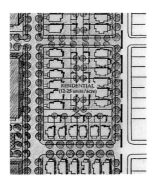

RESIDENTIAL
(12-25 units/acre)

Because the Jackson-Taylor area has been dominated by industry, its streets have suffered from many years of neglect. In some locations, public rights-of-way have been encroached upon or taken over altogether by the food processing businesses that surround them.

One element of the revitalization plan is the return of these rights-of-way to public use, either as streets or open space. Upgraded standards for streets and walkways (below right) are planned to further enhance the district's appeal for pedestrians.

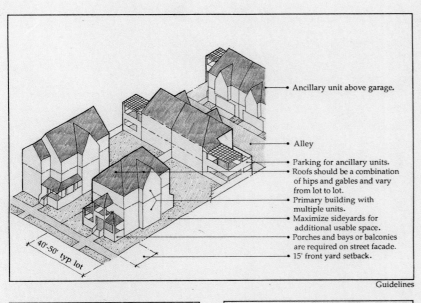

- Ancillary unit above garage.
- Alley
- Parking for ancillary units.
- Roofs should be a combination of hips and gables and vary from lot to lot.
- Primary building with multiple units.
- Maximize sideyards for additional usable space.
- Porches and bays or balconies are required on street facade.
- 15' front yard setback.

40'-50' typ lot

Guidelines

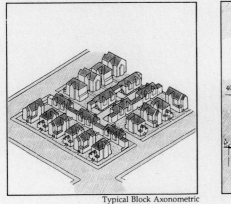

Typical Block Axonometric

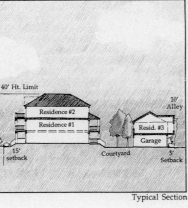

40' Ht. Limit

Residence #2
Residence #1

10' Alley

Resid. #3
Garage

15' setback

Courtyard

5' Setback

Typical Section

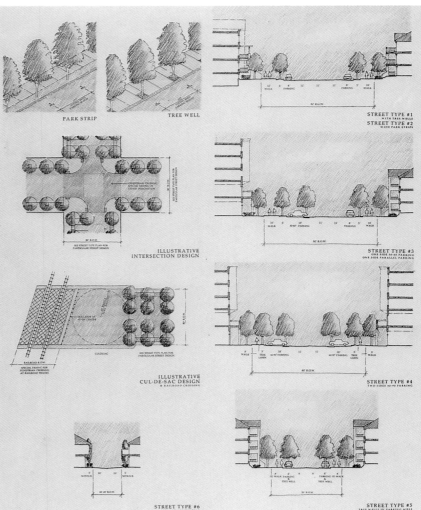

PARK STRIP

TREE WELL

STREET TYPE #1
WITH TREE WELLS

STREET TYPE #2
WITH PARK STRIPS

ILLUSTRATIVE
INTERSECTION DESIGN

STREET TYPE #3
ONE SIDE 30-40' PARKING
ONE SIDE PARALLEL PARKING

ILLUSTRATIVE
CUL-DE-SAC DESIGN
& RAILROAD CROSSING

STREET TYPE #4
TWO SIDES 60-90' PARKING

STREET TYPE #6
ALLEY AT RESIDENTIAL

STREET TYPE #5
TREE WELLS IN PARKING AISLES

Highland District

Tucson, Arizona, 1990

The predominantly brick campus of the University of Arizona (left) is situated near Tucson's historic center. The city's street grid penetrates into the campus, terminating at its central landscaped mall (visible in upper part of plan, below).

Several obsolete one- and two-story housing and service buildings presently occupy the site of the Highland residence halls.

Like Thomas Jefferson's famous campus at the University of Virginia, the Highland District master plan for the University of Arizona could well be described as "an academical village." Instead of building "one large and expensive building" as was the common practice in his day, Jefferson proposed several "small and separate lodges" around a square. Similarly, the designers of the University of Arizona's Highland District suggested a community of low-rise courtyard buildings instead of the high-rise towers that the university had been considering.

Wanting to change from a predominantly commuter school to a residential one, the university had embarked on an ambitious building program to house 3,000 students in a new part of the campus. Administrators knew, however, that they needed to provide a greater sense of community than that which is typically found in most large student housing complexes.

The scheme proposed by architects Elizabeth Moule and Stefanos Polyzoides showed that a group of lower buildings could easily accommodate the same densities as the towers while providing a higher quality of student life. Their initial study for the 18-acre site ultimately grew into a set of urban design guidelines for a "district" including both private residential quarters and more public places where students, staff and faculty could comfortably interact. Other program elements include street level retail busi-

The proposed Highland District (opposite and plan, left) includes twelve residence halls, two commons facilities, a parking garage and two recreational fields. Together these form a major new southern entrance to the campus. Retail stores face the heavily traveled Sixth Street; a continuous pedestrian arcade lines the more pedestrian-scaled Highland Avenue.

The building, landscape and open-space types used in the Highland District are based on precedents observed in Tucson and surrounding desert areas as well as climatically similar regions of the Middle East and North Africa.

Sketches (below) drawn by architects Elizabeth Moule and Stefanos Polyzoides illustrate some of the many specific sources that inspired the design of this project.

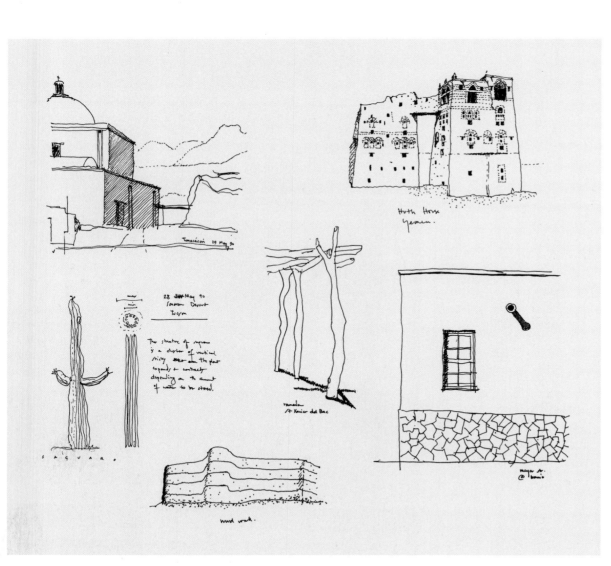

nesses, administrative offices, classrooms, recreational facilities and a large parking garage.

The architects sought out urban design models more suited to Tucson's desert climate than the typical American college campus. The large landscaped quads and sweeping green lawns commonly associated with such campuses have proven inhospitable and difficult to maintain in the hot, dry climate of the southwest.

The Highland District plan evokes a different urban tradition with architectural elements configured to save energy and resources, while rendering the desert environment more habitable. Like the patios and paseos of Mexico or the intricate spatial network of the Middle Eastern casbah, the district's many small "self-shading" courtyards encourage the movement of air, but keep the sun out during most of the day. Masonry is the principal building material. Its mass provides a stabilizing effect that neutralizes the extreme temperature swings between Tucson's hot days and cool nights.

The physical structure of the district plan also reinforces its social goals. Student rooms are organized into clusters around the small, private garden courtyards. The larger and more public courtyards closer to Highland Avenue are surrounded by common spaces, including living and study areas. Each individual residence hall, in turn, is meant to function as a defined and cohesive community within the larger district.

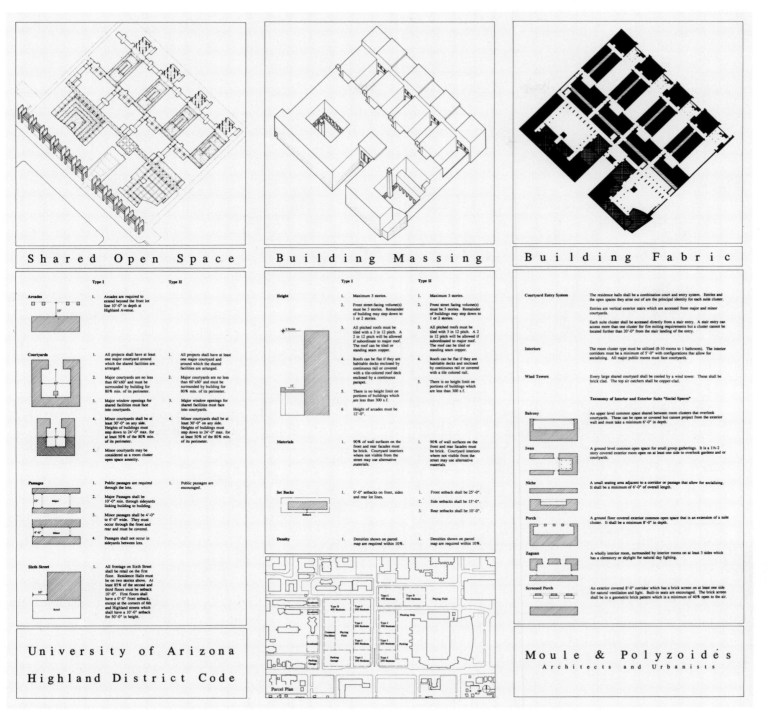

Shared Open Space

Building Massing

Building Fabric

University of Arizona
Highland District Code

Moule & Polyzoídes
Architects and Urbanists

A detailed code (left) was created by the planning team to regulate the implementation of the Highland District master plan. The code deals with the relationship of buildings to adjacent streets, the internal organization of courtyards and passages and the clustering of public and private rooms within each building.

Like the 17th century Mission Tumacacori outside Tucson (detail below), buildings in the Highland District utilize a sequence of walled courtyards to define individual precincts within a larger spatial composition.

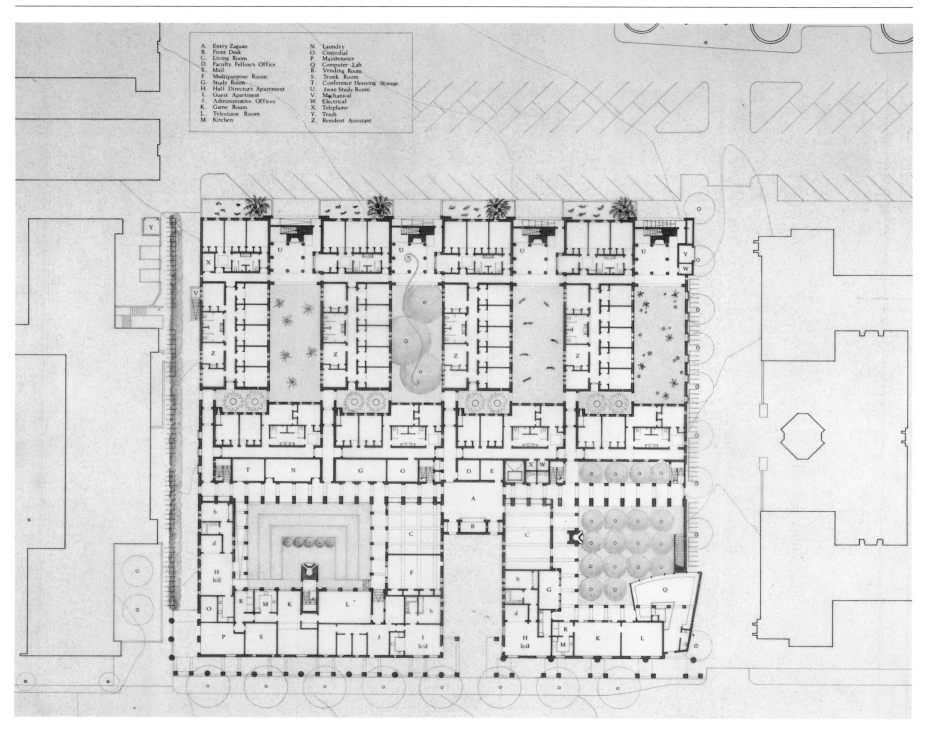

A. Entry Zaguan
B. Front Desk
C. Living Room
D. Faculty Fellow's Office
E. Mail
F. Multipurpose Room
G. Study Room
H. Hall Director's Apartment
I. Guest Apartment
J. Administrative Offices
K. Game Room
L. Television Room
M. Kitchen
N. Laundry
O. Custodial
P. Maintenance
Q. Computer Lab
R. Vending Room
S. Trunk Room
T. Conference Housing Storage
U. Iwan Study Room
V. Mechanical
W. Electrical
X. Telephone
Y. Trash
Z. Resident Assistant

Each of the building's six principal courtyards has a unique character related to its location within the plan (left) and landscape features. Plantings were selected from the most drought-tolerant native species.

The more public front courtyards (below) are surrounded by shared living, recreation and meeting rooms. Several guest rooms also overlook these outdoor spaces. The more private rear courtyards are entirely bounded by student rooms.

Wind towers are used to cool the two front courtyards. Air passing through a water-soaked mesh at the top of the tower is cooled, then drops down the shaft by convection.

Temperatures in outdoor spaces cooled by this process can be up to 20 degrees (F) lower than surrounding, equivalently shaded areas.

This form of passive cooling has been adapted from ancient Middle Eastern examples by researchers at the University of Arizona. The same towers can also be used as outdoor fireplaces in the winter.

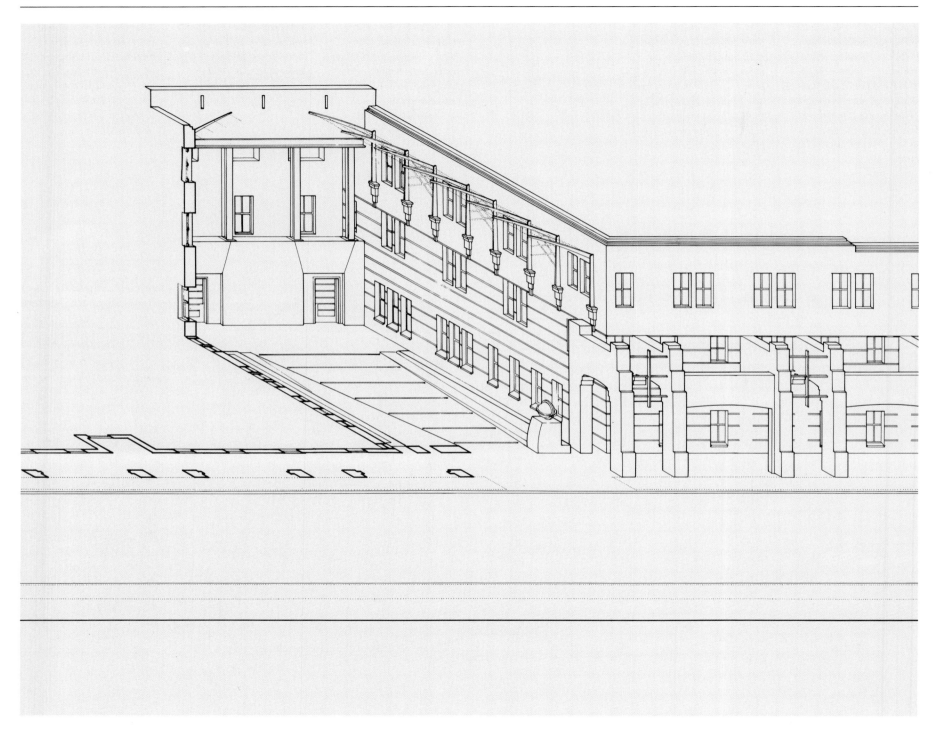

The residence hall's sloped entry court (opposite) is modeled after the "callejon" or dead-end streets found in many Arab influenced Spanish cities. (The example, right, is in Cordoba.) Climbing vines on an overhead trellis help to shade the entry court.

The residence hall's west elevation (below) integrates a pedestrian arcade along Highland Avenue. The building's red brick exterior wall surface, mandated by the new code, relates to the existing architecture of the campus.

The east elevation (bottom) faces across a parking grove to the university's stadium. The massing of this face of the building relates to the giant scale of the stadium.

As the first of 12 planned residence halls in the district, this building will serve as a demonstration of the concepts and physical design criteria set forth in the Highland District Code (page 201).

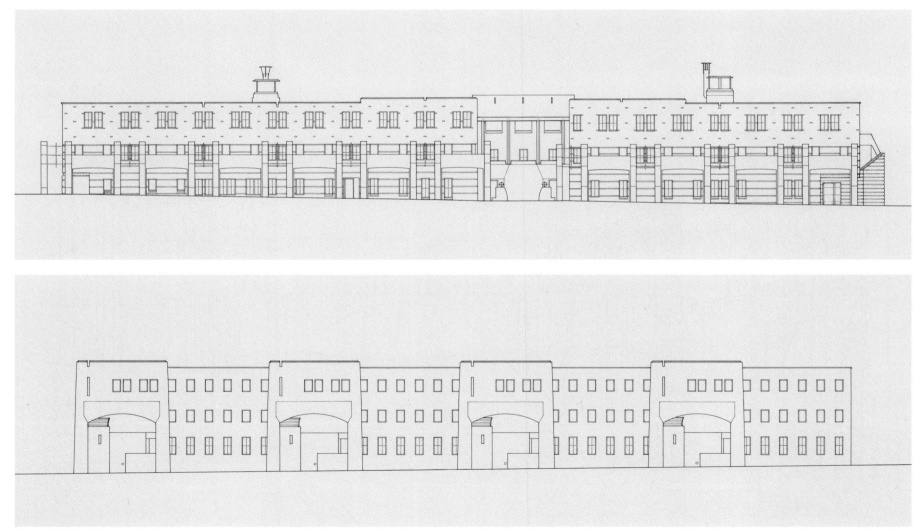

Clinton

New York, New York, 1986

The Clinton community plan (below) defines a network of public and semi-public spaces within the existing city grid. Nearly 1,000 feet in length, this neighborhood's blocks are among the longest in Manhattan.

The proposed plan's new streets and open spaces create a fabric of smaller blocks, thus establishing a more intimate, "residential" scale within the district.

The Clinton Market Square (opposite and center of plan, below) is a public space whose design and usage reflect the working character of the area. During business hours it accommodates truck loading; at other times it functions as the neighborhood square.

In contrast to the anti-growth NIMBY (not in my backyard) attitude held by many community advocacy groups, the proactive residents of Manhattan's Clinton neighborhood countered a city-supported development plan with one of their own. Instead of allowing two new apartment towers to create what *The New York Times* called the "Great Wall on 10th Avenue," the community proposed a master plan more consistent with the scale and character of the surrounding area.

Situated within a city-owned urban renewal district only partially completed before funding ran out in the 1960s, the Clinton neighborhood has existed in a state of bureaucratic limbo for decades. When private developers generated a plan for the site in the late 1980s, the city backed their high-rise proposal even though it would require extensive site demolition and yield only 20 percent affordable housing units.

An alternative scheme created by architects Steven Peterson and Barbara Littenberg saves all the existing, on-site housing units and delivers a much higher percentage of affordable and moderate income units. Their plan preserves more of the neighborhood's authentic urban fabric, including residential, commercial and industrial buildings. Several new mid-block public spaces provide for the functional needs of this "working" district and bring a greater sense of identity and cohesion to the diverse community.

The project site is within Manhattan's Chelsea-Clinton district (above), an area formerly known as Hell's Kitchen. A major goal of the master plan was the preservation of the neighborhood's remaining small-scale buildings; many such buildings were lost to high-rise urban renewal projects in the 1960s.

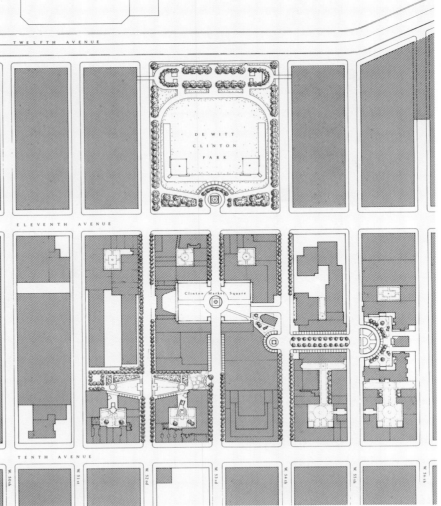

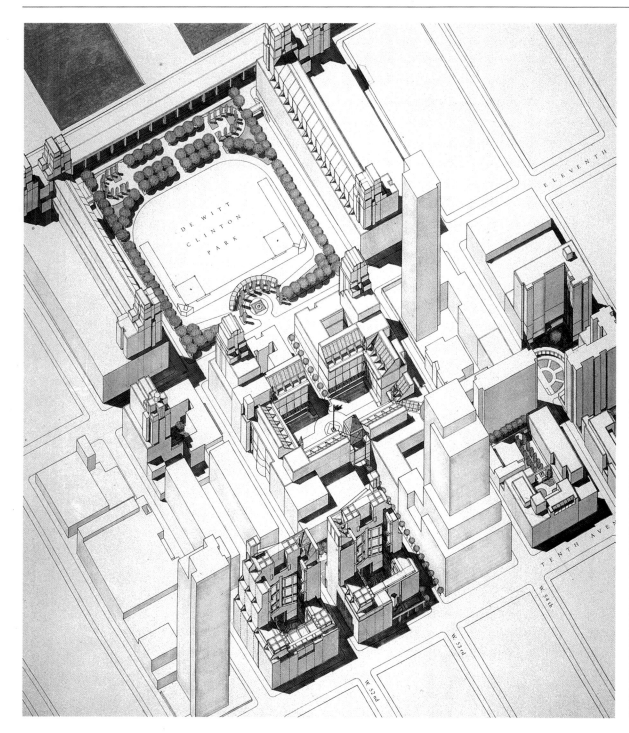

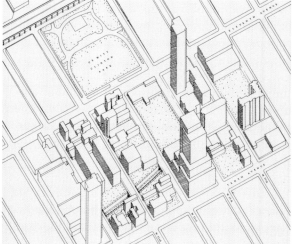

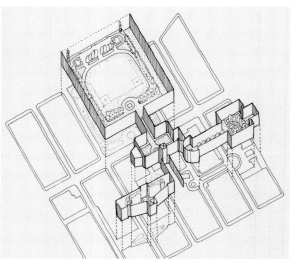

The proposed Clinton community master plan (left) took advantage of several large undeveloped tracts of land in the existing neighborhood (below). New buildings were added which define a network of public open spaces (bottom).

Each of these "public rooms" has its own defined function and identity within the overall plan.

DeWitt Clinton Park (below left, background) will continue to be used for active recreation. Its play fields contrast with the hardscape of Clinton Market Square (foreground), which is intended to feel more like an Italian piazza.

The shape of the two-block long "Triangle Square" (bottom left) was generated by its placement over an existing underground rail right-of-way.

The resulting park creates a mid-block pedestrian passageway and "garden entrance" for the apartment buildings. The inflected walls of the twin buildings help to contain and unify this space.

Smaller internal entry courts (below) will be the most private open spaces within the plan. They will be seen only by residents and guests within the complex.

The twin block apartments
(this spread) are the first
stage of the Clinton master
plan. Of its 652 units, 40
percent are for residents
of low and moderate income.
The remaining market rate
units are on the higher floors
of the complex.

Reversing the usual New
York City norm of tall
buildings on the avenues
and lower ones mid-block,
the form of these apartments
responds to an eight-story
height limit on the Tenth
Avenue edge of the site.

This design also preserves
a group of existing low-rise
buildings (pictured on
page 207) and a gas station
which is notched out of
the corner of one block.
A garden canopy covers the
station (lower right in site
plan, below and foreground
in photo, opposite).

As the first buildings to
be designed according to the
district's urban design
guidelines, the twin block
apartments demonstrate the
validity of the master plan's
organizing principles.

Unlike the many large-scale
object buildings that compete for attention within the
Manhattan skyline, these
buildings have subordinated
their form to the larger
urban structure of the block,
the neighborhood and the
underlying city pattern.

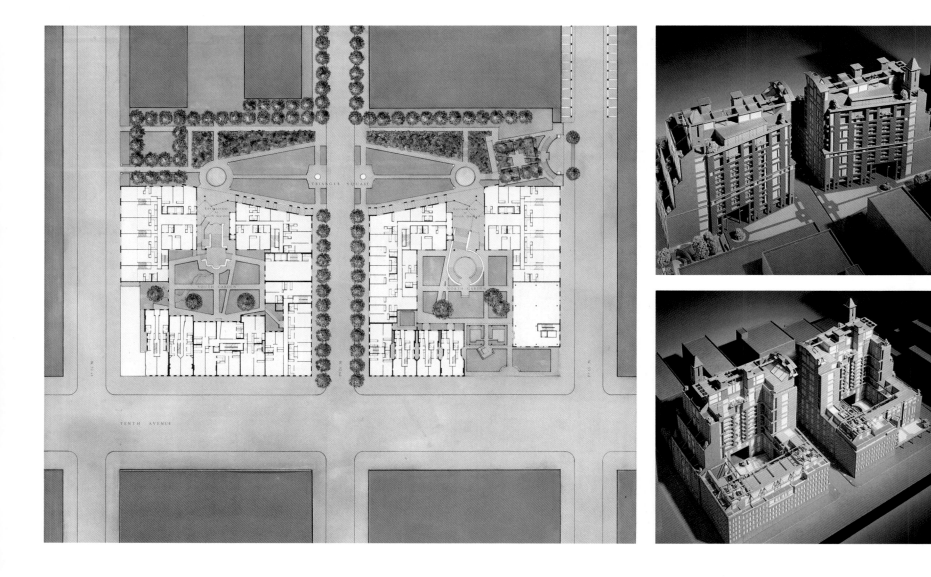

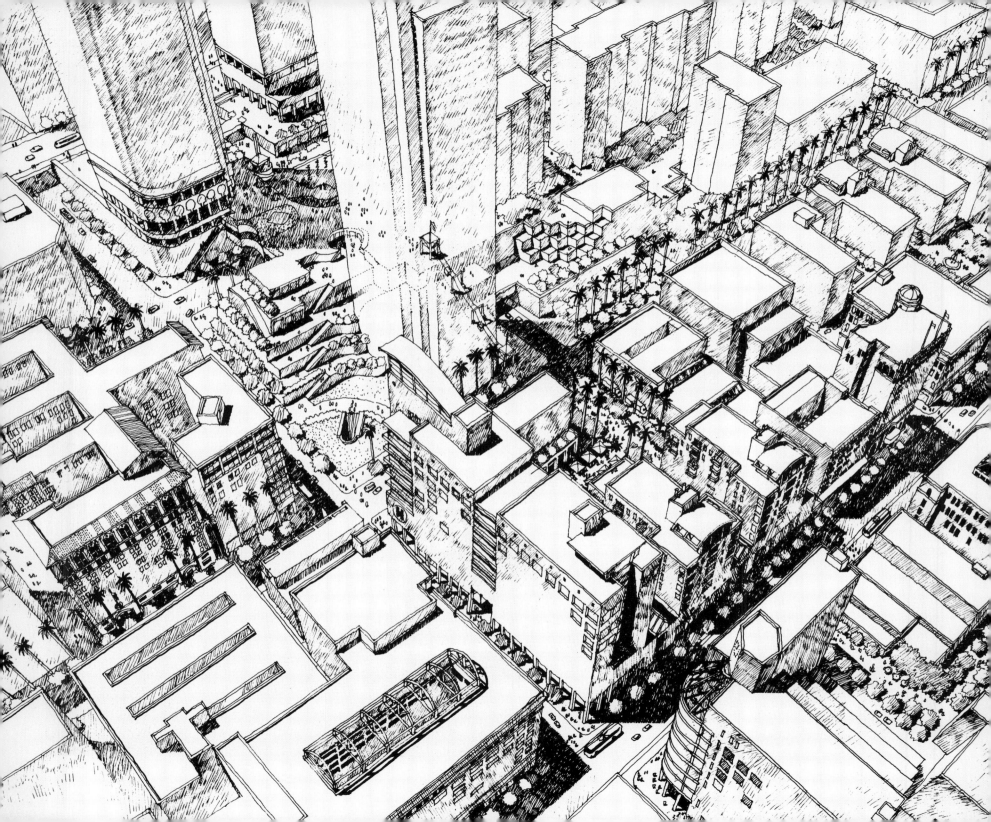

Downtown Los Angeles

Los Angeles, California, 1993

Though it has been called "a city in search of a center," Los Angeles actually does have a well-established downtown. And while it may not be as familiar as some of the region's higher-profile communities such as Beverly Hills or Santa Monica, downtown Los Angeles has historically played a major role in the commerce, government, social life and culture of the vast metropolitan area that surrounds it.

First founded as a Spanish pueblo in 1781, the city of Los Angeles entered a period of rapid growth in the late 1800s. By the 1920s, downtown Los Angeles had become the hub of an extensive inter-urban rail network. Existing towns along rail corridors such as Pasadena and new ones like Hollywood grew rapidly as wave after wave of newcomers populated the region. Just minutes to the ocean or to downtown's many jobs, these "streetcar suburbs" came to symbolize the good life that was available in the Los Angeles area.

The prosperity of Southern California and increasing use of automobiles led to an intensive period of road and freeway building in the postwar era. One unfortunate result of the massive new transportation infrastructure was the decline of the area's trolley car system and with it, downtown's role as a regional hub. The omnipresence of the automobile and the development patterns it fostered eventually blurred both the physical boundaries and the

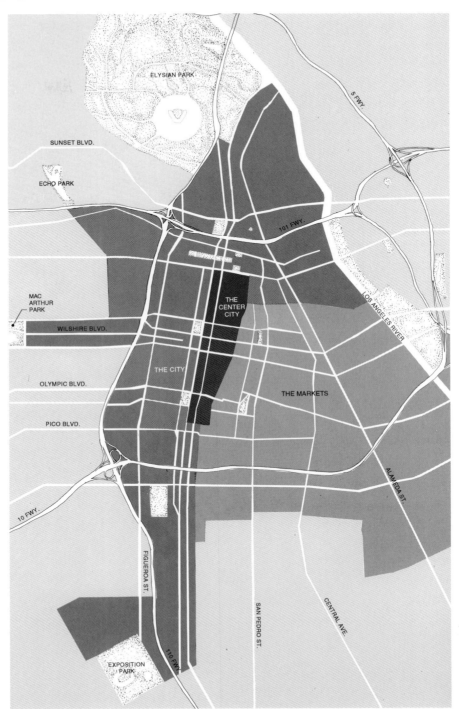

The conceptual plan of downtown (left) defines three distinct yet interdependent parts—The City, The Center City and The Markets. Each has its own history, character and patterns of activity and use.

One of the plan's projects, Grand Central Square/ Phase II (opposite) in The Center City, aims to stabilize the decline of downtown by renovating existing buildings and building new ones for offices and housing. A new public plaza is located next to the Grand Central Market, a popular gathering place. This revitalization effort benefits from several nearby transportation improvements: a recently opened Red Line subway stop and the legendary Angel's Flight funicular railway (visible behind tower in center of illustration, opposite and historic photo, below). It is due to reopen in 1994.

The plan's vision of downtown Los Angeles in 2020 anticipates not just extensive physical changes (highlighted in one possible scenario, right) but social and economic ones as well. Blending policy and design initiatives, the plan defines a physical framework to guide the incremental build-out of downtown. A new development code allows growth to occur in a predictable manner.

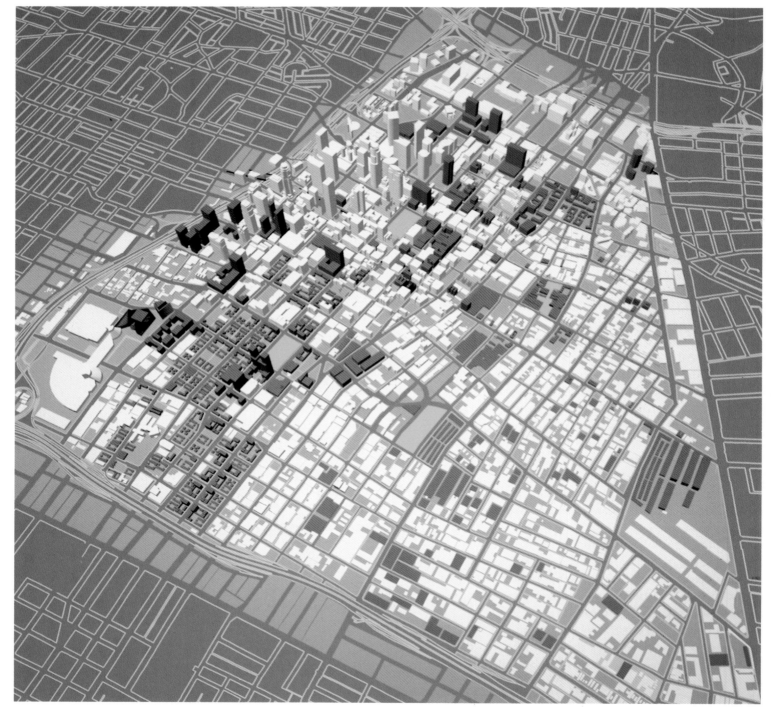

A pattern of intensive high-rise development and land speculation has caused downtown Los Angeles' edges to be dominated by parking lots (left).

Property in these areas, initially cleared for future office towers, often remains in parking use for decades. Though such sites may be zoned for potentially profitable buildings, inflated land prices and weak market conditions act to discourage any form of development.

One goal of the Strategic Plan is to convert such over-entitled areas into viable pedestrian-oriented, mixed-use neighborhoods. Developed incrementally, these places would benefit from their proximity to downtown's employment centers.

identity of downtown and other previously distinct communities within the Los Angeles area.

The current decline of downtown has prompted considerable debate among planners and civic leaders as to whether Los Angeles still needs a dominant urban core at its center. In this era of automobility, in a region with a great number of competing subcenters, some question whether the traditional center of the city should continue to be emphasized.

The recently completed Downtown Los Angeles Strategic Plan argues that a strong urban core is essential to the future economic, social and environmental viability of the region. It promotes a vision of a newly energized downtown as the preeminent center for the metropolitan area's commerce, industry, tourism, culture and government.

The Strategic Plan proposes to accomplish its mission through the reconstruction of a series of safe, clean, pedestrian-oriented, mixed-use neighborhoods and districts housing up to 100,000 new residents. Continuing its role as the economic engine of the region, the revitalized downtown is also expected to support, directly or indirectly, some 1,000,000 jobs.

Its diverse and concentrated mix of people and activities benefit from billions of dollars in past and planned regional infrastructure investment. As one of the most accessible locations in the region, downtown is at the hub of both the

existing freeway network and Los Angeles' ambitious new rail transit system (now under construction).

The Strategic Plan also addresses pressing environmental concerns. It seeks to densify existing, well-serviced urban areas as a way to curb Los Angeles' pervasive suburban sprawl (now over 5,000 square miles). Its compact growth pattern is meant to offset more destructive low-density development that is now occurring at the region's suburban fringe.

The plan was the result of a five-year-long public process directed by a 65-member committee representing a wide range of interests. A team of urban designers led by Los Angeles-based architects Elizabeth Moule and Stefanos Polyzoides included principals from several recognized firms–Andres Duany and Elizabeth Plater-Zyberk, Hanna/Olin and Solomon Inc. Consultants in the areas of economics, transportation, historic preservation, environmental management and social services also participated in the process.

Four collaborative charettes and many months of intensive public discussions culminated in a plan recommending both physical design and policy directives. The document's conceptual structure organizes downtown into three principal parts: "The City" is an area of mixed office, retail, civic, residential and entertainment uses. "The Markets," principally

dominated by a large and diverse concentration of manufacturing and wholesale businesses, includes clusters of housing, retail and a range of social services. In between, "The Center City" spans the historic core of downtown, as well as its theater, garment and jewelry districts.

Several larger physical "frameworks" are meant to guide the transformation of downtown over the next several decades. A transportation framework provides regional accessibility and improvements to internal circulation. A defined hierarchy of street types, stronger pedestrian links and various transit and parking initiatives contribute to this structure.

Downtown's open-space framework includes enhanced streets and sidewalks and the development of several new civic parks and plazas. These elements form the backdrop for much of the plan's new residential development.

A third framework relating to built form proposes guidelines for use, density and building design. A new development code, meant to replace the area's existing zoning, is intended to bring greater clarity and predictability to the process of development in downtown.

Several first steps have been set as preconditions for the implementation of the Strategic Plan. These include the provision of clean, safe streets; changes to key policies and approval processes intended to level the economic playing field between downtown and outlying

Four major parks and several landscaped "avenidas" are the principal elements of the downtown plan's open-space framework (below). The recently redesigned Pershing Square is one of the parks; three more of similar scale are to be newly created.

In addition to these civic-scaled spaces, several smaller parks are suggested to serve the needs of individual districts, neighborhoods and institutions. These parks (not shown in diagram) are to be widely dispersed.

About 60 percent of those coming into downtown Los Angeles each day now arrive in single-occupant automobiles. Planned improvements to regional transportation systems aim to shift many such drivers to other modes of travel.

Proposed alignments for both heavy- and light-rail lines (below) are a central component of the plan's transportation framework. This framework is critical to downtown's future growth and economic viability.

The Red Line's recently opened five-mile downtown section of subway is one part of what will ultimately be a 400-mile regional transit network. By comparison, Los Angeles' inter-urban rail system included over 1,000 miles of track during its heyday in the 1920s.

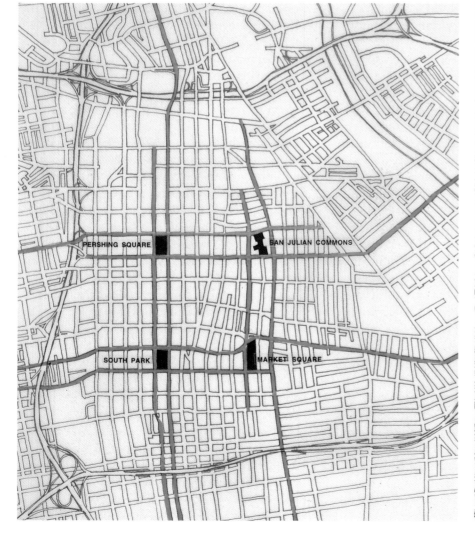

PERSHING SQUARE   SAN JULIAN COMMONS

SOUTH PARK   MARKET SQUARE

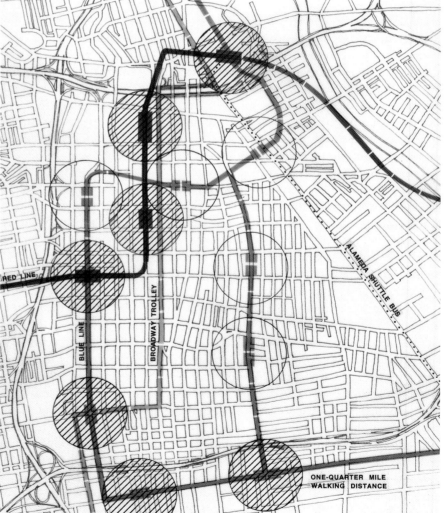

RED LINE

BLUE LINE

BROADWAY TROLLEY

ALAMEDA SHUTTLE BUS

ONE-QUARTER MILE WALKING DISTANCE

Sixteen "catalytic projects" (diagrammatic plan, right and examples, overleaf) are distributed throughout downtown's various districts and neighborhoods.

These multiple-purpose, mixed-use projects combine elements of transportation infrastructure, open space, landscape and buildings. They are intended to stimulate the social, physical and economic transformation of downtown Los Angeles.

areas; and the adoption of new policies aimed at stimulating economic growth.

Later steps include expansion of the area's existing industrial base, new programs for employment development, historic resource preservation, the creation of middle-income neighborhoods and a range of transportation and open-space initiatives. The plan also suggests ways of dealing effectively and humanely with homelessness, poverty and crime.

A series of 16 "catalytic projects" have been proposed as a way to jump-start the cycle of investment and development in downtown. Widely dispersed throughout The City, The Center City and The Markets, these projects combine many elements: transportation infrastructure, expansion of business and public activities in each district, improved linkages and access between neighborhoods and new opportunities for jobs and affordable housing.

The scope of the Los Angeles Strategic Plan is vast—the impact of many of its downtown-wide proposals will be felt across the entire region. Unlike past plans, however, which sought to impose a predetermined end vision, this plan relies on numerous incremental steps to "seed" future growth through joint public/private investment. In today's era of limited resources, such an approach may well be the best way to rebuild Los Angeles' downtown and those of other American metropolitan regions as well.

Most of the catalytic projects (examples, this spread) represent some form of joint public/private partnership. They were chosen both for their immediate benefits and their ability to generate investment in the future.

While each project relates to a particular location, they all address several down-town-wide goals: economic growth, social equity, access to transportation and community development.

Areas of vacant land around St. Vibiana Cathedral (below left) have been targeted for clusters of housing. A new public plaza next to the cathedral is the focus of this project, to be implemented in conjunction with the Catholic Archdiocese of the city of Los Angeles.

Southpark Square (bottom), another catalytic project, is one of four principal civic open spaces proposed in the Strategic Plan. Buildings containing commercial, institutional and residential uses surround the square.

Market Square (below right) combines several retail markets related to downtown's wholesale industries. As the anchor for the newly defined "Markets" area, this in-door/outdoor facility offers fresh produce, fish, meat, flowers and other items seven days a week.

Los Angeles' new convention center (below) now sits isolated at the edge of downtown. This catalytic project integrates that important facility into the urban fabric and life of downtown.

A proposed convention hotel, a shuttle connection to downtown's existing hotel district, pedestrian links to Seventh Street's retail area and upgrades to Figuroa Street (center of illustration) are among the recommendations that are included in this project.

The Broadway theater district, once the showplace for Southern California's thriving film industry, has been in decline since the 1940s. This project organizes several historic theaters into a defined regional entertainment district.

The Architecture of Community

Vincent Scully

The architects who are published in this book believe that the principles shaping their work, among them the establishment of public space, pedestrian scale, and neighborhood identity, are as applicable to center city as to suburban conditions. This may well be true, and there are one or two urban projects to suggest it, but it is a fact that the most characteristic situation with which most of this work deals is a suburban one. In view of the fact, too, that there are a number of active contemporary strategies for the healing of center city that are not mentioned in this volume—the historic preservation of neighborhoods and their inhabitants is one example among many—the book's title, *The New Urbanism*, cannot help but seem overly comprehensive.

The New Suburbanism might be a truer label, because the *new* theme that links these projects is the redesign of that vast area in which most Americans now live, sprawled between the metropolitan center, which is emptying out, and the open countryside, which is rapidly being devoured. The major issue surely has to do with reshaping that sprawl of automobile suburbia into communities that make sense, and *Toward an Architecture of Community*, the book's subtitle, is what this book is primarily about. In that sense, it has to do with architecture at its proper scale and put to its proper use, which is the shaping of the human environment within

the natural world, the building of the human community entire.

All human culture is intended to protect human beings from nature in one way or another and to mitigate the effect upon them of nature's immutable laws. Architecture is one of humanity's major strategies in that endeavor. It shelters human beings and reassures them. Its purpose is to mediate between the individual and the natural world by creating the physical reality of the human community, by which the individual is linked to the rest of humanity and nature is in part kept out, in part framed, tamed, and itself humanized. So architecture constructs its own model of reality within nature's implacable order. It is within that model that human beings live; they need it badly, and if it breaks down they may well become insane.

That is exactly what is happening today, and not only in America, but the pattern, as so often in contemporary history, can be perceived most clearly here. This is so, in part, because Americans have in fact destroyed so many kinds of communities during the past generation. The process began directly after World War II, when the remaining trolley tracks, the very lifeline of town and suburb alike, were apparently bought and torn up by the automobile interests. Public transit had been declining since 1914 in any event as the number of automobiles rose. The Redevelopment of the 1960s completed the

Ideal city for three million (Le Corbusier; 1922), view along main boulevard.

destruction and showed the true shape of the holocaust. The automobile was, and remains, the agent of chaos, the breaker of the city, and Redevelopment tore most American towns apart to allow it free passage through their centers, which were supposed to be revitalized by affluent suburban shoppers thereby. Instead the reverse took place: The automobile created the suburban shopping mall, which sucked the life out of the old city centers everywhere. This is ironic enough, because the existing center-city communities had themselves been destroyed by Redevelopment in order to bring the largely mythical suburbanite shoppers in. To follow I-95 and its various connectors from New England to Florida is to watch that evil process at work from Oak Street in New Haven to Overtown in Miami, at the very end of the road. Their communities physically torn apart, and given no opportunity to form new ones, many of the inhabitants of center city began to lose their minds, as who would not. Many of them were African-Americans from the rural South who had been lured to the big cities to work in war plants during World War II; then the factories moved away with perfect cynicism, seeking even cheaper labor back in the South once more; then, in financial panic, the big cities redeveloped themselves in the manner already described and there its people were, out of work under the Piranesian piers of the

freeway, in a surreal wasteland with homes, churches, stores, and most of all the orienting street grid of the city, all shot to hell.

By contrast, the suburbs, closed off from the urban population by what Frank Lloyd Wright once called "the iron hand of realty," seemed like Paradise, but they were spawning their own neuroses too, fed by endless hours on the road and no connection with much of anything when one got where one was going. Soon fear came to play its part. It rode behind the locked doors of the automobiles and was eminently justified, whether by the nut on the highway, or the sniper on the overpass, or by what happened if the wrong exit was taken off the connector.

Whatever other factors have been involved in this disintegration of community, it is still the automobile—and how much we all love it—which has done the job. It has not only obliterated the community's physical structure but has also made us feel that the community's psychic protection is unnecessary, and that what the car seems to offer in terms of individual freedom is enough. It is a device of deep illusion and may be said to have rendered all of society insane. Indeed, the years to come will soon show us whether the automobile and what we have thought of as civilization can coexist.

Some of us were writing and teaching all this in the 1960s—even then the eventual effects on

American society were predictable enough—and some younger people were apparently listening. Peter Calthorpe, a student at Yale in the 1970s, seems to have been one of them. His "transit-oriented development," as assembled at Laguna West, is an attempt to regroup the suburb into a density which makes public transit feasible. It is shaped by avenues that radiate, like those of Versailles, from a center of public buildings and spaces, among them a "village green." One thinks of the 17th-century grid plan of New Haven, Connecticut, with the great Green in the center. As the grid moved west to shape most of the cities of the continent, the Green, the public space, tended to disappear under the pressure of private greed. Calthorpe now tries to bring it back, reflecting the attempt by many organizations over the past 30 years to preserve or restore public space. One recalls the fight under Margaret Flint of the New Haven Trust for Historic Preservation to preserve the scale and amenity of New Haven's Green itself in 1967. Indeed, the combats of that year—when New Haven's post office and city hall were saved from Redevelopment and after which, by extension, the brutal demolition of low-income neighborhoods was brought to a halt by Senator Lowell Weicker—might be regarded as the true beginning of the contemporary preservation movement, through which, for the first time in the modern period, a popular mass movement

Lever Brothers Headquarters, New York City (Skidmore, Owings & Merrill, architects; constructed 1952).

Whitney Museum of American Art, New York City (Marcel Breuer architect; constructed 1963).

has discovered the means and the political clout to force architects and civic officials alike to do what the informed public wants them to do.

That movement, now boldly led by the National Trust for Historic Preservation, does seem to reflect the yearning to rebuild community which is felt by most Americans today. It now seems obvious to almost everybody–as it did once before, in the 1870s, when the Colonial Revival began–that community is what America has most conspicuously lost, and community is precisely what the canonical Modern architecture and planning of the middle years of this century were totally unable to provide. This was so for many reasons; foremost among them was the fact that the Modern architects of the heroic period (Wright, Le Corbusier, Mies Van der Rohe, Gropius and their followers) all despised the traditional city–the finest achievement of Western architecture, put together piece by piece over the centuries–and were determined to replace it with their own personal, utopian, idiosyncratic schemes. Le Corbusier's Ville Radieuse was the most influential of them all; and it furnished the basic model for American Redevelopment itself. Even the social structures involved were eerily the same: both were "cités d'affaires," cities of business, from which the poor were to be excluded. The German Modernists had advanced equally catastrophic ideas, based upon their concept of

the "zeitgeist," the "spirit of the age," that did not allow anything which had been done before to be done again or even to be preserved. So Hilbersheimer proposed his endless miles of high-rise slabs, his landscapes of hell, out of which the mass housing of the 1950s took shape, much of it to be dynamited as wholly unlivable hardly more than 20 years later.

In all these cataclysmic proposals for the city there was a true hatred for the world as it was socially constituted, but there was also something else, a consuming contempt for it on aesthetic grounds. The Modern architects of the International Style had largely taken abstract painting as their model, and they came to want to be as free from all constraints as those painters were, free from everything which had always shaped and limited architecture before, in part from statics itself (forms must float) and from roofs, windows, trim and so on, but most of all from the restraints of the urban situation as a whole: from the city, from the community. Their buildings were to be free of zoning laws, and from the need to define the street, and from all respect for whatever already existed on and around the site. They were to be free–like Lever House or the Pan Am Building or the Whitney Museum or even the Guggenheim Museum–to rip the old urbanism apart or to outrage it, or, perhaps most truly, to use its order, while it lasted, as a background before

which they could cavort. Most of all they had to be abstract; they could not under any circumstances be inflected toward their surroundings by Classical or vernacular details or stylistic references of any kind. Such would have constituted an immoral act. Here was another madness to complement the others. It is still prevalent today among many architects who, baffled by the complexity of reality, still insist that architecture is a purely self-referential game, having to do with formal invention, linked madly enough with linguistics, or literature, but not at all with the city or with human living on any sane terms. Such architects claim to reflect the chaos of modern life and to celebrate it. Some of them pretend to worship the automobile, and the "space-time continuum," like Marinetti before them idolizing violence, speed, war and Fascism in the end. "Whom Zeus wishes to destroy," said Aeschylus more or less, "he hastens on with madness."

Yet it should be said that there is hardly an architect or critic living today who has not been drawn to Modern architecture during his life and does not love thousands of Modern works of art. But the urban issue has to be faced. The International Style built many beautiful buildings, but its urbanistic theory and practice destroyed the city. It wrote bad law. Its theme in the end was individuality; hence its purest creations were suburban villas, like the Villa

*Glass House, New
Canaan, Connecticut
(Philip Johnson, architect;
constructed 1949).*

*Vanna Venturi House
(bottom), Chestnut Hill,
Pennsylvania (Venturi
and Rauch, architects;
constructed 1962); Trubek
and Wislocki houses (right),
Nantucket Island,
Massachusetts (Venturi
and Rauch, architects;
constructed 1970-1).*

Savoie and Philip Johnson's Glass House. These celebrated the individual free from history and time. One could not make a community out of them. In the Glass House especially the individual human being seems wholly liberated from the entire human community. The secret is technology, a chancy thing; plugged into its heating and lighting devices the existential mortal man can dispense with everything else that once stood between nature and himself. He enjoys the sensation of being wholly alone in the world. His architecture cannot, will not, deal with community issues.

So Neo-Modern architecture, in its present "Deconstructivist" phase, though popular in the schools—why not, it offers the ideal academic vocabulary, easy to teach as a graphic exercise and compromised and complicated by nothing that exists outside the academic halls—has been failing for a long time in the larger world of the built environment itself. Here it is clear that the most important development of the past three decades or more has been the revival of the Classical and vernacular traditions of architecture, which have always dealt with questions of community and environment, and their reintegration into the mainstream of Modern architecture. That development in fact began in the late 1940s with an historical appreciation of the American domestic architecture of the 19th century—which I tried to call the Stick and

Shingle Styles—and it first took new shape in the present with Robert Venturi's shingled Beach House of 1959. Venturi then went on, in the Vanna Venturi House of the early 1960s, to reassess the early buildings of Frank Lloyd Wright, which had themselves grown directly out of the Shingle Style of the 1880s, and he worked his way wholly back into the Shingle Style itself, as in the Trubek and Wislocki houses of 1970. Here Venturi rediscovered a basic vernacular type, very close indeed to the types "remembered" (as he put it) by Aldo Rossi in Italy very soon thereafter. Many other architects then followed that lead, Robert A.M. Stern foremost in time among them. Stern soon learned to abandon his compulsion to invent— his early houses, though based on Shingle Style models, are Proto-Deconstructivist in form—in favor of trying to learn how to design traditional

buildings well, and to group them in ways that make sense. The point became not style but type and, by extension, context. Here again Robert Venturi's work led the way. Wu Hall in Princeton, the Institute for Scientific Information in Philadelphia, and the Sainsbury Wing of the National Gallery in London, all inflect what are otherwise clearly Modern buildings toward the particular "styles" which preexist on each site: Tudorish in Princeton, International Style in Philadelphia, Classical on Trafalgar Square. Each new building thus enhances and completes the existing place on its own terms. The city is healed rather than outraged—poignantly so in London, where the site had actually been blitzed and where early schemes to build upon it lent credence to Prince Charles' remark that Modern architecture had done more damage to England than the Luftwaffe. Now the architect gives up his semi-divine pretension to be Destroyer and Creator and to invent new styles like new religions, and aspires instead to the more humane and realistic role of healer, of physician. Venturi was surely encouraged in this new pragmatism by the work of his wife Denise Scott Brown in neighborhood design and advocacy planning. So, with Venturi, the architect abandons the iconoclasm of much of the Modern movement in favor of the idea that he belongs to a long and continuous architectural tradition, through which cities in the past

Wu Hall, Princeton, New Jersey (Venturi, Rauch and Scott Brown, architects; constructed 1983).

have on the whole been built correctly and in reasonable accordance with human needs.

Out of this view, which is in fact the natural culmination of the vernacular and Classical revival, the work of Andres Duany and Elizabeth Plater-Zyberk derives. It completes the revival by dealing with the town as a whole. It reclaims for architecture, and for architects, a whole realm of environmental shaping that has been usurped in recent generations by hosts of supposed experts, many of whom, like those of the truly sinister Departments of Transportation everywhere, have played major roles in tearing the environment to bits and encouraging its most cancerous aberrations. With these two young architects, and with their students and colleagues at the University of Miami, architecture regains its traditional stature as the means by which cities are made.

I have written elsewhere how, as architecture students at Yale in the early 1970s, Duany and Plater-Zyberk led my seminar into New Haven's vernacular neighborhoods and showed us all not only how intelligently the individual buildings were put together but also how well they were related to each other to make an urban environment—how effectively the lots worked, and the porches related to the street, and the sidewalks with their fences and their rows of trees bound the whole fabric together, and how street parking was better than parking

lots and the automobile could be disciplined, and how, most of all, it could all be done again—and fundamentally had to be done again as all of a piece if it was going to be done right—from the turned posts and the frontal gables to the picket fences, the sidewalks and the trees. Everything that the International Style had hated, everything that the "zeitgeist" had so Germanically consigned to death, came alive again. For me, marinated in Modernism, it was the revelation of a new life in everything. There was no reason whatever why the best of everything had to be consigned to the past. Everything was available to be used again; now, as always in architecture, there were models to go by, types to employ.

So it is important to remember that for Duany and Plater-Zyberk the plan as such did not come first. First came the buildings, the architectural vernacular, because it was after all the buildings which had brought the old New Haven grid up into three dimensions to shape a place. Duany and Plater-Zyberk's critics have never really understood this. It is again a question of types which, with their qualifying details and decoration, have shown themselves capable of shaping civilized places and of fitting together in groups to make towns. Leon Krier was also instrumental in helping us see this, and he became one of Duany and Plater-Zyberk's most important mentors and was to build a beautiful house at Seaside.

Terms like "historicism" are not relevant here—the *zeitgeist* mentality is "historicist," not this one—but ancillary concepts like those relative to symbol are relevant indeed, and no excuse need be made for that fact. Human beings experience all works of visual art in two different but inextricably interrelated ways: empathetically and by association. We feel them both in our bodies and in terms of whatever our culture has taught us. Modernism at its purest fundamentally wanted to eliminate the cultural signs if possible—hence abstraction. It was Venturi himself who, in his epoch-making *Complexity and Contradiction in Architecture* (1966) and his *Learning from Las Vegas* (1972), first brought an awareness of the centrality of symbolism back to architecture, and he was the first to use semiotics as an architectural tool. It was he who introduced literary criticism itself, especially Empson's theory of ambiguity, into the contemporary architectural dialogue. Faced with this, the Neo-Modernists would like to divert it by replacing the relevant primary architectural symbols—those having to do with nature, place and community—with secondary and diversionary ones having to do with linguistics or whatever else may be dredged up out of the riot of sign systems in the human mind.

Not Duany and Plater-Zyberk. Their eyes are on the reality of things as they are. That is why Seaside is so moving. Whatever it may be

Master plan of Venice, Florida (John Nolen, city planner; 1926).

French Country Village, Coral Gables, Florida (Edgar Albright, architect; constructed 1925).

in fact—a resort community, a modern-day Chautauqua—it has beyond that succeeded, more fully than any other work of architecture in our time has done, in creating an image of community, a symbol of human culture's place in nature's vastness. It does this in terms of the densely three-dimensional organization of its building types as they group together, almost huddle together, on the shore of Florida's panhandle, pressed close up to the gleaming white sand, the green and blue sea and the wild skies of the Gulf of Mexico. Therefore, Seaside is not an affair of plan only, not only of two-dimensional geometry, as all too many planned communities in this century have tended to become. True enough, Seaside's plan as such has a distinguished ancestry. It owes a direct debt not only to Versailles and to the whole French classic planning tradition, out of which Washington no less than modern Paris took its shape, but also to the fine American planning profession that flourished before Gropius came to Harvard in the 1930s and destroyed it at its heart. One thinks here especially of John Nolen's work of the 1920s in Florida, so well illustrated by John Hancock in Jean-Francois Lejeune's brilliant publication *The New City: Foundations* (Fall, 1991). All the planning shapes at Seaside are in Nolen's plans for Venice and Clewiston, both in Florida: the grid, the broad hemicycles, the diagonal avenues. And Nolen

was of course not alone in his time. Planners of the teens and twenties like Frederick Law Olmsted, Jr., Frank Williams, Arthur Shurtlief, Arthur Comey, George and James Ford, every one of them with at least one degree from Harvard, also come to mind, as do many others. It is true that one weakness of these planners, a somewhat Jeffersonian preoccupation from early in the century onward with what they called the "congestion" of the cities, was to play into the hands of the Modernist iconoclasts and the automobile freaks after World War II. Otherwise, the New Urbanism, so-called, is in large part a revival of the Classical and vernacular planning tradition as it existed before International-Style Modernism perverted its methods and objectives.

But Duany and Plater-Zyberk differ from Nolen—and so Seaside from Venice—in one fundamental aspect: They write a code that controls the buildings as well as the plan. They therefore ensure that the three-dimensional reality of the town will fulfill the concept adumbrated in its plat—without themselves having to design every building in it. Hence they encourage many other architects and builders to work, as they can do freely enough, within the overall guidelines. Nolen could not normally exert that much control. So his streets are often ill-defined, his axes climaxed by gas stations, the whole inadequately shaped and

contained. Calthorpe so far has been in something of the same fix.

But Duany and Plater-Zyberk had learned not only from Nolen but also from George Merrick, the developer of Coral Gables, upon which he worked most directly from 1921 to 1926, when the hurricane of that year wiped him out but failed to kill his town. Merrick is one of the true heroes of American architecture, and an unlikely one. He was a Florida real estate man of the bad old days of the boom when so many of Florida's lots were resold two or three times in one day and were in fact under water. But not those of Coral Gables, which also has an unusual plan, involving a perimeter of tightly gridded streets that contains and protects a free-flowing English garden within it—its shapes probably suggested by its several golf courses—and all fundamentally at automobile scale: the automobile scale of the 1920s, that is, the scale of "motoring," which is what Coral Gables, though it once had a fine public transportation system, was fundamentally intended for. We can't really blame Merrick for his beautiful renderings of fine boulevards with a few dignified town cars proceeding along them. Who could have foreseen the explosion of the species that was to come? But what Duany and Plater-Zyberk and Robert Davis learned from Coral Gables was not only the general lesson that a fine coherent small city

Rowhouses, Seaside, Florida (Walter Chatham, architect; constructed 1991).

could be made out of suburban elements but also the specific lesson that it took a Draconian building code to do it. That's what Merrick had, a code that shaped first the beginnings of a Spanish or, perhaps better, a Mediterranean-Revival town and then introduced little villages into it that were French or Chinese or South African Cape Dutch or Southern Colonial—all perfectly delightful, especially the Chinese.

With the hurricane of 1926, Merrick went bankrupt and lost control, and the houses, especially after World War II, became more typically suburban—squashed down, spread out, less urbane and less naturally groupable—while the lots became much bigger, so that a certain structure, or scale, was lost. But much of the code held, and a fundamental urban order continued to be maintained. In the end that order was furnished largely by the trees. They shape the streets and cover them over against the sun and are the major architectural elements that make the place special and unified in every way, and disguise the worst of the houses.

Seaside's structure does not derive from its trees. The windy Gulf coast is not sympathetic to them, and the "jungle" will grow up only to the height that is protected by the houses, but the principle of shaping the streets three-dimensionally is written into the code. Streets are as narrow as possible—automobiles can get through them perfectly well but their scale

remains pedestrian—and they are closely defined by picket fences and front porches and by building masses brought tightly up to them. There are no carports and few garages. The cars survive well enough and the street facade retains its integrity. So the important place-maker is the code. It is not "fussy" or "escapist" but essential, and at Seaside it may not have been written strictly enough.

It is curious that the houses there which have been most published in the architectural press—though not in the popular press, which understands the issues better—are those which most stridently challenge the code, as if originality were architecture's main virtue and subversion of community its greatest good. The houses by Walter Chatham at Seaside are the most conspicuous in this regard. Each destroys a type; his own intrudes what looks like a primitivistic cabin, something appropriate to a glade in the Everglades, into a civilized street of humanly scaled windows, flat trim and delicate porches, and so barbarizes it, while his row houses at the town's urban core do the two things no row-house can do without destroying the group: interrupting the cornice line and dividing the individual house volume vertically down the middle. Yet Robert Davis encourages Chatham (whom everybody likes anyway) and continues to give him buildings to do, perhaps valuing his intransigence as an image of the therapeutic

license within the general order—or simply because it is invariably published. To go further, it would be salutary to see what a really fine architect like Frank Gehry—his work almost Deconstructivist but much too genial, accomplished, and untheoretical for that—might be able to do within the code at Seaside. Gehry has shown not only that he knows how to inflect his apparently anarchic buildings toward the places they are intended for but also that he understands and loves American wood frame construction. He might well find a way to reinterpret the tradition and retain civility in ways that Chatham, for example, has not yet been able to do.

Distressing, though, is the tendency of Duany and Plater-Zyberk, when addressing Neo-Modernists, to suggest that they employ the vernacular in their projects only because it is popular with their clients. This buffoonery, genial enough, nevertheless leaves them open to the charge of "pandering" to the public which their opponents are not slow to advance. But the pandering in this case, as in that of Chatham, is to the architectural magazines and the professional club. It makes a joke of everything Duany and Plater-Zyberk have come to stand for, and it denies the historical facts of their rise. That they should seem to need the approval of professional côteries they have far outclassed may be taken as an aberration of

Ambrogio Lorenzetti, Allegory of Good Government (fresco; 1338-40), Palazzo Pubblico, Siena, Italy.

success and an indication of the tight hold (like that of the Marine Corps or the Catholic Church) which the architectural profession exerts on anyone who has ever belonged to it. In any case, another generation—some collaborators, others trained by Duany and Plater-Zyberk, others affiliated with them at the University of Miami and therefore much more liberated than they—will surely carry on the work. Some names that come to mind, and there may surely be others (many mentioned elsewhere in this book), are: Jorge Hernandez, Teofilo Victoria, Maria de la Guardia, Jorge, Mari and Luis Trelles, Rocco Ceo, Rafael Portuondo, Geoffrey Ferrell, Charles Barrett, Victor Dover, Joseph Kohl, Jaime Correa, Mark Schimmenti, Eric Valle, Scott Merrill, Jean-Francois Lejeune, Ramon Trias, Maralys Nepomechie, Gary Greenan, Dan Williams, Monica Ponce de Leon, Richard McLaughlin, Armando Montero, Thorn Grafton, Suzanne Martinson, Rolando Llanes, Sonia Chao, Maria Nardi, Frank Martinez, Ernesto Buch, Douglas Duany, Dennis Hector, Joanna Lombard, Thomas Spain, Roberto Behar, and Rosario Marquardt, whose rapt and noble paintings have helped to set a Mediterranean impress on the school.

It is true that Seaside seems so deceptively *ad hoc* that it can take a good deal of disruption. Could Kentlands? Probably not so much. But

the point is clear. All human communities involve an intense interplay between the individual and the law. Without the law there is no peace in the community and no freedom for the individual to live without fear. Architecture is the perfect image of that state of affairs. Ambrogio Lorenzetti showed it to us in Siena, in his *Allegory of Good Government*. There is the country all rounded and rich in vineyards and grain. There is the city wall cutting into it, behind which the hard-edged buildings of the town jostle each other and shape public spaces where the citizens dance together. A figure of *Security* floats above the gate and guards it. Alongside this great scene an allegory of the town government is painted on the wall. The *Commune* sits enthroned, a majestic figure surrounded by virtues. Below him all the citizens of the town are gathered, each dressed in his characteristic costume and all grasping a

golden cord which depends from the *Commune* itself. The cord is the law which binds them together and which they hold voluntarily because it makes them free. In the center of the scene the figure of *Peace* reclines at her ease.

Seaside, which in fact resembles Lorenzetti's densely towered town more than a little—as does Battery Park City at another scale—embodies this necessary duality well. It is interesting in that regard to compare its houses and their groupings with those at Laguna West, where Calthorpe has pointed out that he was not able to control the architectural situation so completely. It is even more interesting to visit the towns along the Gulf near Seaside which imitate it. The picket fences are there, and they help quite a lot, as do the gazebos and the vernacular architecture as well. But the roads are all too wide, the lots usually too big; the density is not really present, so that the auto-

mobile still seems to be in command and the pressure of the communal law is not really applied. Therefore, these derivations from Seaside are all less convincing as places. They should not be despised for that, because their movement is in the right direction, but the point remains luminous: architecture is fundamentally a matter not of individual buildings but of the shaping of community, and that, as in Paris, Uruk, or Siena, is done by the law.

Still, one cannot help but hope that the lessons of Seaside and of the other new towns now taking shape can be applied to the problem of housing for the poor. That is where community is most needed and where it has been most disastrously destroyed. Center city would truly have to be broken down into its intrinsic neighborhoods if this were to take place within it. Sadly, it would all have been much easier to do before Redevelopment, when the basic

structure of the neighborhoods was still there, than it is today. But, whatever the size of the city as a whole, the "five-minute walk" would have to govern distances and the scale of the buildings themselves should respond to the basically low-rise, suburban-sized environment that, for any number of reasons, most Americans seem to want. It is therefore a real question whether "center city" as we know it can *ever* be shaped into the kind of place most Americans want to live in.

The Clinton neighborhood illustrated in this volume is surely a measurable improvement in that regard over the usual development of Manhattan's blocks, but the scale is still enormous, much larger than that of Vienna's great Gemeindebauten of the period 1919-34, which it otherwise somewhat recalls. It is very urbane, with reasonable public spaces. But in America, unlike Europe, only the rich have normally

chosen to live in high-rise apartments. The poor have almost always aspired to what they have been told every American family rates: a single-family house in the suburbs. Ideally they want Seaside. And since we are no longer Modern architects who act upon what we think people ought to have rather than what they want, we should try to figure out how they can get it. The building type itself should present no problem, especially if its basic visual qualities and its sense of personal identification can be captured in a narrower, higher, perhaps even multi-family type. In fact, some of Duany and Plater-Zyberk's basic models, and those of Melanie Taylor and Robert Orr at Seaside, were the two- and three-family wooden houses of New Haven's modest neighborhoods, a good three stories tall with porches, bay windows and high frontal gables, a 19th century blue-collar Stick-and-Shingle structure that defined city streets with a compelling presence and some density but at a moderate scale.

Here, too, a half-forgotten contemporary project comes to mind: Robert Stern's Subway Suburb of 1976. Stern proposed that the city services from subways to sewage that still existed in the South Bronx, above which the city lay burned, wasted and unwanted, should be utilized to create what amounted to a suburban community of single and double houses laid out according to the existing street

SUBWAY SUBURB

Subway Suburb, South Bronx, New York (Robert A.M. Stern, architect; 1976-80).

pattern. Some of the details Stern employed, and perhaps the house types themselves, were not close enough to their superior vernacular prototypes to be convincing today, but the idea was there. HUD later built a few single-family houses in the area that were snapped up at once despite their lack of psychological and physical support from a community group, and similar houses elsewhere can be seen standing in otherwise tragically trashed ghettos all over the northeast, meticulously groomed behind their chain-link fences. There is reason to believe, therefore, that the Seaside type and related vernacular models, easy and economical to construct, might well be adapted for many urban situations. Such is already being done in dribs and drabs by Habitat for Humanity. But could it be funded as a mass program at urban scale?

Seaside, Kentlands, and Laguna West could be built by developers because there was money to be made out of them. Will it ever be possible to make money by building communities for the poor? Ways may yet be found to do so; some combination of private investment with intelligent government subsidies at all levels

may do the trick. The federal government itself once spent so much money on Redevelopment, at a time when the architectural profession hardly knew what to do with the city, that we may hope it will reorder its priorities and begin to spend some now when the profession is better prepared to spend it wisely.

Urban organizations like Chicago's Center for Neighborhood Technology, of which Michael Freedberg is Director of Community Planning, are watching the work of Duany and Plater-Zyberk and Calthorpe and the others very carefully to see if there is anything in it they can use. In Chicago they sit, of course, at the heart of a wonderful urban-suburban order of the recent past, with the Loop, the community of work, and Oak Park, the community of home, perfectly connected by the elevated suburban train. But that order too is breaking down, with work moving centrifugally to Chicago's periphery so that the existing east-west transit serves it perfectly no longer. In the long run a version of Calthorpe's "TODs" might be of relevance here.

To say that there is much hope in this or any other present model would be overstating the case. But there is a lot of determination. One drowns in the urban situation but works with what one has. It would be sad if Seaside, for one, were not to inspire imitations far from the Gulf. Seaside itself sometimes seems to be

sinking under the weight of its own success. Everybody in the country appears to be coming to look at it, smothering it, ironically enough, in automobiles during the summer. The only thing that can save it, says Duany, is more Seasides, plenty of them, and this is surely true in the largest social sense. The town of Windsor, for example, by Duany and Plater-Zyberk, with two polo fields, is aimed at as rich a clientele as exists. It offers large "estate" houses around a golf course and others along the shore. In the center, however, is a tightly-gridded town, and that is where every client so far has wanted to be. So the rich, who can choose, choose community, or at least its image. How much more must the poor, who must depend upon it for their lives, want community? If Seaside and the others cannot in the end offer viable models for that, they will remain entirely beautiful but rather sad. Perhaps they will in fact do so, because human beings are moved to act by symbols, and the symbol is there. When the great winds rise up out of the Gulf—and the storm clouds roll in thundering upon the little lighted town with its towered houses—then a truth is felt, involving the majesty of nature and, however partial, the brotherhood of mankind.

Project Information

The information and credits in the following listings and other parts of this book were obtained from the submitting firms below and other sources believed to be reliable. However, neither McGraw-Hill nor the author guarantees the accuracy or completeness of any information published herein and neither McGraw-Hill nor the author shall be responsible for any errors, omissions or damages arising out of use of this information.

Planning the American Dream (pp. xxv–xlii)

Photo/Illustration Credits: Todd W. Bressi, p. xxvii top left; Calthorpe Associates, pp. xxxi, xxxiii; Dover, Correa, Kohl, Cockshutt, Valle, pp. xxxiv–xxxv, p. xxxvii right top and bottom, p. xxxviii; Andres Duany and Elizabeth Plater-Zyberk, pp. xxx, xxxii, p. xxxvi bottom right, p. xxxix; ©Jeff Goldberg/Esto, p. xli top and bottom left; ©Anton Grassl, p. xl bottom center; Gruen Associates, p. xxviii top right; ©Gabriel Gualteros, p. xl bottom right; Kohler Co., p. xxvi bottom, p. xxvii top right; New York State Office of Parks, Recreation and Historic Preservation, p. xxvi top; Millard Arnold, Norfolk Redevelopment and Housing Authority, p. xl bottom left; Regional Plan Association/Dodson Associates, p. xxxvi top left (pair); John Kriken, Skidmore Owings & Merrill, p. xl top left; Ezra Stoller ©Esto, p. xxviii bottom

right; Stan Ries, p. xl, top right; Sasaki Associates, p. xli bottom right; Jeff Westman, p. xxviii top left; Wurster Bernardi & Emmons, p. xxix

Seaside (pp. 2–17)

Project Location: Walton County, Florida, approximately 40 miles west of Panama City on County Road 30A
Project Area: 80 acres
Developer: Robert Davis, Seaside, Florida
Submitting Firm: Andres Duany and Elizabeth Plater-Zyberk, Architects and Town Planners, Andres Duany (principal), Elizabeth Plater-Zyberk (principal)
Charette Team: Daniel Broggi, Ernesto Buch, Victoria Casasco, Robert Davis, Andres Duany, Elizabeth Plater-Zyberk, Luis Trelles, Teofilo Victoria
Consultants: Leon Krier (architecture, urban design); Barrett, Daffin & Carlin (civil engineering), Daryl Rose Davis (interiors, colors), Douglas Duany (landscape)
Project Status: Approximately 70% complete; all residential lots sold with 225 residences built. Civic and commercial areas 30% complete.
Photo/Illustration Credits: ©Steven Brooke, p. 7 bottom left, p. 8, p. 12 top right, p. 13 top, p. 14, p. 15 top left, p. 16 left, p. 17; Peter Katz, p. 3 bottom, p. 6, p. 7 right, p. 9, p. 10 left, p. 12 left and bottom right, p. 15 right and bottom left, p 16 right, top and bottom; Rolando Llanes

and Rafael Portuondo, p. 3 top; ©Michael Moran, p. 2, p. 7 top left, p 10 right, top and bottom, p. 11, p. 13 bottom

Laguna West (pp. 18-29)

Project Location: Immediately south of Sacramento, California, city limits east of Interstate 5 at Laguna Boulevard
Project Area: 1,045 acres
Developer: RiverWest Development, Sacramento, California, Philip Angelides (president), Susan Baltake, Les Hock, Brian Vale
Submitting Firm: Calthorpe Associates, Peter Calthorpe (principal); Philip Erickson, Mark Macy, Joseph Scanga
Consultants: Ken Kay Associates (landscape), Ken Kay (principal); Fehr & Peers Associates (transportation); AKT Developments (land planning, secondary area), Jack Mixon; Spink Corporation (civil engineering)
Project Status: Town center infrastructure, village green, town hall completed; employment center 10% complete; secondary area (single-family residential) 20% complete; 80 compact single-family houses in town center under construction; elementary school and church starting construction fall 1993
Photo/Illustration Credits: Catherine Chang, Philip Erickson, p. 22, p. 23 bottom; Peter Katz, pp. 27-29; Paul Okamoto, Joseph Scanga, Cleve Brakefield, p. 26; Joe Scanga, p. 18, p. 23

top, p. 25; Rick Williams, Joe Scanga, p. 24; ©Peter Xiques, pp. 20-21 (model by Isabel Kirkland)

Kentlands (pp. 30-45)

Project Location: Gaithersburg, Maryland, 4 miles west of I-270 between Great Seneca Highway, Darnestown and Quince Orchard Roads
Project Area: 356 acres
Developer: Joseph Alfandre & Co., Inc., Rockville, Maryland, Joseph A. Alfandre (president), Robert N. Talbert (vice president), Candy McCracken, Sue Whelan, Steve Wilcox, William A. Winburn IV; The Great Seneca Development Corporation, Jeff Campbell, Mike Cody, Page Lansdale
Submitting Firm: Andres Duany and Elizabeth Plater-Zyberk, Architects and Town Planners, Andres Duany (principal), Elizabeth Plater-Zyberk (principal), Mike Watkins (town architect), William Lennertz (project manager)
Charette Team: Charles Barrett, Keith Bowers, Chester Chellman, Raymond Chu, William Dennis, Andres Duany, Douglas Duany, Tarik El Naggar, Manuel Fernandez-Noval, Jay Graham, Alex Krieger, Doug La Rosa, William Lennertz, Mark Lucy, Leon Nitzin, Patrick Pinnell, Elizabeth Plater-Zyberk, Kathy Poole, Dhiru Thadani, Estela Valle, Mike Watkins, David Wolfe
Consultants: Garr Campbell (landscape);

Rodgers & Associates (civil engineering)
Project Status: Old Farm and Gate House neighborhood (referred to as School district in text) substantially complete; Hill district 25% complete; Lake district 10% complete; 280 rental units and 150 condominiums complete; school, day-care center and church complete; clubhouse and regional shopping center to open fall 1993
Photo/Illustration Credits: Joseph Alfandre & Co., p. 31 bottom; Harry Connolly, p. 30, pp. 38-39; Charles Barrett, Manuel Fernandez-Noval, pp. 32-33, p. 34 bottom, p. 35; ©Alan Karchmer, p. 36, p.37 right, pp. 40, 43-44, p. 45 right; Peter Katz, p. 37 left, top and bottom, pp. 41-42, p. 45 left, top and bottom

South Brentwood Village (pp. 46-51)

Project Location: Immediately south of downtown Brentwood, California, bounded by Walnut Boulevard, Balfour Road and State Highway 4
Project Area: 140 acres
Developer: South Brentwood Associates, Atherton, California, Thomas E. Lodato (president) with Kaufman & Broad, Dublin, California
Submitting Firm: Calthorpe Associates, Peter Calthorpe (principal), Rick Williams (project manager); Catherine Chang, Joseph Scanga, Matt Taecker

Consultants: Carlson, Barbee & Gibson (civil engineering)
Project Status: Approved for construction; expected to commence fall 1993
Photo/Illustration Credits: Peter Katz, p. 47 top; Paul Okamoto, p. 48; Rick Williams, pp. 50-51; Rick Williams, Catherine Chang, p. 46

Bamberton (pp. 52-59)

Project Location: Vancouver Island, British Coumbia, approximately 20 miles north of Victoria on the Trans-Canada highway just south of the town of Mill Bay
Project Area: 1,560 acres
Developer: South Island Development Cooperative, Victoria, British Columbia; David C. Butterfield (president)
Submitting Firm: Andres Duany and Elizabeth Plater-Zyberk, Architects and Town Planners, Andres Duany (principal), Chip Kaufman (town architect), Juan Caruncho (project manager)
Charette Team: Charles Barrett, Juan Caruncho, Walter Chatham, William Dennis, Andres Duany, Manuel Fernandez-Noval, Chip Kaufman, Dana Little, Rod Lovely, Tom Low, Alan Shulman, Estela Valle
Consultants: J.D. Tait & Associates, Inc. (project management), Edwin Tait (principal), Joseph Van Belleghem (principal), Tony Boydell, Darlene Tait; Glatting Lopez Kercher Anglin, Inc. (transportation), Walter Kulash; White

Mountain Survey Company, Inc. (civil engineering, transportation), Chester Chellman; Guy Dauncey, Roger Colwill, Randy Hooper (sustainability); Stanley Associates (water quality)
Project Status: Permits pending; 20 year estimated build-out
Photo/Illustration Credits: Charles Barrett, Manuel Fernandez-Noval, pp. 52, 57-59; Peter Katz, p. 53 top, p. 54 left

Windsor (pp. 60-77)

Project Location: Approximately 8 miles north of Vero Beach, Florida, on highway A1A between the Atlantic Ocean and the Indian River
Project Area: 416 acres
Developer: Galen and Hilary Weston, Toronto, Ontario; Geoffrey and Jorie Butler Kent, Vero Beach, Florida
Submitting Firm: Andres Duany and Elizabeth Plater-Zyberk, Architects and Town Planners, Andres Duany (principal), Elizabeth Plater-Zyberk (principal), Geoffrey Ferrell (project manager), Xavier Iglesias (project manager)
Charette Team: Charles Barrett, Juan Caruncho, Andres Duany, Tarik El Naggar, Geoffrey Ferrell, Peter Jefferson, Robert Trent Jones, Jr., Dony Marin, Scott Merrill, Desmond Muirhead, Felix Pereira, Elizabeth Plater-Zyberk, Craig Roberts, Estela Valle, Hector Valverde, Kamal Zaharin

Consultants: Robert Trent Jones, Jr. (golf course); Stan Smith (tennis courts)
Project Status: Under construction; public infrastructure 35% complete; tennis courts, tennis pavilion and golf course complete; beach club to begin construction fall 1993; 8 residences complete, 8 under construction
Photo/Illustration Credits: Aerial Concepts, p. 61 bottom; Charles Barrett, p. 70, p. 72 (except photo), pp. 73-75; Charles Barrett, Manuel Fernandez-Noval, pp. 62-65; ©Steven Brooke, p. 68 left, p. 69; ©Thomas Delbeck, pp. 60, 66-67, p. 68 right, top and bottom; Thomas Spain, p. 71

Communications Hill (pp. 78-87)

Project Location: San Jose, California
Project Area: 500 acres
Sponsoring Organization: City of San Jose Planning Department, Pat Colombe (principal planner)
Submitting Firm: Solomon Architecture and Planning, Kathryn Clarke (principal), Daniel Solomon (principal); Elizabeth Hartman, David Horsley
Consultants: Phillips Brandt Reddick (urban planning, collaborating), N. Teresa Rea (principal-in-charge), Chris Beck, Michael Horst; Nolte & Associates (civil engineering), Maury Abraham, Deborah Amshoff, Sam Nash, Bert Verrips; Deakin/Harvey/Skabardonis (transpor-

tation), Elizabeth Deakin; The SWA Group (forestry, horticulture), Walter Bemis
Project Status: Specific plan adopted; first phase proceeding to development agreement in 1994
Photo/Illustration Credits: Air Flight Service, p. 79; Kathryn Clarke, p. 80 right, p. 81, p. 86 top right; Philip Rossington, p. 84; Elizabeth Hartman, p. 86 left and bottom right, p. 87; David Horsley, p. 80 left, top and bottom, p. 82 left, top, middle and bottom, p. 83; Thai Nguyen, p. 78; ©Peter Xiques, pp. 82, 85

Rosa Vista (pp.88-95)

Project Location: Mesa, Arizona, at the intersection of Baseline and Ellsworth Roads
Project Area: 30 acres
Developer: Homefree Village Resorts Inc., Denver, Colorado, Craig M. Bollman, Jr. (president)
Submitting Firm: Andres Duany and Elizabeth Plater-Zyberk, Architects and Town Planners, Andres Duany (principal), Juan Caruncho (project manager)
Charette Team: Charles Barrett, Juan Caruncho, Andres Duany, Manuel Fernandez-Noval, Chip Kaufman, Dana Little, Max Underwood, Estela Valle, Kamal Zaharin
Consultants: Cavco Industries, Inc. (manufactured housing, technical support); Genesis Marketing Group, Inc. (marketing)
Project Status: Preliminary zoning approval;

construction expected to commence May 1994, complete build-out projected for October 1994
Photo/Illustration Credits: Charles Barrett, Manuel Fernandez-Noval, p. 88, pp. 92-93; Juan Caruncho, p. 91

A New Village in the Suburbs (pp. 96-99)

Project Location: Southwest Dade County, Florida, at the intersection of 120th Street and 122nd Avenue, west of the Florida Turnpike
Project Area: 100 acres
Developer: Aura Group, Miami, Florida, Martin Greenberg (president), Brandon Lurie (vice president)
Submitting Firm: Dover, Kohl & Partners, South Miami, Florida, Victor Dover (principal), Joseph Kohl (principal); Carol Dufresne, Robert Gray, Dana Little
Consultants: Holland & Knight (legal counsel, land-use), Sam Poole
Project Status: Permits pending
Photo/Illustration Credits: Maricé Chael, p. 98 left; Victor Dover, p. 97 top; Joseph Kohl, p. 98 right, top and bottom, p. 99; Dana Little, p. 96

Wellington (pp. 100-116)

Project Location: Palm Beach County, Florida, south of State Road 80, west of the existing Wellington planned unit development
Project Area: 1,500 acres
Developer: Corepoint Corporation, West Palm

Beach, Florida, Alberto Vadia, Jr. (president)
Submitting Firm: Andres Duany and Elizabeth Plater-Zyberk, Architects and Town Planners, Andres Duany (principal), Elizabeth Plater-Zyberk (principal), Scott Hedge (project manager)
Charette Team: Charles Barrett, Chester Chellman, Andres Duany, Manuel Fernandez-Noval, Geoffrey Ferrell, Scott Hedge, Jorge Hernandez, Chip Kaufman, Jean-Francois Lejeune, Elizabeth Plater-Zyberk, Rafael Portuondo, Jorge Trelles, Luis Trelles, Kristin Triff, Kamal Zaharin
Consultants: Williams, Hatfield & Stoner, Inc. (engineering), Tony Nolan, James Eberhart, Jean Lindsey; David Plummer & Associates, Inc. (transportation), David Plummer (principal), Kahart Pinder; White Mountain Survey Company, Inc. (civil engineering, transportation), Chester Chellman; CZR Incorporated (environmental), David Nickerson, Jr.
Project Status: Unbuilt
Photo/Illustration Credits: Charles Barrett, Manuel Fernandez-Noval, pp. 100, 104-109; Peter Katz, p.101 bottom

Cité Internationale (pp. 118-125)

Project Location: Downtown Montréal, Quebec, bounded by Boulevard Rene Lévesque, Rue University, Bonaventure Autoroute, Rue William and Rue St. Urbain

Project Area: 100 acres
Sponsoring Organization: City of Montréal
Submitting Firm: Peterson/Littenberg Architects, Steven Peterson (principal), Barbara Littenberg (principal), Loren E. Cannon (associate), Tim Eckersley, John Gilmer, Zon Sollenberger
Project Status: Pending
Photo Credits: Steven Peterson, p. 119 top, left and right

Downtown Hayward (pp. 126-133)

Project Location: Downtown Hayward, California, bounded by A Street, Foothill Boulevard, D Street, Grand Street
Project Area: 125 acres
Developer: City of Hayward, John Bush (redevelopment director), Lou Garcia (city manager)
Submitting Firm: Solomon Architecture and Planning, Daniel Solomon (principal, project director); Mallory Cusenberry, Thai Nguyen
Consultants: Deakin/Harvey/Skabardonis (transportation), Elizabeth Deakin (principal), Alex Skabardonis (principal); Freedman, Tung & Bottomley (urban design, focal point), Michael Freedman (principal), Colette Parsons
Project Status: Specific plan adopted by city; 3 block area has been acquired by city for housing, city in negotiations with BART for joint development project
Photo/Illustration Credits: Mallory Cusenberry,

p. 127 top, p.133 middle left; Thai Nguyen, pp. 126, 128-132, p. 133 bottom left and bottom right (with Daniel Solomon); Pacific Aerial Surveys, p. 127 bottom; Daniel Solomon, p. 133 top right; Gary Strang, p. 133 top left

Riviera Beach (pp. 134-141)

Project Location: Riviera Beach, Florida, between the Intracoastal Waterway and Old Dixie Highway
Project Area: 1,600 acres
Sponsoring Organization: Riviera Beach Community Redevelopment Agency, Don DeLaney (executive director)
Submitting Firm: Mark Schimmenti Architecture and Town Planning, Mark Schimmenti (principal), Dona Lubin (project manager), Carl Levin, Mike Sardinas
Collaborating Firm: Dover, Correa, Kohl, Cockshutt, Valle (urban design), Victor Dover (principal), Jaime Correa (principal), Joseph Kohl (principal), Erick Valle (principal), Dana Little
Consultant: Geoffrey Ferrell (urban code)
Project Status: Approved by redevelopment agency board and regional planning authorities; municipal permits pending
Photo/Illustration Credits: Jaime Correa, p. 137; Victor Dover, p. 138 right, top and bottom, p. 139 left, top and bottom; Manuel Fernandez-Noval, p. 135 (coloration); Joseph Kohl, p. 135

bottom right, p. 136, p. 139 right, top and bottom; Dana Little, p. 138 left, top and bottom; Carl Levin, p. 140 left; Dona Lubin, p. 140 bottom right; Mike Sardinas, p. 140 top right; Mark Schimmenti, p. 134

Rio Vista West (pp. 142-145)

Project Location: Mission Valley, San Diego, California, bounded by Friars Road, Stadium Way and the San Diego River
Project Area: 95 acres
Developer: CalMat Properties Co., San Diego, California, Donald A. Cerone (vice president)
Submitting Firm: Calthorpe Associates, Peter Calthorpe (principal); Matt Taecker (project manager), Joseph Scanga
Consultants: T & B Planning Consultants, Inc. (implementation), Douglas Boyd, Karen Ruggles; Douglas Newcomb, Inc. (landscape); Bement Dainwood Sturgeon (civil engineering); Entranco-Federhart (transportation)
Project Status: Permits pending; selected as model project for San Diego's TOD guidelines
Photo/Illustration Credits: Peter Katz, p. 143 bottom right; Marvin Rand, p. 143 top; Joseph Scanga, Matt Taecker, pp. 142, 144-145

Lake West (pp. 146-153)

Project Location: West Dallas, Texas, bounded by Westmoreland Road, Singleton Boulevard, Hampton Road and the Trinity River

Project Area: 500 acres
Sponsoring Organization: Dallas Housing Authority, Jack Herrington (exective director)
Submitting Firm: Peterson/Littenberg Architects, Steven Peterson (principal), Barbara Littenberg (principal); Loren E. Cannon (associate); Blake Middleton, James Papoutsis
Consultants: Carter & Burgess, Inc. (engineering, planning), John H. Mason; Selzer-Volk-Borne (architecture, collaborating), Leonard Volk (principal); Real Estate Research Corporation (marketing)
Project Status: 900 units completed
Photo Credits: Dallas Housing Authority, p. 147 bottom; Steven Peterson, p. 150 left

Downcity Providence (pp. 154-159)

Project Location: Downtown Providence, Rhode Island, centered on the southwest corner of Kennedy Plaza
Project Area: 162 acres
Sponsoring Organizations/Individuals: Capital Grille; Citizen's Bank; City of Providence; Edwards and Angel; Fleet Bank; Gilbane Properties, Inc.; Hinkley, Allen, Snyder & Comen; H. James Field, Jr.; Johnson & Wales University; KPMG Peat Marwick; National Trust for Historic Preservation; Omni Biltmore Hotel; Point Gammon Corporation; The Providence Foundation; Providence Journal; Providence Washington Insurance Co.; Rhode

Island Port Authority
Submitting Firm: Andres Duany and Elizabeth Plater-Zyberk, Architects and Town Planners, Andres Duany (principal), Tom Low (project manager)
Charette Team: Andres Duany (principal), Charles Barrett, Buff Chace, Walter Chatham, Manuel Fernandez-Noval, Robert Freeman, Randall Imai, Michael Kinerk, Tom Kohler, William Lennertz, Dana Little, Tom Low, George Rolfe, Jonathan Rose, Iskandar Shafie, Sharon Stanford, Yarmir Steiner, Douglas S. Storrs, Anne Tate
Consultants: Michael Kinerk (marketing); Alex Krieger (urban design, preservation); Tom Kohler (management); Gibbs Planning Group, Inc. (retail), Robert J. Gibbs (principal), George Rolfe (retail); Jonathan Rose (housing)
Project Status: Plan accepted, municipal zoning revisions pending
Photo/Illustration Credits: Charles Barrett, Manuel Fernandez-Noval, pp. 154, 158, p. 159 bottom; Peter Katz, p. 155 top, p. 157 top; Andres Duany, p. 155 right

Orange Tree Courts (pp. 160-163)

Project Location: Downtown Riverside, California, bounded by Main, Fifth, Orange and Sixth Streets
Project Area: Approximately 1.5 acres
Sponsoring Organization: City of Riverside

Redevelopment Department, Marguerite Gulati (director)
Submitting Firm: Elizabeth Moule and Stefanos Polyzoides, Architects and Urbanists, Elizabeth Moule (principal), Stefanos Polyzoides (principal), Xiaojian He; competition scheme by deBretteville & Polyzoides, Peter deBretteville (principal), Stefanos Polyzoides (principal), Bob Knight
Project Status: Unbuilt
Photo Credits: Peter Katz, p. 161 top and right

Atlantic Center (pp. 164-167)

Project Location: Downtown Brooklyn, New York, between the intersections of Fulton Street and Flatbush Avenue, Atlantic and Flatbush Avenues, Atlantic and Carlton Avenues and Green and Carlton Avenues
Project Area: 24 acres
Developer: Rose Associates, Inc., New York, Jonathan Rose (president)
Submitting Firm: Calthorpe Associates (master plan, residential areas), Peter Calthorpe (principal)
Collaborating Firms: Skidmore Owings & Merrill, Raul de Armas (master plan, commercial areas), David M. Childs (architectural design, office buildings), Michael Keselica (project manager); Simmons Architects, Harry Simmons, Jr. (architectural design, residential buildings)

Consultants: Lee Weintraub, Weintraub & diDomenico (landscape)
Project Status: Modified scheme approved for construction; expected to begin spring 1994
Photo Credits: Jim Horner, p. 166 left; Peter Katz, p. 165 bottom, left and right, p. 167 top

Mashpee Commons (pp. 168-177)

Project Location: Mashpee, Massachusetts, at the intersection of Routes 28 and 151
Project Area: 294 acres
Developer: Fields Point Limited Partnership, Mashpee, Massachusetts, Buff Chace (managing general partner), Douglas S. Storrs (vice president), A. John Renz (vice president), David W. Burke
Submitting Firm: Andres Duany and Elizabeth Plater-Zyberk, Architects and Town Planners, Andres Duany (principal), Elizabeth Plater-Zyberk (principal), William Lennertz (project manager)
Charette Team: Charles Barrett, Stephanie Bothwell, Buff Chace, Chester Chellman, William Dennis, Andres Duany, Douglas Duany, Tarik El Naggar, Manuel Fernandez-Noval, Scott Hedge, Randall Imai, Alex Krieger, William Lennertz, John Montague Massengale, Alick McClean, Elizabeth Plater-Zyberk, A. John Renz, Douglas S. Storrs, Ann Tate
Consultants: White Mountain Survey Com-

pany, Inc. (civil engineering, transportation), Chester Chellman; Dufresne/Henry (civil engineering); Ropes & Gray (legal counsel, land use)
Project Status: In progress; core commercial areas 50% complete; 2 residential neighborhoods approved, permits pending for remaining 5 neighborhoods
Photo/Illustration Credits: Charles Barrett, Manuel Fernandez-Noval, pp. 170-173; Craig Studio, p. 169 bottom; Steve Dunwell, p. 174 left and right top, pp. 175-176, p. 177 bottom left; Peter Katz, p. 177 left top and right; ©Nick Wheeler/Wheeler Photographics, p. 168, p. 174 bottom right

Playa Vista (pp. 178-191)

Project Location: West Los Angeles, California, between Marina del Rey, Playa del Rey, the San Diego Freeway and the Westchester Bluffs
Project Area: 1,087 acres
Developer/Submitting Firm: Maguire Thomas Partners, Los Angeles, California, Nelson Rising (partner-in-charge), Douglas Gardner (project manager), Randy Johnson (chief financial officer), John McAlister (public policy), Tom Ricci (marina project manager), Joel Stensby (construction manager)
Collaborating Firms: Elizabeth Moule and Stefanos Polyzoides, Architects and Urbanists, Elizabeth Moule (principal), Stefanos

Polyzoides (principal), Kevin Reed (project architect), Liza Kerrigan, Robert Levit, Dion McCarthy, Doug Myhr, Michelle Nycek, Geoffrey Siebens; Moore Ruble Yudell (architects), Buzz Yudell (principal-in-charge), Charles Moore (principal designer), John Ruble (principal designer), Linda Brettler, Beth Elliot, Doug Jamieson, Kerry Hogan, Wendy Kohn, Gavin Monk, Mark Peacor, Curtis Woodhouse; Andres Duany and Elizabeth Plater-Zyberk, Architects and Town Planners, Andres Duany (principal), Elizabeth Plater-Zyberk (principal), Charles Barrett, Chester Chellman, William Dennis, Tarik El Naggar, Manuel Fernandez-Noval, Geoffrey Ferrell, Manuela Haselau, Chip Kaufman, William Lennertz, Dony Marin, Estela Valle, Hector Valverde; Legorreta Arquitectos (architects), Ricardo Legorreta (principal), Gerardo Alonsa, Noé Castro, Victor Legorreta; Hanna/Olin, Ltd. (landscape architects), Laurie Olin (principal-in-charge), Dennis McGlade (principal), Robert Bedell (associate-in-charge), Lucinda Sanders (associate), Margaret Fahringer, Frank Garnier, Marsh Kriplen, Kim Ogle, Elaine Rosenberg, Karen Skafte, Robert Stigberg, George Workman
Consultants: Psomas and Asssociates (civil engineering), Sharon Kaplan, Jacob Lipa, Wayne Smith; Barton-Aschman Associates, Inc. (transportation), Fred Dock, Mark Medema

Project Status: City council approval of first phase; preliminary engineering and continued planning in progress for subsequent phases
Photo Credits: ©Tom Bonner, p. 186 bottom right, p. 191 bottom right

Jackson-Taylor (pp. 192-197)

Project Location: San Jose, California, bounded by East Hedding, North 6th, East Empire and North 11th Streets.
Project Area: 75 acres
Sponsoring Organization: City of San Jose Planning Department, Laurel Prevetti (senior planner)
Submitting Firm: Calthorpe Associates, Peter Calthorpe (principal), Shelley Poticha (project manager), Rick Williams (project designer), Catherine Chang, Joseph Scanga, Cindy Sterry
Consultants: Bay Area Economics (economics), Dena Belzer
Project Status: Approved by city council; first phase proceeding
Photo/Illustration Credits: Shelley Poticha, p. 193 top right (pair); Canan Tolon, Catherine Chang, p. 192

Highland District (pp. 198-205)

Project Location: University of Arizona campus, Tucson, Arizona, adjacent to the intersection of Highland Avenue and Sixth Street
Project Area: 18 acres

Sponsoring Organization: Residence Life, University of Arizona, Jim Van Arsdel (director)
Submitting Firm: Elizabeth Moule and Stefanos Polyzoides, Architects and Urbanists, Elizabeth Moule (principal), Stefanos Polyzoides (principal), Kaitlin Drisko, Bob Knight, Robert Levit, Michelle Nycek, Cynthia Phakos
Consultants: Michael Van Valkenburgh Associates (landscape), Michael Van Valkenburgh (principal), Julie Bargman; WLB Group (civil engineering), Mike Byrne; FKM Architects (architecture, collaborating); Turner-Schaller Engineering (structural engineering), Mark Turner (principal); Adams & Associates (mechanical engineering); Monrad Associates (electrical engineering)
Project Status: Master plan approved; first phase buildings construction to start winter 1993.
Photo Credits: Stefanos Polyzoides, p. 201 right, p. 205 top

Clinton (pp. 206-211)

Project Location: Midtown Manhattan, New York, bounded by West 50th Street, 10th Avenue, West 56th Street and 12th Avenue
Project Area: 38 acres
Sponsoring Organization: Clinton Preservation Local Development Corporation, John Glynn (executive director)
Submitting Firm: Peterson/Littenberg Architects, Steven Peterson, Barbara Littenberg

(principals), Loren E. Cannon (project associate), Stephen Moser (project architect)
Consultants: Robert Silman & Associates (civil engineering); Michael Kwartler & Asociates, Michael Kwartler, Dennis Ferris (zoning); Allee, King, Rosen & Fleming, Deborah Allee (environmental)
Project Status: Pending
Photo Credits: Steven Peterson, p. 207; ©Jock Pottle/Esto, p. 210 right, top and bottom, p. 211

Downtown Los Angeles (pp. 212-219)

Project Location: Downtown Los Angeles, California, bounded by Alameda Street and the Santa Monica, Harbor and Hollywood Freeways
Project Area: Approximately 2,720 acres
Sponsoring Organization: City of Los Angeles, Community Redevelopment Agency
Submitting Firm: Elizabeth Moule and Stefanos Polyzoides, Architects and Urbanists, Elizabeth Moule (principal), Stefanos Polyzoides (principal); Xiaojian He, Adrian Koffka, Geoffrey Siebens
Collaborating Firms: Andres Duany and Elizabeth Plater-Zyberk, Architects and Town Planners, Elizabeth Plater-Zyberk (principal), Scott Hedge; Solomon Architecture and Planning, Daniel Solomon (principal), Amy Miller; Susan Haviland, Architect; Peter deBretteville, Architect

Consultants: Hanna/Olin, Ltd. (landscape), Bob Hanna (principal), Shirley Kressel; Telemark Community Builders (implementation), Will Fleissig (principal), Marty Borko; Cordoba Corporation (economic planning), Maria Mehranian, Brent Barnes, Robert Vasquez ; Michael Dear, Jennifer Wolch (social services, homelessness); Carson Anderson (historic preservation); Kaku Associates, Inc. (transportation), Dick Kaku (principal), Pat Gibson; Barton Aschman Associates (transportation), Brad Williams; Korve Engineering (transportation), Michael Bates

Project Status: Final report adopted by sponsoring organization, municipal approvals pending

Photo Credit: ©Linda Saltzman, p. 215

The Architecture of Community
(pp. 221–230)

Photo/Illustration Credits: Art Resource, pp. 228–229; Victor Dover, p. 226 top right; Rollin La France, p. 224 bottom; Michael Moran, p. 227; ©Robert A.M. Stern Architects, p. 230; John Nolen Papers, Rare and Manuscript Collections, Cornell University Library, p. 226 top left; Ezra Stoller ©Esto, p. 223, p. 224 top left; Venturi, Scott Brown and Associates, Inc., p. 224 top right; ©Paul Warchol, p. 225

241

Contributors

Project contributors (opposite) at the First Congress for the New Urbanism, October 8, 1993: (clockwise from lower right) Elizabeth Plater-Zyberk, Elizabeth Moule, Joseph Kohl, Geoffrey Ferrell, Jaime Correa, Barbara Littenberg, Mark Schimmenti, Erick Valle, Steven Peterson, Victor Dover, Stefanos Polyzoides, Daniel Solomon, Andres Duany and Peter Calthorpe. Not pictured: Kathryn Clarke; editorial contributors Todd W. Bressi and Vincent Scully. Photograph by Adam Auel.

Todd W. Bressi is associate editor of *Places, A Quarterly Journal of Environmental Design* and teaches urban design in the Hunter College graduate urban planning program. He is editor of the book *Planning and Zoning New York City* and writes frequently on urban design and planning for several publications, including *Metropolis, Planning* and *New York Newsday*.

Peter Calthorpe has practiced architecture since 1972 and formed Calthorpe Associates in 1983. After attending Antioch College, he studied architecture at Yale University. Calthorpe has lectured widely throughout the U.S., Europe, Australia and South America and has taught at the University of California (Berkeley), University of Washington, University of Oregon and University of North Carolina. Calthorpe is the coauthor of *Sustainable Communities* and author of *The Next American Metropolis*. He has received numerous honors and awards and has been cited by *Newsweek* as one of 25 "innovators on the cutting edge."

Jaime Correa holds masters degrees in both architecture and city planning, and certificates in Urban Design and Historic Preservation from the University of Pennsylvania. He is a partner of the Atelier for Architecture and Urbanism, Inc. and the Office for Urban Counterprojects, both in Miami. Correa is an instructor in the graduate program in suburb and town design of the University of Miami.

Victor Dover and **Joseph Kohl** are principals of Dover, Kohl & Partners in South Miami, Florida. Each holds a bachelor of architecture degree from Virginia Polytechnic Institute and a master of architecture degree from the University of Miami where they have both taught. Dover lectures widely at conferences and community meetings on redevelopment and growth management. Kohl is recognized for his advanced work in electronic media and computer-assisted visualization.

Andres Duany and **Elizabeth Plater-Zyberk** completed undergraduate degrees in architecture and urban planning at Princeton and both went on to receive their master of architecture degrees from Yale University. In 1980 they founded their Miami-based architecture and town planning practice. Their firm has designed over 70 new towns and community revitalization projects. Duany and Plater-Zyberk have received numerous awards including University of Virginia's Thomas Jefferson Award and two State of Florida Governor's Urban Design Awards. The firm has been recognized internationally for its urban planning and architectural design work. Duany and Plater-Zyberk have both taught at major universities and lectured in the U.S., Canada, Europe, the Caribbean and Japan.

Geoffrey Ferrell received his bachelor of architecture degree from the Oregon School of

Design and holds a bachelor of science degree in public policy from Willamette University. He has worked with Duany and Plater-Zyberk as a town planner and code writer. Ferrell was an adjunct faculty member of the University of Miami's graduate program in suburb and town design and is coauthor of the publication *The City Is an Investment in Our Future.*

Elizabeth Moule and **Stefanos Polyzoides** are Los Angeles–based architects and urbanists who have been partners since 1990. Moule received a bachelor of arts degree in art history from Smith College and a master of architecture degree from Princeton University. She also studied at the Institute for Architecture and Urban Studies in New York. Moule has taught at many U.S. universities as a visiting critic and is the author of various articles on architecture and urbanism. Polyzoides was born and raised in Athens, Greece, and received both bachelor and master degrees in architecture and urban planning from Princeton University. He is associate professor of architecture at the University of Southern California and has written extensively on the urban and architectural history of Southern California.

Steven Peterson and **Barbara Littenberg** founded their New York architecture and urban design firm in 1979. Their work has been published and exhibited in the U.S. and internationally. Peterson and Littenberg have jointly won numerous professional awards and international design competitions. Peterson holds bachelor and master degrees in architecture from Cornell University. He has taught at Cornell University and Harvard University and is the author of several articles. Littenberg holds a bachelor of architecture degree from Cornell University and is associate professor of architecture at Yale University. She has taught at Columbia University, Harvard University and the Rhode Island School of Design.

Mark Schimmenti, an architect and urbanist, has practiced in New York, Tokyo, San Juan and Miami. He holds bachelor and master degrees in architecture from the University of Florida and is associate professor of city and town design at the University of Virginia. Schimmenti has taught at several schools of architecture and lectured before numerous professional organizations and community groups. His professional practice specializes in the creation of master plans and comprehensive design guidelines for cities, neighborhoods and new developments.

Vincent Scully received both his undergraduate and doctoral degrees from Yale University where he has taught since 1947. Scully's books include *The Shingle Style and the Stick Style*, *American Architecture and Urbanism*, *The Earth, the Temple, and the Gods* and *Architecture: The Natural and the Manmade* among others. He is currently the Sterling Professor of the History of Art Emeritus and the William Clyde DeVane Professor of Humanities Emeritus at Yale University.

Daniel Solomon and **Kathryn Clarke** are principals of the San Francisco firm of Solomon Architecture and Planning. The firm's work has been widely published and won numerous awards. Solomon holds a bachelor of architecture degree from Columbia University, a bachelor of arts degree from Stanford University and a master of architecture degree from the University of California (Berkeley). He is a professor of architecture at the University of California (Berkeley), where he has been a faculty member since 1966. Solomon has written many articles and regularly lectures in the U.S. and abroad. Clarke holds a bachelor of architecture degree from Virginia Polytechnic Institute and State University where she has been assistant professor. Clarke has lectured at the University of California (Berkeley) and is currently an adjunct professor at California College of Arts and Crafts.

Erick Valle received his master of architecture degree from the University of Miami where he is assistant professor of urban design. Valle established and is director of the school's computer visualization lab.

Acknowledgments

Consistent with the collaborative spirit of the New Urbanism, this book reflects the input and participation of a great many individuals. Foremost among these are the architects whose work is represented in these pages: Peter Calthorpe, Kathryn Clarke, Jaime Correa, Victor Dover, Andres Duany, Geoffrey Ferrell, Joseph Kohl, Barbara Littenberg, Elizabeth Moule, Steven Peterson, Elizabeth Plater-Zyberk, Stefanos Polyzoides, Mark Schimmenti, Daniel Solomon and Erick Valle. Their work and ideas are what this book is all about. I am indebted also to Todd W. Bressi and Vincent Scully whose eloquent written contributions help to place this emerging movement within its proper social, historic and academic context.

There are many others to whom I owe thanks. Nancy Bruning, a writer and editor of considerable talent, skills and experience, worked closely with me in the writing of this book. By the end of the project we were literally finishing each other's sentences. Clifton Lemon, a graphic designer with an unerring eye for elegance and clarity, was both patient and uncompromising through the duration of this project. He put up with a client that was both author, fellow designer and friend—undoubtedly the toughest possible combination.

Many friends provided the support and encouragement that convinced me to take on and complete this task. Perhaps they knew that by writing this book, I might eventually stop talking about it. Ron Morgan, Pam Kinzie, Tom Sargent, Jeffrey Westman, Adam Gross, Carter Bravmann, David Pearson and Julia Bloomfield are among this group. Others played important roles in the chain of events that led me to this project. A past client, Nathaniel Taylor of California's S.H. Cowell Foundation, inadvertently launched this endeavor by requesting information about "new and innovative" communities around the U.S. His inquiry, in turn, led me to Chip Kaufman, who is affiliated with Andres Duany and Elizabeth Plater-Zyberk on several of their west coast projects. Chip first introduced me to many of the key concepts and projects that ultimately found their way into this book. Mark Schimmenti, a longtime friend (also a contributor), deserves special mention. In many ways, Mark was my guide to the New Urbanism, generously giving time, knowledge and advice in support of this effort.

Many others helped to smooth my way through various stages of the project. Alexandra Anderson, Cynthia Cannell, Ed Marquand, Blair and Helaine Kaplan Prentice, Owen Edwards, Dayna Macy and Jacki Merri Meyer helped me to understand many of the complexities of the publishing process. Their advice was invaluable. Many friends reviewed the book and book proposal at different stages. Lon Dubinsky, Steve Weissman, Ann Lewnes, Christopher Scholz, Christine Azevedo, Andy Harris, Irwin Kaplan, Harrison Rue and Wayne Berg provided insights, ideas and criticism, all of which affected the ultimate form and content of this publication. Joel Stein, my editor at McGraw-Hill, was an advocate for this book from our first conversation onward. His vision and patience were central to this project's ultimate realization. Jane Palmieri, also of McGraw-Hill, was responsible for the detailed editing of the book. Her professionalism, good sense and warmth made one part of the publishing process much less traumatic than I expected it to be.

During the course of my research, I worked closely with the staffs of the firms whose work is represented in this book. These people are the unsung heroes of the New Urbanism and, as such, deserve special recognition. In particular, I would like to thank Joseph Scanga, Shelley Poticha, Matt Taecker, Philip Erickson, Catherine Chang and Lyssandra Williams of Calthorpe Associates; Robert Gray of Dover, Kohl & Partners; Xavier Iglesias, Marilyn Avery, Richard Shearer, Tom Low, Juan Caruncho, Scott Hedge, Mike Watkins, Kamal Zaharin, Iskandar Shafie, Dana Little, Estela Valle, Enid Duany, Marjie Tracy, Oscar Machado and Tony Lopez of Duany and Plater-Zyberk; Robert Levit, Xiaojian He and Michele Marquez of Moule and Polyzoides; Peter Szilagyi of Peterson/Littenberg; and Gary Strang, Philip Rossington and Patricia Mc-Brayer of Solomon Architecture and Planning.

Several other individuals connected with "the movement"–Deborah Berke, Charles Barrett, Scott Merrill, Billy Winburn, Doug Storrs, Jean-Francois Lejeune, Dan Cary, Christopher Kent, David Mohney, Robert Gibbs and Rick Williams–provided detailed information about many of the projects mentioned herein. They generously shared their firsthand knowledge of the early days of Seaside, Laguna West, Mashpee Commons, Windsor and other projects. Their observations and anecdotes could easily fill another volume.

Many superb visual images, both photographic, diagrammatic and illustrative have been reproduced in this book. I wish to thank all of the photographers, architects, draftspersons and artists who have lent their work to this effort. Special thanks go to Thomas Delbeck, to Peter Macchia of Modern Effects who did most of the color copy photography and to my longtime friend, Erica Stoller, who provided both historic and contemporary images from Esto's extensive archives.

There are several others, mostly close friends, whose contributions are harder to quantify but of no less importance. I'm thinking of Paco Underhill, Peter-Ayers Tarantino, Janet Marie Smith, Carl Seville, Howard Zweig, Judd Allyn, Hilary Hillman, Barbara Al-Haffar, David Paeth, James Barron, Bill True and Burt Stern. There are others, I'm sure, that I will only remember after the book has gone to press. To them, my sincerest apologies.

Finally, I wish to thank my father, Dr. Max Katz, who made sure that I didn't starve while finishing this project and my mother, to whom this book is dedicated. She encouraged me to pursue this project but, sadly, did not live to see it completed.

About the Author

Peter Katz is a design and marketing consultant based in San Francisco, California, and Seattle, Washington. He has directed real estate-related projects throughout the U.S. and the Pacific Rim. Katz studied architecture and graphic design at The Cooper Union for the Advancement of Science and Art in New York, receiving a bachelor of fine arts degree and the Royal Society of Arts (London) honor award upon graduation. Katz lectures frequently on urban issues to university audiences and citizens' groups.